CIVILITY AND SUBVERSION

The book provides a sophisticated alternative to existing accounts of the role of the intellectual in modern democracy. Arguing that society suffers from a systemic deliberation deficit, Jeffrey Goldfarb explores the potential of the intellectual as democratic agent, at once civilizing political contestation and subverting complacent consensus. The sentimental leftist view of the intellectual as guardian of democracy and the demonizing rightist view of the intellectual as obstructor of progress are both shown to be inadequate. Instead, intellectuals are portrayed as special kinds of "strangers" who pay careful attention to their critical faculties, uniquely equipping them to address the most pressing issues of today. Professor Goldfarb deploys classical and contemporary social theory to analyze a diverse set of intellectuals in action, from Socrates in fifth-century Athens to Malcolm X and Toni Morrison in twentieth-century America, and, drawing on personal acquaintance, the political dissidents in communist and post-communist Central Europe.

JEFFREY C. GOLDFARB is Professor of Sociology and Co-Chair of the Committee for Democratic Studies at the Graduate Faculty of the New School for Social Research in New York City. He is the author of numerous essays and scholarly articles as well as six books, including *After the Fall* (1992), *Beyond Glasnost* (1989), and *On Cultural Freedom* (1982). In addition to his scholarly work on cultural and intellectual life, he has been actively involved in democratic movements in Eastern and Central Europe, particularly Poland, since before the fall of communism. He was co-founder, along with Adam Michnik, of an international clandestine network of oppositional intellectuals, the Democracy Seminar. He draws on this first-hand experience in *Civility and Subversion*.

CIVILITY AND SUBVERSION

The Intellectual in Democratic Society

JEFFREY C. GOLDFARB

CAMBRIDGE
UNIVERSITY PRESS

PUBLISHED BY THE PRESS SYNDICATE OF THE UNIVERSITY OF CAMBRIDGE
The Pitt Building, Trumpington Street, Cambridge CB2 1RP, United Kingdom

CAMBRIDGE UNIVERSITY PRESS
The Edinburgh Building, Cambridge, CB2 2RU, United Kingdom
http://www.cup.cam.ac.uk
40 West 20th Street, New York, NY 10011-4211, USA   http://www.cup.org
10 Stamford Road, Oakleigh, Melbourne 3166, Australia

© Jeffrey C. Goldfarb 1998

First published 1998

Printed in the United Kingdom at the University Press, Cambridge

Typeset in 11/12½ Baskerville [CE]

A catalogue record for this book is available from the British Library

ISBN 0 521 62220 4 hardback
ISBN 0 521 62723 0 paperback

In memory of my father
Benjamin Goldfarb, 1915–1997

Contents

Acknowledgments

This inquiry is about the importance of serious intellectual discussion. Talk also has been my primary method of investigation. Conversations with Talal Asad, Eugene Halton, Ira Katznelson, Marcin Krol, Elzbieta Matynia, Alberto Melucci, Adam Michnik, David Plotke, Robin Wagner-Pacifici, Terry Williams, Dmitri Shalin, Ann Snitow, Eviatar Zerubavel, and Ari and Vera Zolberg were important in helping me develop this project, as were discussions with students in my classes on intellectuals, media and civil society, and the sociology of culture at the New School for Social Research in New York City, and in seminars on the problems of democratic culture at the Democracy and Diversity Summer Graduate Institute in Cracow, Poland. Further, I would like to acknowledge my debt to my teacher, Donald Levine, whose insights into the work of Georg Simmel have provided me with a way to think about the democratic intellectual with engagement, but, I hope, without ideology.

Some years ago, in the preface to my book *The Cynical Society*, I acknowledged my debt to my father, a private intellectual, for what he taught me about politics. Here, I dedicate this work to his memory, with a sense of loss, and with profound appreciation for what he taught me about living a meaningful life.

CHAPTER I

Introduction: the intellectuals at century's end

I believe that intellectuals have played crucial roles in the making of democracy and in the ongoing practices of democratic life. I further believe that the diminution of intellectual activity presents a major threat to democracy in our times. Intellectuals are central democratic actors, and when they leave the political stage, democratic performance ends in failure. I have such beliefs, and judge that they are especially pressing nowadays, because I perceive that intellectuals are particularly able to address one of the most pressing needs of democracies: the need to deliberate about common problems.

Intellectuals help societies talk about their problems. They contribute to a democratic life when they civilize political contestation and when they subvert complacent consensus; when they provide enemies with the discursive possibility to become opponents and when they facilitate public deliberations about problems buried by the norms of civility. This is the primary thesis of this inquiry. Intellectuals are key democratic agents as they stimulate informed discussion about pressing social problems, fulfilling this role by cultivating *civility* in public life and promoting the *subversion* of restrictive common sense.

In order to explore this primary thesis adequately, we will consider in this investigation the dilemmas and complexities of intellectual action in democratic society. I will attempt to depict the intellectual as a distinct type of social actor (chapter 2) and show how he or she establishes a field for social action in public (chapters 3 and 4). As our inquiry progresses, the figure of the intellectual in democratic society will be more fully described. The full account of the democratic intellectual in contemporary societies is presented in the conclusion.

This will not be a straightforward formal inquiry. I will present a sociological definition of intellectuals by considering how they have

defined themselves in their actions in society. This will lead us to a
consideration of Socrates as an archetype of the classical intellectual
in a classical democracy (chapter 2), and to an examination of the
intellectual in communist and post-communist Europe (chapters 5,
6, and 10). These cases will be explored as comparative counter-
points to the investigation of the situation of the intellectual in the
United States.

Our understanding of the intellectual in democratic society will
emerge as we view intellectuals in action: grappling with the eclipse
of public life with the development of mass society, as John Dewey
and Walter Lippmann did in the first part of this century (chapter 3);
attempting to subvert the restrictions of power and hierarchy, as
C. Wright Mills and Edward Said have in the second part of the
century (chapter 4); constructing and reconstructing our political
vocabularies, as intellectuals in a sort of liberal cosmopolitan
conspiracy have done, as they reintroduced the ideal of civil society
with the defeat of actually existing socialism (chapter 5). The
autonomy of cultural life from political and economic power will be
shown to be a requisite of a free intellectual life, a requisite worth
cultivating, a primary concern of intellectuals in action in post-
communist Europe (chapter 6), but the autonomy of cultural institutions, such as the American university, I will maintain, has its
dangers when it is too complete, leading to the sublimation of
political contestation, as can be observed in the controversies over
political correctness (chapter 7). Yet, even with the problems of the
American university, we will observe intellectuals working on major
American social problems, such as the problems of race, both by
subverting cultural conventions, as did Malcolm X (chapter 8), and
by carefully working on establishing more reflective civilized discussion of media events, as did a group of academics in reaction to the
confirmation hearings of Clarence Thomas (chapter 9). Developing
the proper balance between civility and subversion, I will argue, is a
crucial problem facing democratic intellectuals, and we will take a
look at the situation of feminism in the new democracies of Central
Europe as one in which this balance is being weighed (chapter 10).

THE DELIBERATION DEFICIT

This account of intellectuals in democratic society is a reaction to
the problems of our day. Mine is not simply a description of what

intellectuals have done. I will make no attempt to give a descriptive survey of the situation of intellectuals in contemporary societies.[1] Instead, I will attempt to demonstrate what intellectuals do when they are supportive of democratic life. The inquiry is self-consciously a combination of empirical and normative investigation into the situation of democracy and intellectuals. I believe that they (we) are especially able to address the problems of our political culture, but, in order to do so, we must take them (ourselves) more seriously, facing the unique problems of our day.

Of the problems we face, the poor quality of public discussion in contemporary democracies is a key to my concerns. We, of democratic societies, are experiencing a *deliberation deficit*. It is not that there is no exchange of information. Obviously the opposite is the case. Ours is a world of the electronic superhighway, with huge data banks on matters public and private. But information does not automatically yield informed discussions. We are flooded by discrete facts about everything and everybody, through new and old technologies. Information has become a primary basis of power and wealth, a central characteristic of post-industrial society. The thoughtful consideration of the problems facing democracies by their citizenries and their representatives, though, has become ever harder to sustain. We know very well how to process information, and we are getting better and better at it, but we have an exceedingly difficult time thinking about the information we process, especially with each other. Thus, my sense that intellectuals are important, that they matter. If intellectuals do not provoke serious talk about the problems we face, no one will.

Without such talk, democratic polities function undeliberately. Everyday political practices become strategic campaigns of mass manipulation – a situation all too well known in contemporary democracies. Political programs are formulated to appeal to popular prejudices, both in their form and in their content. They promise something for nothing, and they are presented in easily digestible packages, following made-for-television formulas. The general populus makes political decisions as it chooses brands of soap. Cynicism and confusion seem to be the general rule of the political game from Moscow to Lima, from Milan to Tokyo to Dallas. The intellectual confrontation with cynicism today presents distinctive dilemmas and opportunities, as we will observe in the conclusion of our inquiry.

I will attempt to show in the chapters that follow how intellectuals support democratic society by making it possible to deliberate about specific problems, how they make it possible to go beyond the prevailing political confusions and cynicism. I will resist the theoretical temptation to assign a singular role for intellectuals, good for all places and for all times. What intellectuals do to support democracy, I will maintain, is situationally specific. None the less, I do believe that reasonable sustained consequential discussion about complicated social, political, and cultural problems is a key component of the intellectual's role, particularly as he or she contributes to the constitution of democratic life, and that this discussion is pressingly needed in contemporary democratic societies.

Serious discussion is being marginalized at best, silenced at worst. When repressive regimes reign, the silencing of discussion is commonplace. But often in liberal democratic polities, such as the United States, the free market works toward the same effect, especially as it functions through the electronic media. Commercial television and radio broadcast news sensation and shouting heads.[2] The distinctions between tabloid journalism and serious journalism are becoming ever more difficult to make. Scandal and gossip which arguably are the appropriate fare for the former are becoming staples of purportedly more serious programs. This does not only mean that journalism standards have lowered. It means, as well, that the very notion of such standards is being cast into doubt. The fundamental distinction between news and entertainment is becoming difficult to maintain. And when it comes to broadcast discussions, talk radio has perfected the form of the discursive boxing match. The aims are not to reason and illuminate, but to ridicule and entertain. There are tame talk shows on commercial and public television and radio, and there are distinguished journals of opinion in the so-called print media, not to mention the ancient medium of books. Yet these are becoming marginalized, reaching elite "opinion makers" but apparently not the broad general public.

Such a situation, perhaps, is not all that unusual. It not only is present in the United States, but can be observed world-wide. Indeed, in some sense, it is not even anything particularly new. After all, at the same time that *The New York Times* was developed as a newspaper of record (at the close of the nineteenth century), yellow journalism was perfected as a popular form, and the great French treatises of the enlightenment appeared at the same time that the low literature of Grub Street developed (in the second half of the eighteenth century). Popular entertainments are always more prevalent, refined arguments always more restricted in their appeal. Yet, the problem lies with the present uncertain relationship between the entertaining and the serious, and how this uncertainty distorts public deliberations and decisions. One end result is the prevailing mediocrity of political decisions observable world-wide.[3]

Intellectuals can, I believe, provide, as they have provided in the past, a corrective for this kind of situation, contributing an informed critical intelligence in public life. This has been the distinctive role of intellectuals since the times of Socrates, as I will show below. The pressing question is: will they do so in the future? Addressing this question is no simple task. It requires a much clearer understanding of who the intellectual is and what her or his roles are in complex societies: a task I will turn to in the next chapter. It further requires an understanding of the consequences of specific intellectual interventions in different places and on different issues. There was a time when social thinkers could imagine a leadership role and function of intellectuals in society, from Lenin's vanguard of the proletariat to Mannheim's free-floating adjudicator of competing class interests, to Benda's disinterested guardians of truth.[4] Now such accounts are unconvincing, even for those who have adhered to one of these positions until quite recently. With the fall of communism, vanguards have lost their appeal, even to radical revolutionaries such as the Zapatistas of Mexico.[5] With the intellectuals' products, knowledge and cultural imagination becoming the bases of power in post-industrial societies, the notion that the intellectuals do not have interests of their own as do other groups in society is ever more difficult to sustain. And, as for truth as an autonomous force in society, independent from competing narrow interests, in the world of multiculturalism and postmodernism, this seems little more than a quaint claim for privilege. With such rather common generalized starting positions in doubt, an account of the intellectual in democratic society requires careful examination of intellectuals at work in specific contexts, with an understanding that their work and its effects are quite likely to be different in different contexts.

Yet, there are a number of general issues which I think we ought to examine. These issues comprise a common set of sociological problems which intellectuals face at century's end. The most basic among these emanate from the fundamental tensions faced by the intellectual in democratic society.

Intellectuals have a paradoxical status in democratic societies. On the one (enlightened) hand, democracy requires the cultural excellence intellectuals do contribute, their special knowledge, their creative capacities and their communicative skills. On the other hand, the egalitarian one, in democracies intellectuals and their "cultural excellence" are viewed with suspicion. Intellectual position is established through hierarchies of judgment. There is such a thing as a good and a bad argument, a fine and a mediocre piece of work, and intellectual power depends upon such judgment. Yet, democracy inculcates an inherent suspicion of hierarchy as a matter of fundamental principle. This conflict, it seems to me, is an ongoing part of the democratic experience, a central problematic of democratic life, making the intellectual's position in democratic society a perpetually uncertain one. Intellectuals have a love-hate relationship with democracy, and democracy has a love-hate relationship with intellectuals.[6]

On the side of love, or at least mutual dependence: democracy is the rule of the people, and to be a viable form of governance it requires an informed and critical citizenry. Democrats need both the expertise and the normative insights provided by the cultural activities of intellectuals in order to pursue the ideal of wise governance. Further and more importantly, they need the opportunity for public deliberations that intellectual contestation opens. In a democracy, an informed public must be capable of making critical judgments, sometimes about complicated matters. Thus intellectuals should take part in public life, and their fellow citizens, or at least their representatives, ought to be informed about the fruits of intellectual activities. Otherwise, some form of tyranny or oligarchy is likely to be more powerful and pervasive. For, if a democratic polity does not draw upon all the sources of available information and good judgment, it will be weakened. The makers of the American Revolution and Constitution – the founding political elite – clearly adhered to such a republican vision, as Gordon Wood has brilliantly underscored.[7]

But Wood has just as clearly demonstrated the instability of the elite's vision. Democracies may not hate intellectuals, but they are often deeply suspicious of them. The American founders expected a natural aristocracy, an intellectual elite (themselves), to lead in public affairs, replacing the corruption and incompetency of the old hierarchy with a new, i.e. definitely late eighteenth century, sort of meritocracy. Instead, an egalitarian dynamic, described by Tocqueville as a "providential force," overturned both the old hierarchy and the republican dreams of a new, democratically sanctioned one. When push came to shove, the yeoman farmers, mechanics, and craftsmen chose from among themselves, or from among others, people like Andrew Jackson or Martin Van Buren, who most clearly represented their interests, judgments, and prejudices. The democratic tension between enlightened intellectual ideals and egalitarian ideals, then, dates back to at least the early years of the world's oldest democracy, and it has been with us ever since.

For many observers of the American scene, including de Tocqueville, this situation leads to cultural gloom. They fear that since democracy is egalitarian, and culture, as the arts and sciences, is hierarchical, cultural excellence will necessarily be undermined by a democratic ethos. For the more populist minded, the problem is viewed in a mirrored fashion. They worry that an intellectual elite will dominate popular opinion and customs. The sociologist Herbert Gans holds such an opinion,[8] as do (more famously) such conservative political figures as former Vice-President Dan Quayle, William Bennett, and Pat Buchanan. Both left-wing and right-wing populism share a suspicion of intellectual elitism. On the left, where Gans is a very moderate player, such elitism is seen as a force which privileges the privileged, who have a clear interest in the status quo. On the right, the intellectual elite is viewed as a cosmopolitan force which denigrates the common beliefs and folkways of ordinary people.

Intellectuals have tried to face this problem from almost every angle. Some, such as Gans, have adopted the populist position. Others, such as Hilton Kramer on the right[9] but also Irving Howe on the left,[10] have opted for a more elitist position, defending cultural refinement in the face of populist mediocrity. Yet, the intellectual contribution does not end simply with taking sides, and clearly and forcefully articulating one position or the other. Intellectuals contribute to public debate by adding depth to the consideration of the problem. Thus, the American historian Richard Hofstader confronted the problems of populist anti-intellectualism in two of his major books, *Anti-Intellectualism in American Life* and *The*

Paranoid Style in Politics, and the French sociologist Pierre Bourdieu has explored how cultural elitism subverts democracy in his *magnum opus, Distinctions.*[11]

Such scholarly interventions do, though, present problems of their own. Their form restricts their audience. They are, for the most part, accessible only to a highly trained public, those with a high level of literacy and a high degree of training. The clear writings of Hofstader, ironically the anti-populist who has the literary capacity to reach a general audience, as opposed to such technical writings as those of Bourdieu, do have more potential public impact. But this is qualified by national variations. Thus, roughly speaking, the French have a much greater tolerance for theoretical abstraction than do the British or the Americans, epitomized in the post-war period by the intellectual celebrity of Jean-Paul Sartre, while the British value clarity, typified by the work of Orwell, and the Americans go for a more prophetic tone, exemplified by the writings of Walter Lippmann. Clearly, the way intellectuals write and the way the general public reads affect the way intellectuals struggle with populist skepticism and with elitism.

In the following chapters, I will explore this struggle, as it is shaped by public expectations in different places and in different times, and around different issues. But we must realize that beyond the variations are a set of formal similarities, emanating from inherent problems of large-scale complex societies, as their members attempt to communicate with each other. Beyond the tensions intellectuals face in democratic societies which are a result of their paradoxical position, there are the immense problems of mass media and mass culture.

INTELLECTUAL ACTION IN MASS SOCIETY

Whether one is British, French, or American, or of any other post-industrial society, it is striking that the role of the written word has receded as radio, the telephone, and television have become major media for societal communication. There are some indications that literacy may be making a momentary comeback with the increased importance and popularity of the personal computer, but it would seem that any increased importance of writing and reading for the general public will be soon a thing of the past once a new generation of computers with enhanced audio and video capacities are in place.

Whether or not writing and reading make a modest rebound, it is clear that the centrality of the writer as a popular communicator is a thing of the past. No pamphleteers of our day will have the impact of those during the American Revolution. The great twentieth-century novelists have not been the mass entertainers that Dickens and Twain were, and it even seems doubtful that the novelists of the next century will be as central to the popular culture as were Hemingway and Fitzgerald in their day. This presents serious problems for modern intellectuals, who have been best known as writers of a critical temperament.

It can be argued, of course, that this does not automatically spell the end to the intellectual in democracy. Many intellectuals of the past were not primarily writers. Perhaps the greatest of them all, Socrates, did not even leave any written legacy. In nineteenth-century America, public lectures and debate were major forms of intellectual exchange. Therefore, it should not necessarily be alarming that television, radio, and film have become major media of societal communication. It should even be expected that some of our major intellectuals use or appear on these media. The rise of the electronic media does not necessarily spell the end to intellectual life as we have known it.

Yet, there are serious problems which must be addressed. Those, such as Andrew Ross and Stanley Aronowitz, who believe critical intellectual life is sustained by the popular media must face the fact that the way the mass media are organized and the way they function present very significant constraints on public discussion and on the possible activities of critical intellectuals.[12] Public deliberations and intellectual activities have been defined by the powers of the mass media, with sound bites replacing reasoned argument, with successful media manipulation overwhelming principled politics, and with media celebrity confused with famed accomplishment. This has often overpowered critical intellectuals.

Critics of mass culture and mass politics have been concerned with these problems for a long time. The critique of the masses clearly involved at first a conservative response to democratic developments. Ortega y Gasset opens his classic, *The Revolt of the Masses*, with the image of the unwashed suddenly encroaching upon the institutions of civilization.[13] The mere fact that crude "others" were sitting next to the more refined in theaters and other cultural institutions was the source of alarm. Later criticisms of mass society and culture, though, were directed toward something quite different, what I am trying to highlight here as a fundamental problem of the intellectual in contemporary democratic societies. The criticisms of the mass media and of mass culture by thinkers such as Max Horkheimer and Theodor Adorno, Jurgen Habermas and Hannah Arendt, focus not so much on those untutored who took part in public life, but on the constrained organization and the control of publicity operating through the institutions of the mass culture industry.[14]

From the point of view of this inquiry, the mass media present a special problem. Although they do provide the intellectuals with the possibility to reach a broad audience, they make it difficult for intellectuals to speak their own truths clearly and criticize the wrongs they see or advance the rights they can imagine. Given democratic desires to address their works to a general public, intellectuals must use mass media. But these often frustrate their efforts because the media change the meaning of intellectual works in one way or the other, or make it impossible for certain ideas to reach an audience or even be imagined. The logic of media communication often dominates the logic of intellectual criticism.

Before the advent of the mass electronic media, the intellectual, as writer, controlled his or her mode of production to a much greater extent than the intellectual of the media age does. Now, whether in print or on film or on the airwaves, the imperatives of the media constrain what and how things can be addressed to a general public. Consider this as it relates to the pressing problem of the politics of cultural identity, an issue I will explore throughout this investigation.

The relationship between the politics of identity and democracy is extremely complicated. Confronting these complications through the institutions of the mass media is extraordinarily difficult. This is not always the result of bad intentions, although such intentions are sometimes evident, for example in Serbian and Croatian television accounts of inter-ethnic relations when Yugoslavia broke up. In such situations, coarse repressive control rules the air, and identity politics is a cultural war. Short of such war, the identity politics of the mass media ranges from highly constrained speech situations to circuses, this even with the good intentions.

Critical intellectuals, with limited degrees of success, do attempt to resist these constraints and to avoid such circuses, but this is far from easy. It often seems the case that identity politics plus the mass media equals irrationality, not the normal province of intellectuals. They sometimes can be heard, but often only faintly, and their impact on public life is imperceptible. They are overwhelmed by the discourse of the mass media. A prominent American case indicates the depth of the problem.

The relationship between Native Americans and other Americans has been a deeply troubled one, often distorted by romanticism. The stories of Cowboys and Indians and of the old west are an important part of American popular mythology. The ideal movie image of the cowboy, the generic John Wayne, as the rugged individualist, fighting for what he knows is right, against the barbarians, without the support of civilization, for many Americans is the quintessential American hero. In recent years, though, the racism of the myth, along with other explicitly racist imagery, has met disfavor, and Hollywood amends have been attempted. The Cowboy–Indian encounter has turned toward the Indian's favor in the Kevin Costner blockbuster film, *Dances with Wolves*. Costner is a new-age hero, discovering a glorified Indian way of life. The Sioux, with whom he comes to live, are presented as noble savages. They are understood as the very opposite of the white man's image of them, not heathen but in a God-given state of nature, more civilized than the white man. The Sioux are at peace with the world, while the white man aggressively fights against it. No realistic Sioux–white man encounter is presented. The film has no more historical veracity than the old cowboy movies of the past. Instead a new mythology and demonology are represented. The white man is not the lonesome cowboy but the brutalized soldier, straight out of a liberal's image of Vietnam.[15]

In *Dances with Wolves*, white identity is constructed through the reversal of stereotypes. It does contribute to the audience's self-critical awareness, by questioning the old myths and demons, but the difficult confrontation between fundamentally conflicting cultural worlds is avoided. In earlier American movies, white identity and the American way of life were affirmed with the subjugation of the red savage. Human progress, the triumph of individualism and self-governance, and the advance of civilization were melodramatically portrayed in those films. In new-age Hollywood, all of that is denied, also in a melodramatic way. But in turning away from the old stereotypes, new stereotypes of the other are constructed, and the old ideals are left unappreciated.

The dominant social groups of the United States have never figured out how to live with Native Americans in a way that is consistent with the ideals of American democracy and the ideals of the Native Americans. *Dances with Wolves* does not help. It is possible that this is the result of an individual's or group of individuals' failings. In fact, Costner, an established Hollywood star, played the leading role, directed and co-authored the film. Its inadequacies surely are, at least in part, a result of his personal limitations. Yet, in that his failure is far from unprecedented, it cannot be entirely his responsibility. The film addresses racism in a cautious and ultimately racist manner. This is part of a long tradition of Hollywood, dating back to *To Kill a Mockingbird* and *A Gentleman's Agreement* and including more recent work such as *Mississippi Burning* and *The Last of the Mohicans*. Sensitive topics are presented in ways that will not offend. Members of subordinated groups are depicted in non-threatening roles. When they stand out as individuals, they are presented as unblemished heroes, "credits to their race." Hollywood has not gone much beyond the white hat, black hat conventions of the earliest Westerns. Such an approach to commercial film is not a necessity. There are exceptions to the rule; Spike Lee's *Do the Right Thing*, but not his *Malcolm X*, is a striking one, in my judgment. Yet, the rule is an institutionalized fact of life. The marketing concerns of the film industry, together with a relatively narrow set of privileged world-views, make for a severely limited range of cultural expression on the issues of identity politics in Hollywood.

Should we expect something else? Perhaps not. The American film industry lives, after all, according to its name. It is an industry, a big business focused upon a bottom line. Yet, it is most difficult to find a way to reach a broad public where the logic of the bottom line does not operate. Television fictional programming and news also operate within tight financial constraints, as do the newspaper business, and magazine and book publishing. A critical intellectually cogent public discussion of identity issues through any of these faces distorting constraints.

There are, of course, worse incidences of media distortion than *Dances with Wolves*, from the Lindbergh kidnapping to the strange case of O. J. Simpson. Yet, the case of this film is revealing because it is not just a clear instance of media excess. *Dances with Wolves* was a film that attempted to work against stereotype. It did start from a position of intellectual critique. It did attempt to add another dimension to our consideration of the history of the west, questioning our very understanding of what civilization means. But in it, criticism was channeled through a Hollywood form, substituting one canned vision for another.

The media not only dominate public discussion because of their inherent power to reach and inform a broad audience, overshadowing more conventional intellectual activity, they also set limits on the terms of public discussion and the content of discussion. The range of opinion deemed suitable for broadcast becomes the range of opinion opened to the broad general public. There is a kind of mass-media-determined definition of the situation at work: that which appears through the airwaves is real and consequential, that which does not, is not.

The intellectual who wishes to address social problems faces, then, the formal problem of dealing with the issues at hand, through and against the mass media, and the more straightforward substantive task of addressing pressing social, political, economic, and cultural forces. Some, such as Noam Chomsky, would have us believe that there is a simple set of problems facing us here.[16] The mass media and the corporate powers are identical, and therefore "television lies," as it was put in the entirely different context of the shipyards in Poland during the strikes which led to the Solidarity trade union movement. But television lies not only because of the ideological agenda and power of those who control it, whether they are multinational corporations or party elites. The logic of the media, their *modus operandi*, makes "truth telling" very difficult. It necessarily simplifies. It depicts visually with great power, but reasons weakly. And even when it attempts to be non-ideological, its objectivistic form more readily serves power than undermines it.[17] So whatever the issue at hand is, the intellectual must deal with its substance and with the consequences of the mass mediation of the problem. This makes the political engagement of intellectuals a highly problematic one.

INTELLECTUAL ENGAGEMENT AND IDEOLOGY

The obstacles to intellectual engagement come in two general forms. They arise from institutionalized factors of complex societies in a democratic age, as I have indicated thus far: from the strength of the media and its power to limit the public agenda and from the suspicions intellectuals face in democracies; they also are a consequence of the limited capacities and misdirected will of intellectuals themselves. While there is a great deal of resistance to intellectuality in the mass media of democratic societies, potential intellectuals often quit even before they meet resistance. They avoid public engagement as a matter of convenience, or because of a confusion concerning their potential role in society. Many potential intellectuals have misunderstood their relationship with politics. Central to this misunderstanding and to an abdication of intellectual responsibilities, in my judgment, is a confusion of political commitment with ideology.

Some intellectuals over-commit in their ideological engagement, while others attempt to avoid ideology at all costs, turning away from public responsibilities in the name of disinterested science, art, and scholarship. Both in the case of the overly committed, the tendentious partisans, such as those condemned by Julian Benda in his classic *The Treason of the Intellectuals,* and in the case of the scientists, artists, and scholars who believe that they must remain confined in their specialized realm, the intellectual flees from public responsibility. While the ideologist confuses theory with politics,[18] the disengaged intellectual fears such confusion and retreats to insignificance or to apology for the way things are. They both contribute, even if in very different ways, to the "de-intellectualization" of public life. The ideologist imagines that all political problems can be solved with the help of the true theory, i.e. his or her ideology. The disengaged intellectual either imagines that the fruits of science will, in some unforeseeable future, solve political problems in an objective way, or withdraws from general public concerns, acquiescing to the status quo.

I realize I am raising controversial issues here. My position, following the insights of Hannah Arendt, depends upon making a strong distinction between political ideas and principles on the one hand and ideology and its politics of coercion on the other.[19] It is predicated on a conviction that between ideology and indifference there is a possibility of principled critical action. This is not the conventional position. Usually people either imagine that all political ideas are in a sense ideological, or they believe that ideologies are bad ideas associated with a political-intellectual position to which they are opposed. The potential contribution of the intellectual to democratic society becomes apparent, in my judgment, only when we distance ourselves from both of these positions.

I will attempt to show how some intellectuals establish this distance, while others succumb to ideology or to intellectual disengagement. This will be central to my primary goal: to attempt to demonstrate that intellectuals can make a difference in a democracy when they do not succumb to ideology or resign from their public responsibilities.[20] To accomplish this, I should make clear here the distinction I want to draw between the ideological engagement of intellectuals and their political engagement.

Intellectuals with an ideological attitude are always looking for the correct interpretation of history, even of contemporary history. They somehow imagine that, if they get it right, political problems will be resolved. They then can magically unite the past, the present, and the future, as part of a grand narrative, using their "true" understanding. Political action simply involves bringing their discovered truth to the people, whether they are the toiling masses, people of color, or the victims of patriarchy, or for that matter, on the other side of the political spectrum, those with individual initiative, the religiously correct, or the racially and nationally pure. Fascist and communist intellectuals are the archetypes of ideological intellectuals. But intellectuals of the contemporary left and right of less apparent totalitarian ambitions also have made the ideological move. This is observable among market liberals of the former Soviet bloc as well as among self-proclaimed radical democrats in the former free world.[21]

In contrast, there are intellectuals who hold these and other positions who do so in a politically engaged principled fashion and act in very different ways. Politics is understood as being more about persuasion and less about truth. There is no illusion that a correct understanding of history will automatically decide pressing political and social issues. The end of intellectual intervention is to inform public debate and policy decision. There is an awareness that the worlds of intellectual inquiry and political action are separate, though problematically related. Political problems are resolved not when the intellectual comes up with theoretical answers, but through the messy give and take of political conflict, compromise, and consensus. Ideas and interests are understood as not being necessarily correlated.

When we analyze the problem of ideology, we make fine distinctions in order to discern the potential for the successful political engagement of intellectuals. We see how frustrated principled poli-

tical engagement leads to ideological assertiveness and political
inconsequentiality, and how a movement away from ideology leads
to intellectual empowerment and democracy. It is my hope that
while it will become clear that it is a matter of judgment where
principled political engagement ends and ideology begins, it will also
become clear that the consequences of such judgments are great.
They therefore should be debated in public discussions. I further
hope that this inquiry will stimulate such discussions. It is in and
through such discussion that the intellectual plays a key role in
democratic societies.

DISCURSIVE POLITICS: CIVILITY VERSUS SUBVERSION

Yet, public discussion, given the problems inherent to democratic
societies, the problems of the mass media, and the problems of
political engagement, is no easy matter. To address this situation,
critical intellectuals have responded in two alternative ways. Some
have attempted to work through and beyond the mass media,
seeking to create improved public discussions, and others have
attempted to work against or at least apart from them, seeking
alternative public discourses. The hope of the former is that the
central debates can be improved with direct intervention. Intellectual columnists, such as Walter Lippmann in the past and the
numerous page writers of the present, are attempting this sort of
intervention, as are the producers of independent television doc-
umentaries. On the other hand, those who try to constitute
alternative public discourses do so in the hope that new centers of
discussion and insight will compete with the dominant mass-
mediated centers of public discourse, leading toward alternative
grounds of political and social action or toward a challenge to the
common sense of the mass media. Thus, for example, during the
McCarthy period, the alternative intellectual journal *Dissent*
managed to inform a democratic socialist opinion which was neither
a Stalinist nor a McCarthyist apologetic, forming the grounds for an
intellectual New Left and for later progressive social movements
which were not primarily occupied with the problems of communism
and anti-communism. Feminist writing and the writing of African
American intellectuals, often at first on the margins of academic
discourse, have played a similar role in the last twenty years in
opening up the possibility of public discussion and action. They have

changed the way we think about and act on the relationship between gender, race, and public life. We will explore these issues more fully in chapters 8, 9, and 10 below. At this point, it is important to observe that those who work through the established media do so using a mode of discourse which is shaped by the media's requirements, while those who attempt to be apart from dominant media address each other in their own vernacular. The danger of mediated discourse is that it may disallow originality. The danger of the discourse of the alternative public is that it may become accessible only to like-minded marginals.

Both those who seek to improve existing public debate and those who attempt to constitute alternatives do so by utilizing either a strategy of consensus formation, a civil approach, or a strategy of subversion, a rude approach. Those who seek consensus and civility are often at odds with those who seek rudely to subvert what they view as oppressive convention. Some of the most interesting and important intellectual debates have been about this. The conflicts, for example, between advocates of black power, such as Malcolm X, and advocates of the broad integrationist civil rights movement, such as Martin Luther King Jr., were not only about competing political goals.[22] They may even have been primarily conflicts in rhetoric and its ends, with Malcolm seeking to disrupt the propriety which included a deeply entrenched racism, while King attempted to change the normative order so that it would become improper to be overtly racist.

With hindsight, we may appreciate that both the subversion and the newly forged consensus contributed to changes in race relations in America. Yet, in the course of political and intellectual action, those who sought to disrupt the racist order of things viewed the civility of a King worthy of open mockery and distain, and, from the point of view of those who sought to forge a more just normative order through a transformed society wide consensus, the subversive rudeness of a Malcolm was treacherous. Rude disruption opens up the discursive order. It provides the possibility of a voice to the previously silenced. Yet, if there is no commitment to an ongoing discussion, subversive disruption can make discussion impossible. This is not a trivial issue, keeping in mind that these strategies can lead to strongly opposing evaluations of political and cultural developments, and that such evaluations can lead intellectuals and others to ideological excesses, democratic commitments, or political withdrawal. In important ways, democratic prospects lie in the balance. We will see how the relationship between the civil and the subversive defines fields of intellectual contestation, through considerations of the eclipse of the public (chapters 3 and 4) and considerations of confrontations of race (chapters 8 and 9) and gender (chapter 10).

INTELLECTUALS AND THE PROSPECTS FOR DEMOCRACY

I will attempt, then, to show in the following chapters that the way intellectuals are affected by the problems of democratic societies and the way they act or do not act in these societies are still of importance, even with the suspicion of intellectuals in democracies, the immense power of the mass media, and the temptations of ideology. Yet, although I believe that intellectuals play a key role in the ongoing life of democratic societies, it is certainly not the case that the intellectuals in any way make up a new ruling class. I do not want to be misunderstood. Intellectuals are far from the primary agents of history, as the Marxists once imagined the proletariat to be. Indeed, societies seem to be able to do without, ignore, and even repress intellectuals without much immediate observable detrimental effect. China today has been able to introduce radical and successful economic reforms, maintaining a very tight grip on the intellectual critics of the regime, while Russia has been open to intellectual criticism, and threatens to descend into economic and political chaos. America has a long and strong anti-intellectual tradition, while France glorifies its intellectual critics, but France is not, therefore, more (or less) successful as a democracy. And, while intellectuals apparently played a key role in fostering the collapse of communism, throughout the old Soviet bloc, when the old guard was pushed off the political stage, the intellectuals soon followed.

Yet, each of these cases, from contemporary China and Russia, to the French and the American political traditions, to the revolutionary events in East and Central Europe, would have been fundamentally different, and would have developed with less democratic potential, if it were not for the active public intellectuals on the political scene. Indeed, they were fundamentally shaped by intellectual activity. Critical intellectuals opened up public space. In the democracy movement in China and in the pursuit of Glasnost in Russia, they created the first fields for free public action. As a central part of the enlightenment traditions of France and the United States, they formed the great democratic traditions of the modern world. And they created the democratic movements of Eastern and Central Europe. Intellectuals, in each of these cases, helped constitute free public realms for critical speech and action which are a crucial part of democratic political experience. A primary task of this investigation will be to account for this contribution of intellectuals. I will attempt to substantiate the positions taken thus far by portraying the modern intellectual as a distinct social type and by investigating the role characteristics of the intellectual in contemporary societies. I will consider the intellectual as an ideal type and use the ideal type to investigate critically the activities of intellectuals as they face central political problems of our day.

CHAPTER 2

Who are the intellectuals?

Intellectuals are ambiguous characters. In societies with strong democratic traditions, such as the United States, they are the objects of popular and elite suspicions.[1] In societies with stronger aristocratic traditions, such as those of Central Europe, they are often the objects of veneration and high hopes.[2] Yet, despite the attention they often get, it is not at all clear who they actually are, and what they actually do. For my contention that intellectuals play a key role in democratic societies to be persuasive, I must clearly specify who it is I think is playing this important role.

The uncertainty about the intellectual's identity is an important sociological fact. It animates intellectual and anti-intellectual life as they function in societies. Sartre's popularity, his position as a celebrity in post-war France and then in much of the world, was predicated on a vague romanticism about the critical intellectual in battle against the regressive forces of injustice, inauthenticity, and Americanism. George Wallace's popularity as a national figure and Presidential candidate in the late sixties and the seventies, in parallel contrast, was based on a similarly vague paranoia directed against "pointy headed intellectuals" and their bureaucratic bedfellows.

Indeed, even some of the most interesting scholarly accounts for and against intellectuals represent their subject with a great deal of ambiguity and imprecision. Thus, Russell Jacoby's fascinating account of *The Last Intellectuals* makes sense only through the lens of a critical nostalgia for left-wing intellectual giants of previous generations, from Lewis Mumford to Irving Howe.[3] His sense of loss sometimes seems to be primarily a reaction against the present generation's style, breadth, and literary capacities. On the other side of the political spectrum, Paul Johnson directs his anti-intellectual venom against intellectuals, while he reserves for praise "men of letters" who are for him, but not for anyone who does not share his prejudices, clearly of another species.[4] Both Jacoby and Johnson, along with many other observers of the intellectual scene, have a sense of what an intellectual is, derived from a common-sense imagination of the social type and their own political and cultural standards. They do not, though, provide a way of thinking about intellectuals as actors which would help us discern, beyond partisan position, their role in democratic society.

Yet, clear scientific precision is not very helpful either. Attempts to operationalize a definition of the intellectual tend to rob the status of its uniqueness. When we define the intellectual as the user of a particular form of speech, or "discourse," as did Alvin Gouldner, or as those who use ideas and symbols in the pursuit of their careers, as did Seymour Martin Lipset, the special character of the intellectual in modern society is missing.[5] Although Jacoby likes this character and Johnson does not, they agree that it includes much more than a mode of professional employment and even more than the way certain people write and talk with each other.

Jacoby and Johnson, and we their understanding readers, grasp that intellectuals are public figures. Intellectuals seem to know, or at least purport to know, what they are talking about, and they do so in a way that reaches out to those who are not expert. Style, a little out of the ordinary, is connected to an intellectual stance. Bohemia seems to be a natural setting for the intellectual. If not in a bohemian enclave, certainly cities are where intellectuals are most likely to be found. We expect our intellectuals to question the conventional, to lead, as Socrates advised, the examined life. They may be conservative, as were the literary modernist critics of mass society, and they may be progressive, as were Jacoby's heroes, but they are never ordinary in their beliefs and actions.

I have presupposed such an image thus far. I assumed that the reader would realize that I was referring to these sorts of people when I maintained the difficult proposition that intellectuals are key players in the pursuit of democracy. Clearly, I was not simply referring to white-collar workers, clerks, professionals, and scientists. But a proper investigation of the importance of intellectuals in democratic society requires going beyond implicit images and beyond narrow operationalized "scientific" conceptions. We therefore turn in this chapter to a consideration of the intellectual as a sociological figure, positioned in society in specific ways, facing a set of recurring social, political, and cultural problems. The identity and the problematic position of the intellectual, at least in the West, begins with Socrates. I can think of no better way of coming to an understanding of who intellectuals are and the problems they face than returning to his case. Socrates' trial reveals the ideal type of the intellectual.

THE CLASSICAL INTELLECTUAL AND HIS PROBLEMS

Socrates presents the dilemmas of the intellectual and the struggle for cultural autonomy, and illuminates how these dilemmas and this struggle define the intellectual as a social figure.[6] Socrates' trial has enduring significance. He is very much of our world, but distanced from us. His tribulations could have happened yesterday, but they are very hard to perceive and, as is so much that relates to intellectuals, are filled with ambiguity.

Socrates' trial and conviction for corrupting the Athenian youth in some ways were not surprising. He was a difficult figure, who asked difficult questions. He was a man who followed the demands of his intellect no matter where they took him. For him, popular opinion was always suspect, as was common sense. He was a teacher who was hard on his students, the citizens of Athens. He was the sort of person who particularly benefited from the democratic freedoms of Athens, but was relentless in his criticisms of the prevailing order. He radically questioned authority in the most infuriating way. He was a subversive. Although it is not surprising that the established authority had trouble with this, it is stunningly tragic that the polity most known for its cultural refinement and sophistication condemned to death the individual who most clearly represented its distinctive qualities. The episode begs for explanation and has been explained from a multitude of perspectives.

From the point of view of a democratic patriotism, in a sense the egalitarian position, an ethos sympathetic to the concerns of the Athenian citizenry, Socrates got what he deserved.[7] He benefited from the freedoms of Athenian democracy, while he persistently questioned their worth. He openly clashed with the democracy, while he acquiesced to aristocratic tyranny, i.e., during the oligarchic rule of the Four Hundred in 411 BC and of the Thirty in 404 BC. He openly ridiculed the gods of the city, the beliefs and principles of his fellow citizens, while the youth who had studied with him turned against their democratic polity. Indeed, included among his most prized students were the dictator Critias and the treacherous plotter Alcibiades, two of the leading young aristocrats to subvert democracy in 411 and in 404. In that it was only five years before the death of Socrates that the Athenian empire fell and the citizens of the city were terrorized, it is not surprising that a persistent critic of the city's ways was called upon to answer for his seditious positions and his relationship with the internal enemies of the state.

Yet, from the point of view of the refined culture of Athens, the aristocratic elitist view, the surprise is great. For cultivated elitists, those who value most the goods of education and refinement, the trial and execution of Socrates was a profound defeat of excellence at the hands of mediocrity.[8] For such people, who included most of Socrates' famous disciples, the greatness of Athens was best represented by the life of Socrates. He personified the Greek spirit, the ideal of *Paideia*. He pursued truth no matter where it took him. He examined life no matter what the consequences. His city failed him. Athens, the "school of Greece" as Pericles put it, turned against the most striking characteristic of Greek culture for which the city was most famous – its self-conscious awareness and examination of its own problems. The city failed when it turned against its most distinctive identity, and it moved to execute its most prominent critical thinker. Apparently the limits of popular prejudice, the baseness of the *demos*, overwhelmed the accomplishments of the best and the brightest.

There is room, of course, between the simple aristocratic and the simple democratic accounts of Socrates' fate. More sophisticated democrats realize, often through carefully studying the experiences of antiquity, as in the case of the American founders, that the rule of the people requires certain conditions for it to proceed in a favorable way. Primary among these conditions is freedom of expression. Even if Socrates mercilessly criticized the ways of the city and presented his criticism to the young with the intention of turning them away from the ways of their ancestors, there are those democrats who understand that democracy is distinguished from popular tyranny only by tolerating dissenting opinions, even those that question the existence of democracy. Likewise among those with an aristocratic sensibility, there are some who understand that the death of Socrates is a tragedy and not a simple representative defeat of excellence at the hands of the mob. Plato may have imagined a republic ruled by philosopher kings, and he and Socrates may have reasoned that the discipline of Sparta was preferable to the disordered rule of the many in Athens, but there are many of a more moderate aristocratic bent who realize that kings are rarely philosophers and that the excellence of Athens is not separate from its democratic openness.

Critical thinkers, our intellectuals, are needed in democracies, as Socrates was needed in Athens, but they are often hard to take; witness his fate. Democracies are often disorderly and seem to be ruled by the logic of the lowest common denominator, a logic most evident in our mass media, but democracies, nonetheless, support the critical and the unconventional, and the intellectually challenging, with much greater regularity than other regimes; witness Socrates' long career. While he may have faced execution in Athens at the age of seventy, in Sparta he would never have had a chance to corrupt the youth or the chance to have asked his questions for such a long time.

The case of Socrates has a clear sociological dimension. If we can agree that we refer to a character such as Socrates when we imagine a critical intellectual, we are now in a position to clarify more concretely the intellectual's sociological identity. Socrates set himself apart from his fellow citizens on the grounds of his reason, but he did not withdraw from his fellow citizens as he disagreed with them. He, in fact, sought them out, wherever he could find them, and confronted them with telling and disturbing questions. Socrates was in a sense a permanent stranger on his native grounds. Georg Simmel, in his classic sociological essay "The Stranger," observed that the stranger is characterized by his simultaneous presence and absence. The stranger lives in a place and time, but he is not of that place and time, in his own mind and in the mind of others.[9] The case of Socrates reminds us that this is characteristic of the intellectual. He is not a stranger because he is from another place, but because he listens to his critical reason with an abnormal degree of diligence.

In his own defense as reported in Plato's *Apology*, Socrates tells "why he is not like other men" in a typically subtle fashion, explaining "why I am called wise and have such evil fame." He refers to the witness of Chaerephon, described as an early friend of his and of his accusers, a man who unlike Socrates fled the city during the tyranny of the Thirty. Socrates reports that Chaerephon had gone to Delphi and asked the oracle whether there was anyone wiser than Socrates, and the prophet answered that there was no wiser man. Socrates relates this story as a puzzle because, as he reveals, "I know that I have no wisdom, small or large." He then explains his odd position: he knows he is not wise, yet a god, who does not lie, maintained that there is no one wiser. He thus realizes his responsibility to find a wiser man and present the evidence to the oracle. He reports that he followed this strategy and went to a man with a great reputation for wisdom. They engaged in a serious conversation, which revealed that the man really was not wise. Socrates displayed his judgment and earned the hatred of the man and of a few other people who listened to the conversation. Socrates concluded: "Although I do not suppose that either of us knows anything really beautiful and good, I am better off than he is – for he knows nothing, and thinks that he knows; I neither know nor think that I know." In this modest way and with frequent repetition of the experience, Socrates came to know the nature of his wisdom, "wisdom such as may perhaps be attained by man," and he came to earn the hatred of many whom he met.

Socrates knows that he knows nothing. He is always searching and displays a disdain for those who end the search too early. His special knowledge, which man is sometimes capable of, is the knowledge gleaned from careful investigation. Received wisdom and common sense are never taken for granted. Public opinion, what everyone knows, Socrates does not necessarily accept, and this is the basis of his superior philosophical position and the hatred of those who believe that the authority of common opinion should be honored. Socrates defends himself by explaining his position, but this position explains both why he did what he did and why Athens did what it did.

The case of Socrates represents the dilemma of the intellectual in democratic society. The autonomy of the intellectual is a definitive attribute of intellectual identity and is an achievement of democratic society. It is built into the ongoing procedures of democratic life. Free discussion among citizens is required for the rule of citizens to work at all, and it provides opportunity for specialists in discussion, such as Socrates, i.e., the intellectuals. The outcome of free debate yields public decision. But what people commonly decide upon is not necessarily what those who are most dedicated to free inquiry would decide. They may disagree. How their dissent is treated varies. It will be tolerated to some degree, but to what degree is an open question. The great achievement of Athenian democracy is that it tolerated Socrates and then his students for so long. The tragedy of Socrates is that the toleration was not without limits.

Socrates very much lived his life in his city. He talked and reasoned with all sorts of people in all sorts of places. When he was given a choice between exile and execution, he chose the latter. His disciples were quite different. After the death of Socrates, many of them, including Plato, fled the city. When things quieted down, Plato returned and established his academy, an intellectual elite nurtured with a philosophy set apart from ordinary citizens. The academy was in the city as was Socrates, but not of the city in the way of Socrates and the earlier sophists. Plato and his colleagues dealt with the tension between the intellect and the *demos* by withdrawing from the *demos*. Intellectual independence was forged with marvelous results: Greek philosophy reached its zenith, while the tensions between the results of political freedom and cultural freedom were minimized through a separation of philosophy from practical politics. The talk Plato provoked, in contrast to Socrates, was esoteric, cut off from the citizenry.

In more complex societies than Athens, we observe the intellectual who is situated among his compatriots, as was Socrates, and we observe, as well, those who are more distant, in our society also frequently in the academy. What seems to be strikingly unique in modern societies is that the critically engaged intellectual as well as the cloistered one have had regularized and, to some extent, stable roles. Socrates was a self-described gadfly who flourished by the strength of his personality and the power of his intellect. People like him, the modern intellectuals whom Johnson condemns and whom Jacoby mourns, became in modern societies a regular part of the social landscape. This distinctiveness emerges from the actions of intellectuals within the distinctive social formation of modernity.

THE INTELLECTUAL AND MODERNITY

The position of the intellectual is to a certain extent a matter of individual will. It requires a stance of independence in the fashion of Socrates. Yet more is involved than individual character. The intellectual is embedded in a social context, not simply set against a social order. While Socrates' critical disposition is his definitive quality, he acted on this disposition in Athens, a city distinguished by its openness to critical inquiry. He consistently questioned received wisdom in a society that generally accepted such questioning. For much of human history, this acceptance has been particularly noteworthy. With modernity, the exception has become more the rule. With the advance of social differentiation, the expression of competing opinions has increasingly become a normal part of social life. This did not come about simply as a straightforward victory of the intellectual against the powers that be, Galileo versus the Church, but with a significant transformation of the powers, as part of modernization.

In pre-modern societies, the relationships among religious, political, economic, and intellectual life were intimate. There was no strong distinction between the cleric and the intellectual, nor was there a strong distinction between the economic agent and the political actor. The cultural worlds of the arts and the sciences were not clearly set apart from religion. The system of legitimate coercion (the state) was not set apart from the system of production and exchange (the economy). In modern society all this changed. Most strikingly, the state and the economy developed considerable institutionalized autonomy, differentiated from each other and differentiated from religion. With modernity, there is an advance of a division of labor, of societal differentiation. The modern intellectual entered the historical stage with a normal social role in this social environment.

The competing accounts of the emergence of the modern order, of classical and contemporary sociologists, provide different explanations for the emergence of the new kind of differentiated social order, and they provide as well competing diagnoses of the promise and problems of modernity. Karl Marx believed that the complexities of the modern order were ultimately related to the distinctively capitalist mode of production. Max Weber, in contrast, seemed to believe that the modern order was ultimately based on a rational orientation to the world. Georg Simmel thought that the key to the modern order was in its utilization of money as a universal abstract means of exchange, while Emile Durkheim thought that it was social and moral complexity which defined the modern social order. Talcott Parsons, a student of these and other "classical sociologists," tried to develop a highly complex synthesis of their views. In his early work, this gave special attention to the nature of social action. In his middle years, emphasis was placed on the way specific social structures are formed to serve distinctive functions for the overall survival of complex society. And in his later years, the earlier problematics of social action and of structural functionalism were addressed through the framework of systems theory. Niklas Luhmann has developed this mature Parsonian position in his own version of systems theory. In turn, Jurgen Habermas has attempted the most systematic response to their position with his lifeworld critique of systems analysis. All of these thinkers have struggled with defining the distinctive attributes of the modern social order. While their theories conflict on primary as well as on secondary issues, they all agree that the contemporary order of complex societies is highly differentiated in comparison with the societies that have preceded them.[10] The intellectuals' autonomy in modern societies emerges as a part of this societal differentiation.

Intellectuals, as we know them, are relatively recent societal characters, appearing in this context of social differentiation. As a distinct identifiable social group, not as extraordinary individuals such as Socrates, they entered the historical arena in the modern era. In contrast to priests and prophets, they have been distinguished by their separation from religious authority. They are figures of the enlightenment, of modern culture. Intellectuals have been a regular part of the modern scene.

The social differentiation of the sphere of cultural activities is the fundamental ground on which the modern intellectual stands. Recent studies in social history have turned away from this. They have explored in great detail the developing autonomy of the political sphere, i.e., the building of the nation-state, and of the economic sphere, i.e., the development of capitalist economies and work-forces, but they have tended to underplay the significance of the developing autonomy of the cultural sphere of the arts and the sciences.[11] In fact, the developing autonomy of the arts and sciences, the development of the secular arts and of the modern sciences, has long been understood as a definitively modern manifestation: scientific investigation set apart from religious dogma, the movement from morality plays to secular theater, the movement of painting from the church and the palace to the bourgeois home, and so forth. Causation has become particularly a matter of contestation in the recent studies. They have, in my opinion, become stuck in an idealist versus materialist debate. Does the secularized modern outlook foster the economic and political developments, or does the political economy yield the new outlook? I must confess that I am relatively agnostic about these matters, believing that understanding the whole configuration of modernity as it is mutually supportive and in conflict with itself is a much more interesting theoretical problem, with more pressing practical implications.

I believe, therefore, that the central questions about modernity to be addressed are: how is the autonomy of the cultural sphere limited and supported by the autonomy of the political and the economic spheres, and, how does cultural freedom limit the autonomies of the polity and the economy? In more straightforward practical language: how does cultural freedom provide a basis for critique of the practices of the nation-state and of capitalism? And, how do the imperatives of the nation-state and capitalism repress the possibilities of cultural critique? The critical theories of the Frankfurt School, of Adorno, Horkheimer, and Benjamin, were focused on these questions, as is the work of their most brilliant student, Jurgen Habermas.[12] From a radically different perspective, the work of Michel Foucault also addresses these problems, with a pessimistic sense that the critical reasoning which the "Frankfurters" tried to keep alive was part of the problem and not grounds for hope.[13]

With these questions about cultural autonomy and these theoretical traditions in mind, we perceive the intellectual as a key modern figure, socially grounded in the autonomy of the cultural sphere. The intellectual is an agent of the cultural autonomy of modernity. That autonomy is not a given. It must be constituted and reconstituted through the independent actions of intellectuals. These actions often conflict with the powers: economic, political, and cultural. A significant measure of the nature of a particular modern social order is revealed by how this conflict is manifested: from the absolute repression of totalitarianism to the persistent soft constraints of liberalism. In such situations, intellectuals often go beyond their immediate social domain, turning toward a broader public.

THE INTELLECTUAL AND THE PUBLIC

Thus far in attempting to answer the questions raised in this chapter, I have turned to antiquity and the case of Socrates to show that intellectuals are strangers who are "strange" not because they are necessarily from elsewhere, but because they are abnormally diligent in the attention they pay to their critical faculties. I then turned to the central problematic of modernity, social differentiation, to go on to show that in modern complex societies these strangers in our midst have a permanent home. The institutions and practices of autonomous culture, the sciences and the arts, allow for those who are specialists in distinct cultural pursuits, as was Socrates, to get on with their work with general social acceptance, at least in liberal polities. Yet, something is still missing in my sociological portrait of the modern intellectual. The institutions of the arts and sciences may be able to provide a home for figures such as Plato and his academicians, but there are things that Socrates did which are not easily confined to these institutions. Even more to the point, when we think about intellectuals, as did Johnson and Jacoby, we do not have in mind artists and scientists as artists and scientists. We have a sense of something else. As Jean-Paul Sartre once put it: an atomic scientist is not an intellectual when working on atomic physics, but is an intellectual when signing a letter of protest against nuclear arms.[14] He suggests what we know implicitly, that to be an intellectual is to be something other than a technician, an expert, or even a scientist, a scholar, or an artist. Intellectuals are those who use their expertise, their access to special knowledge, and their capacity to manipulate symbols, for broader public purposes. Just as Socrates went out into the agora to do his philosophy, modern intellectuals address themselves to a broad public when they are acting as intellectuals. This way of thinking about intellectuals and politics is an enlightenment legacy, classically addressed in Kant's essay "On Answering the Question, 'What is Enlightenment?'"[15] We should realize that there are two problematic parts in the formulation, the individual critical agent whom we call "the intellectual," and the arena of his or her activity, "the public." Intellectuals ultimately establish their identity in public.

We must recognize that the very possibility of such public address has been problematic. The existence of an independent public sphere has been a matter of historical struggle. In modern society, unlike antiquity, the public developed as a differentiated sphere in social life, structurally distinct from the state, the economy, and the expert professions.[16] As Kant took pains to explain, the free speech of public discussion is set apart from bureaucratic state activities. While individual responsibilities toward authority should be fulfilled, he argued that authority should respect the free exchange of ideas that occurs outside of authoritative relationships. In such a way, the enlightened fruits of free discussion, an informed public opinion, would then inform authority. In complex mass societies, such a relationship between free discussion and public opinion is no simple matter, as we have already observed in the previous chapter. With the development of a culture industry, in publishing, the mass media, and the information industries, it has become increasingly difficult for the free exchange of ideas in public to avoid the constraints of political and economic imperatives. And with the development of expertise and the control of information as bases of power, discussion has all too often been confined to highly restrictive groups. Addressing a general public, drawing upon the special sensibilities of the intellectual life, and overcoming the specific constraints of complex societies raise the question of the active role of the intellectual.

In order to understand more fully who the intellectuals are, we must understand more precisely what roles they play in society. This is not only an empirical issue. It is as well a normative one. When intellectuals specify what their role is, as in the case of Kant, they are in fact formulating a position about what it ought to be. And as they do this, they support or undermine the formation of an independent public; they create or destroy the possibility for other strangers who pay special attention to their critical capacities to flourish; they in fact contribute to or weaken the capacity of a society to deliberate and act democratically. I concede that my account of the intellectual combines empirical generalization and normative concerns, specifically because our understandings of the intellectual's role of the past have reached a dead end.

THE ROLE OF INTELLECTUALS

Concerning the historical role of the intellectuals, there has been great ambivalence among Marxists. They identify the subject of history as the proletarian, not the intellectual. Yet, intellectuals have played major roles in Marxist parties and politics. Marx, Lenin, Stalin, and Mao viciously attacked the duplicity and lack of resolve of intellectuals as servants of capital and, to use a phrase of Althusser, its state ideological apparatus. Yet, these men were in no sense workers. As Paul Johnson has observed, it is even questionable whether Marx ever set foot in a factory. Indeed, the importance Marx ascribed to a "scientific" theory, and its connection with communist politics, gave rise to the concept of a special role for "engaged intellectuals." Lenin developed this into an organizational theory with Party vanguards and democratic centralism, and Lukacs justified the arrangements on the highest philosophic grounds.[17] Intellectuals were often condemned by Marxists (Gramsci is the great exception), but just as often, they dominated Marxist politics. Their publics were manipulated in such a way that they themselves became invisible as intellectuals. Instead they were party leaders, activists, and organizers, or, when they were in power, bureaucrats, censors, and "cultural workers." They devised a theory, an official ideology, which became a substitute for politics, turning the social world into an oppressive intellectual creation, protecting party intellectuals from critical inspection. Of course new critical intellectuals, from liberals to Catholics to Marxist humanists, struggled to articulate opposition.

The starting point for Karl Mannheim's sociology of knowledge, his sociology of intellectuals, was the tension among groups of intellectuals.[18] Mannheim based his account of intellectual activity on a more realistic appraisal of the connection between intellectuals and their publics. According to Mannheim, intellectuals spoke from a variety of societal positions to the interests of a range of classes variably connected to party positions. He recognized what Sartre's aphorism did not: Sartre's scientist-intellectual might just as easily be the pro-bomb Edward Teller as the anti-bomb Robert Oppenheimer. Mannheim, sometimes called "the bourgeois Marx" because of his more even-handed approach, argued that all knowledge was socially grounded, and that all class interests and class-based parties had intellectuals who justified their positions. Although he grappled with these issues with subtlety and sophistication, he tried to overcome the relativistic implications of his position by means of an ultimately unsuccessful notion of relationalism. He proposed that intellectuals could distance themselves from prevailing and limited class positions, and develop a sort of historic compromise among the limited sorts of knowledge available to those with more engaged partisan interests or understandings. Thus, for Mannheim, intellectuals played one of two roles. Normally they expressed, both consciously and unconsciously, the clashing and limited interests and understandings of specific classes. But they could go beyond these by utilizing a sociology of knowledge, drawing upon their understanding of the structures of historical development and the social structure of class and political interests. Intellectuals could then reconcile the variety of interests and develop a more scientific worldview and politics.

Given his trust of the free-floating intellectuals, which had a social grounding specifically located in his cosmopolitan Central European Jewish background, it is not surprising that when Mannheim fled to England he became a strong advocate of rational state planning, i.e., the welfare state. He had started his political-intellectual career as a minor official in the short-lived Béla Kun regime in Hungary, that is, as a Marxist-oriented partisan intellectual. Then he moved to Germany, where he observed the factionalism of liberal democracy and argued for an intellectual synthesis of the partial truths of the factions. When he moved to England, he called for an enlightened rule of experts. Mannheim did not go as far as George Lundberg and earlier social scientists, who really did think science could save us,[19] but his career pointed in the direction of another notion of the role of the intellectual – that of expert technician in a technocracy. Metaphorically speaking, Oppenheimer and Teller were not only intellectuals in their roles as opponent and proponent of nuclear arms; in this older sense, they were intellectuals when working together on the building of the world's first atomic bomb.

Much of present-day policy research follows this position. The public for the work of "intellectuals" is the government, an agency, a foundation, or a corporation. The so-called intellectual is commissioned to do a feasibility study or develop a program to solve a social problem. What such studies have in common is that the fundamental parameters of inquiry are defined by someone other than the intellectual. His or her public is the powers.

I realize I am now stretching my argument. Government experts and policy scientists rarely consider themselves intellectuals, nor do many observers consider them so. Indeed, since the enlightenment, a distinction has been made between intellectual activity and state service. This has led to expert disdain for the intellectual. Expert wisdom suggests that "intellectuals are people who speak a great deal on matters about which they know little."[20] Apparently taking Sartre quite seriously, this position implies that scientists should keep to physics, both Oppenheimer and Teller. Kant would agree. He underscored that the enlightened critical thinker, in league with other enlightened critical thinkers, should engage in public debate apart from his or her official capacities. One is not an intellectual when one's activity is defined by the state.

Yet, it must be recognized that the divide between an independent public sphere and the state is not always easily drawn, and the alternative intellectual roles discussed thus far – partisan, detached, and expert intellectuals – blend into one another in any individual career (like Mannheim's) or any intellectual profession, especially in the social sciences. The roles are the subject matter of the sociological literature on intellectuals, a literature which strangely overlooks a major achievement and promise of modernity, to wit, democracy. The partisan intellectual argues for a party position, often as an ideologist in the name of a "superior" theory, archetypically Marxism. The detached intellectual, in the name of a superior objective understanding, promises a resolution of political conflict through scientific means. The expert promises to substitute science for political conflicts and deliberations. Oddly, public deliberation and the rule of the people are absent from these accounts.

I am pointing to two problems: the inadequate self-understanding of intellectuals regarding their role in society; and the same misunderstanding on the part of professional observers regarding the intellectual world. All the discussion of intellectuals as the new class, whether it is viewed with hope (e.g., in some of the work of Alvin Gouldner) or with dismay (e.g., in Konrad and Szelenyi on Eastern Europe), sees the intellectual project as that of legislation, as Zygmunt Bauman has put it.[21] Bauman maintains that with postmodernity comes the new role of interpretation, which he seems to understand as being a diminished task. I believe, to the contrary, that the new task is neither new nor less preferable to legislation, and it involves a lot more than interpretation. We observe it in the life of Socrates, and we can observe it in our own times. It is most apparent among intellectuals who seek to support democracy.

It is at this point that the special role of the intellectual to foster deliberation in democratic society becomes clear. The democratic intellectual addresses the paradox of democracy and culture, between democracy's egalitarianism and culture's hierarchy. Seen from this point of view, partisan, detached, and expert intellectuals have mistakenly come down strongly on the side of hierarchy rather than democracy. What appears to be simply a description of a social role is, in fact, an anti-democratic political stance. For anti-democrats, such as Socrates and Plato, this would not be a problem. In our democratic age, it is. The vanguard Marxist claims a superior knowledge based on Marxism's special insights into history's subject, the proletariat. The more open, detached intellectual claims special knowledge based on his or her power of scientific synthesis, and the policy expert makes similar claims for his or her objective science. Missing from each of these positions is an appreciation of the intellectual's contribution to democratic deliberations.

Thus, for example, James Coleman in his presidential address to the American Sociological Association, in 1992, called for the scientific reconstruction of the microstructure of society, based upon his careful objective appraisal that the family is no longer functional.[22] When I heard Coleman's address, I happened to be reading Paul Johnson's *Intellectuals*. Although I was in strong disagreement with much of Johnson's book (which condemns modern intellectuals for their secular immorality), I found his observations about the impracticality of intellectuals strangely applicable to Coleman's proposal. His cost benefit analysis of the family seemed to be oddly lacking in common sense, and practically deaf to the moral and ethical concerns voiced by ordinary people, about both the relationship between generations and the relationship between genders. These issues are highly politicized and problematic, and cannot be resolved by social engineers. And intellectuals, either as feminist social theorists or as policy analysts, should not claim a special knowledge for their resolution.

Yet, such intellectuals will no doubt not be silent, as the life and death of Socrates demonstrated. They will speak as clearly and forcefully as they can. Free and often contentious public discussion is what intellectual life is all about, and this is good for both culture and democracy. A key intellectual role in democracy, the role I will examine in the remainder of this study, then, is talk. Talk is what Socrates literally did with his life, and stimulating informed talk, public deliberation in an age of information, is what intellectuals, in contrast to professionals, can contribute to the public good.

Caution at this point is in order. In a certain sense, "talk is cheap." As deficits rise, as international conflicts escalate, as economies go from bad to worse, intellectuals drone on, substituting their apparently meaningless and empty debates for substantive action. Democracies seem to bog down in endless discussion, satisfying to the speakers' egos, perhaps, but basically an excuse for inaction. And yet, I still maintain that talk is the lifeblood of the democratic body politic. Political problems do exist between people, and the only way they can be identified, let alone addressed, is with talk; the more the better.

The *cheapness* of talk is most apparent when polities need to address technical problems, for example the building of a telecommunications system, and they talk about it instead of facilitating the problem's resolution. Talk's *preciousness* is most apparent when misunderstandings or conflicting interests exist between significant parts of the population, for in a democracy, the only way these conflicting interests can be adequately resolved, and these misunderstandings overcome, is through free and open discussion.[23] This is why free speech is a crucial basis for democratic politics, despite the fact that free speech is often foolish speech. And this is why I believe that intellectuals are crucial actors in democratic societies.

The communist experience further indicates that free speech is not a luxury of rich liberal democracies. Together with the absence of a free market and free democratic decision making, the limits on free speech deprived communist society of the information about itself which is necessary in complex economic, political, and social life. Without free speech, technical as well as normative problems cannot be addressed efficiently. Complex society needs free speech a great deal.

Despite its importance, free public discussion does not come easily. Although the offices of the government censor can be closed without much problem, i.e. where the prevailing powers choose to do this, unofficial limits persist on the free exchange of ideas and opinions, especially about society's most troublesome dilemmas. In Poland, for example, people with different opinions about the proper relationships among Church, state, and nation may have a hard time engaging one another with mutual respect and toleration. A law, passed after the fall of communism, which officially codified the proper morality for the mass media clearly did not help, threatening to substitute censorship by the Church for the previous censorship by the communists. But talking about sensitive problems is never easy, even without such blunders. Americans, as another example, have been trying to talk about race with many failures and despite periodic, but limited, successes.

When these issues are kept in the foreground, it becomes clear that a major role of the intellectual in democratic society is to encourage free discussion about difficult issues. Intellectuals, no doubt, do serve as expert advisors, sometimes with great insight;

take, for example, James Coleman's studies on education.[24] But their expert opinion ideally begins political discussion, or sustains it in a more informed fashion; it does not end it. (If it does, the political order would be better defined as a technocracy rather than a democracy.) Nor does their reasoned partisan positioning end all political contest, whether they identify with liberals, conservatives, or radicals. Rather, it directs debate. And attempts to resolve debate through comparison, generalization, and synthesis, as in Mannheim's relationalism,[25] at best resets the terms of discussion and contest. Generally, the tensions between egalitarian democracy and hierarchical culture are only momentarily resolved in public deliberations, decision making, and action.

THE INTELLECTUAL DOES NOT EQUAL THE IDEOLOGUE

We are now in a position to answer directly the question posed in this chapter. *The intellectuals are special kinds of strangers, who pay special attention to their critical faculties, who act autonomously of the centers of power and address a general public, playing the specialized role in democratic societies of fostering informed discussion about pressing societal issues.* We have come to this approach to the intellectual by considering: the classical position of the intellectual and the contribution of sociology to understanding the structural situation of the intellectual in modern society; the intellectual as stranger and as an agent in differentiated society, with a special relationship to the public. I have drawn upon the contributions of sociology to understand this structural situation and to present an understanding of the relation of the intellectual to the public. In the next two chapters, we will consider the question of the public more intensively, but before doing so, I should more directly address the issue of why I think the present approach to the intellectual in democratic society is the most fruitful one.

In attempting to be true to the complexity of history and the complexity of our times, we must recognize that people who have been called intellectuals have played a wide variety of social roles in a wide variety of places and times, with results that have not been always desirable. They certainly have not all been primarily talk provokers, as advocated here. They have not all been, perhaps even most have not been, agents of democracy. As intellectuals have dreamt of the wonders of freedom and enlightenment, of democracy and science, and have addressed, in the mode of Kant, the major problems of their day, they have been key political and cultural agents of the horrors of this century: the totalitarianisms of the left and the right, the genocides of Europe, Asia, and Africa. They also have been among the heroic resisters of twentieth-century horrors. The present approach to the intellectual role is formulated in such a way so that we can understand the intellectual's role as he or she avoids the totalitarian tendency. We are seeking to understand the distinctively democratic role of intellectuals as they avoid the pitfalls of ideology and totalitarian temptations.

We inherit understandings of the intellectuals, roles that are implicated in ideological excesses. They are variations on the theme of the intellectual as the bearer of truth, the intellectual as the philosopher king. The theme comes in heavy and light versions. "Totalitarian heavy" has the intellectual as the vanguardist, the ideologically partisan intellectual. Armed with the truth of history or biology, of communism and anti-communism, of religious revelation or scientific fact, the totalitarian intellectual is willing to exact incredible suffering in the here and now, rationalized by a vision of an idealized future. Hannah Arendt analyzed the horrors wrought by the totalitarian ideologist with telling cogency in her classic work, *The Origins of Totalitarianism*. Here, I am trying to map out the intellectual alternative. I am seeking to portray the kind of intellectual that Arendt and many like her have been, as they have sought to broaden our understanding and our capacity to talk about the problems we face as democratic citizens.

The immediate objects of Arendt's critique were the vanguardist ideologues of totalitarian parties, a group which has receded from the public stage in recent years. But the way we usually think about intellectuals still often is grounded in vanguardist notions or in oppositions to vanguardism which include the mark of the object of critique, i.e. "totalitarian elite."

From the point of view of the political left and the right, politically engaged intellectuals are labeled as ideological, for either critical or apologetic reasons. On the left, the ideology is in the ideas that support the status quo. This takes the form of actively apologetic rationalizations for the way things are and of practical supports for the prevailing way of doing things. Thus, from the point of view of a critical left, both the technical intellectuals and the more theoretical justifiers of the way things are, i.e. both the reformist liberals and the conservatives, are represented as ideologists. For the right, all who dare to question radically the existing order of things are similarly labeled as ideological. Their denial that the way things are is the way they pretty much must be is viewed as being irrational.[26] The primary object of ideological critique of the right is that of Marxism and things that seem to be associated with Marxism and its history. This takes on the form of criticisms of past practices and ideas, that, for example, retrospectively Rousseau and Plato are often labeled as precursors of totalitarian ideologists. It also comes in the form of prognosis. Thus, the intellectual who questions the logic of the market is viewed as being ideological. For the left, in contrast, the ideological is in the positive connection political ideas have with the prevailing political order. But both the left and the right share, nonetheless, a fundamental approach: political ideas are reduced to their apparent social consequences. The ideas of intellectuals and their identity are judged as they serve social functions of promoting or inhibiting social change.

But when all intellectual ideas about public life are identified as being ideological, the role of the intellectual is identified as being that of an ideologue, for better and for worse. This is a variation on the themes of Marx and Mannheim. The problem with this position, from the point of view of the present inquiry, is that it makes the distinction between ideologist and any other intellectual role difficult to perceive. Viewing intellectuals as ideologists makes it difficult to see that the heirs of Socrates are not just a variety of philosopher kings, each peddling his or her particular philosophy. Plato is not Socrates' only student. The idea of the intellectual as an agent of deliberation seeks to present an alternative to this closed state of affairs. Put another way, I am proposing here an approach to the intellectual which considers the role of the intellectual when ideology again ends, but this time including "the end of ideology" ideology of the fifties and sixties.[27]

Often in those debates the proponents of the end of ideology presented alternative notions of the intellectual and his or her responsibilities, while they condemned the ideologists. They sought to substitute the expert and technician for the ideologue, the ideal of detachment for that of commitment.[28] Ideology was something of a holdover, to be expected in the developing world, but in retreat in the truly modern social orders. The alternative to ideology was technocracy.[29] It was overlooked that not all political ideas are ideologies, and that the grounds for fundamental complaint and contestation, for social criticism, have not disappeared with the defeat of Nazism, and the failures of actually existing socialism. They presented a critique of the intellectual as ideologue, but could only imagine the expert as the alternative. When the young intellectuals of the New Left provoked the cultural and political explosions of the sixties, the limitations of the end of ideology position became strikingly apparent. Young intellectuals supported the development of new social movements: the civil rights movement, the anti-war movement, the feminist movement, and the ecology movement among others in the West. These experiences suggest that there was and is a need for a conception of the intellectual that involves something different from both that of an expert and that of an ideologist.

This has led to the notion that the intellectual serves as the voice of social movements, that the role of the intellectual is to have an organic relationship with critical social forces which question the existing order of things, to clarify the position of these forces, give clear articulation of their true vision. Such an outlook, drawing from the reflections of Gramsci, has been most forcefully presented by Edward Said in recent years, whose work will be carefully reviewed below (chapter 4). Alberto Melucci, a major theorist of the new social movements, explains the limitations of viewing intellectuals as organic agents of social movements, when he observes: "intellectuals who claim to represent the good conscience or the true ideology of a movement have always participated in preparing the way for the advent of the Prince, only to end up as either his victims or his courtiers."[30] Said goes through extensive critical analysis of policy intellectuals, expressing open disdain for them as servants of the powers. He and others who understand the role of the intellectual as that of expressing the insights and articulating the voice of critical social movements, opt instead for alternative powers, of the so-called subaltern, failing to see that theirs is still the position of the philosopher king.[31] It still involves the presentation of historical truth to the masses. Without power, it does not replicate totalitarianism, and with the commitment to perpetual critique, to an attitude that the role of the intellectual is to always question, its potential for the justification of or subjugation by tyranny may be avoided.[32] Nonetheless, the connection between the intellectual and democracy is not made directly.

I suggest that key to that connection is deliberation in public. The characterization of the intellectual presented in this chapter points us to a consideration of the turn to the public in modern society. We now follow this path of inquiry as it was explored by two of the great American intellectuals of the first half of the twentieth century, as they debated the relationship between the intellectual and the public, seeking a new civility for the complex society of the twentieth century.

CHAPTER 3

The civil intellectual and the public

Although it is natural for intellectuals to turn to the public, this does not come easily in modern democracies. The close interaction between the intellectual and his or her audience, as revealed in the case of Socrates, is replaced by distanced industrial and post-industrial processes: mass communications, public relations, the mass media, the cultural industry. In one sense, this is a very democratic development; mass culture includes more people in intellectual exchange. The political commentators on talk radio and television present their criticism to a much broader audience than classic intellectual writers, from Zola to Sartre, ever did. Yet, something is missing in this democratic development.[1] While the new forms of public exchange are more democratic in that they are more inclusive, they are less democratic in that they are less participatory, less deliberative, and more manipulative. Democracy's self-rule of the people comes up short on the self and strong on the rule.

Some, such as those of the realist school of democracy, from Joseph Schumpeter to Robert Dahl, view this turn as inevitable. They understand that democracy can practically function in complex societies of the twentieth century only through a politics of elite competition and action, with the "people" taking a necessarily passive role. It is argued that the institutions of modern democracy necessarily should distance the citizenry from the actual practices of governance and policy debate. Officials are elected through free and fair elections. They rule. Democracy is defined as polyarchy.[2]

There is much to recommend this position. By considering democracy as it can be realized, it presents a practical alternative to modern tyranny. The pursuit of more ideal forms of democracy, with more direct forms of participation, it is cogently pointed out, has all too often led to tyrannical excesses or extreme inefficiencies.

The problem with the realist position, though, when it is applied to the situation of intellectuals and the public, is that it apparently takes the public out of the democratic game. Democracy becomes an elite enterprise. Consequential public discussion appears to include the policy considerations of the governing elite on the one hand, and mass manipulation on the other. When the intellectual stays within the circles of authority, the autonomy of the intellectual from the powers is open to serious question. Intellectuals in such a situation may influence the powers that be, but their standing, independent of the powers, is then uncertain, as is the standing of democracy. Yet, from the point of view of realism, there is the question as to whether there is an alternative, whether the intellectual can play a positive role beyond the governing circles in highly complex political systems.

These are issues that intellectuals face both theoretically and actively. Intellectuals find themselves situated between the ideals of democracy and elitist realism. They must conceive of themselves and democratic practice in such a way that the competing claims of the quality of cultural criticism and egalitarian ideals are addressed. In the United States, this has been the pressing concern of some of our leading intellectual figures. John Dewey and Walter Lippmann, two of the most prominent public American intellectuals of the first part of the twentieth century, have confronted the complexities of the relationship between intellectuals and the democratic public, both in their writings and in the way they acted: Dewey as a major academic philosopher, Lippmann as a renowned journalist. Dewey and Lippmann directly engaged each other in their published work. They wrote about the problems of our public life before the cold war and its aftermath. Yet, they addressed the problems in such a way that they seem to speak to us directly. They attempted to constitute informed democratic publics in the way they conducted their careers and formulated their social commentaries and criticisms. They attempted to be true to the ideals of democracy and realistic in the pursuit of their particular political and intellectual aims. We turn to a consideration of their major works on the problem of democratic culture as a way of investigating the complex relationship between intellectuals and the democratic public.[3]

By considering their works, we will observe intellectuals attempting to conceive of a civilized way to address the social problems of a complex society. They do so both in the substantive diagnosis of their times and in their dialogue. We will discover that the positions of Dewey and Lippmann are each wanting, but that the tension between the positions they mapped out reveals the dilemmas with which the democratic intellectual must work. Dewey's criticisms of Lippmann and Lippmann's criticisms of Dewey will be taken seriously. Although they are arguing opposing positions, I maintain that they are both right in their critical thrust. The discursive intellectual struggles to overcome the limitations of the elitist critique of the democratic position and the democratic critique of the elitist position. In their life and in their work, they point to an alternative to the ideologue. In their debate, the limits of the position of the expert also become apparent, as do, unintentionally, the limits of civility.

Walter Lippmann was one of the first modern pundits.[4] He was of the chattering class, a relatively conservative voice from "inside the beltway." He was a man of great erudition and contradiction. He started his political career as a founding member of the Harvard Socialist Club. For the bulk of his life, he interpreted current affairs for the popular press in the voice of a refined elitist, while at the same time he wrote books showing that the masses were incapable of making critical judgments. He was a Jew who understood all too well the anti-semitism of Hitler and the anti-Jewish quotas at Harvard. He was a man of the establishment, but he closed his career as an opponent of the establishment's follies in Vietnam, supporting the anti-war movement. He wrote elegantly, in a clear, accessible voice, the position of an unembarrassed elitist. When it came to the role of the public in democratic cultural life, Lippmann was a super-realist.

John Dewey was Lippmann's opposite.[5] He was a populist professor, a scientist with anti-elitist views, a democrat who wrote opaquely, but for the popular audience. His politics were highly idealistic and radical, while his philosophy was highly realistic and practical. His was a theoretical position which had been criticized in Europe for its justification of capitalism and the life of the cash nexus, while he was, in fact, on the socialist fringe of the American political consensus. He was a man of the academy, who took clear public positions, who had his greatest impact on the theories and practices of primary and secondary education. He was a radical democrat. He believed that the only answer to the problems of democracies took the form of more democracy, including the increased participation of the public in political life.

Lippmann and Dewey were intellectual giants, who had related and competing intellectual concerns. Their lives and their works tell a great deal about democracy and the intellectual, and their relationship in deliberation. Each addressed the problems of the intellectual in mass society and the intellectuals' ambivalent and ambiguous confrontation with the democratic public. They were both in their ways democrats, but their ways were opposites, and this they confronted. Neither was an ideologue. Two of their major works, Lippmann's *Public Opinion* and Dewey's *The Public and its Problems*, actively engage each other, considering directly the problems of the intellectuals and the democratic public.[6] Dewey's book can be read as a direct response to Lippmann's. Their inquiries, for all their differences, highlight together the centrality of public opinion in the life of democracies and the troubled relationship intellectuals have with public opinion. They further deal with the central problem of leadership and the intellectual's relationship to it in a democracy.

LIPPMANN'S PUBLIC OPINION

Public Opinion is a deeply pessimistic work. It builds on Lippmann's experience as an anti-war activist, who converted to the Wilsonian cause of making "the world safe for democracy," joined the government effort, and observed directly the manipulation of war propaganda and the cynicism of the Versailles Treaty. Lippmann became a democrat of the realist school. He learned his realism before, during, and after the First World War. He began his public life as a socialist idealist. His practical experiences led him to become convinced that even eighteenth-century ideals of liberal democracy were impractical. Rule of the people had become rule by the manipulators of the people, utilizing the people's emotional response to public affairs. It concerned him when he saw the lies of the official propaganda become the basis of public policy. This undermined not only the ideals of democracy, but also, in Lippmann's judgment more significantly, the effectiveness of democratic rule. In *Public Opinion*, Lippmann goes beyond his personal experiences to offer a full critique of democracy as a responsible form of governance, at the same time that he is trying to support the institutions of an actually existing democratic polity.

Lippmann's critique is based on what he takes to be an advanced understanding of political psychology. He observes that the individual acts "not on the basis of direct and certain knowledge, but on pictures made by himself or given to him." This opens the field to propaganda which is the "effort to alter the picture to which men respond, to substitute one social pattern for another" (p.16). Propaganda compromises our capacity to understand and to take part in public affairs and diminishes the power of public opinion. Ideally, public opinion is the force behind or, more precisely, the empowering agency of democratic governance. But when public opinion is informed by concerted distortions of public affairs, democracy is undermined and made less effective. Democracy becomes a mere appearance. The real form of governance is mass manipulation. Such a democracy, as mass manipulation, is also empowered by ignorance, not intelligence. This is Lippmann's greatest concern.

Lippmann's frustrated idealism, an idealism which has just about been destroyed in our political world, is striking. The raw manipulation of information by those in authority appears as scandalous only to those who do not take it to be a normal matter. Since his day, we have become much more accustomed to official secrets and official deceptions. Lippmann's thinking is influenced by the implications of official distortions and deceits, in a way that we in our cynicism are not so influenced. His offended idealism leads him to wonder about the viability of democracy. He becomes deeply concerned that "democracy in its original form never seriously faced the problem which arises because the pictures inside people's heads do not automatically correspond to the world outside" (p.19).

He observes the problem as it is strikingly manifested in modern times. The politically relevant environment goes well beyond the circles of social life which are immediately observable to any one individual. People become dependent upon false sources of information, emerging from manipulated stereotypes, and make their decisions poorly. What becomes important for the aspiring political leader is not an ability to deal with the problems of the day in their complexity, but the capacity to present the problems in a simple way so the public may become convinced that it is able to understand them. Leaders become those who are expert in simplifying public relations procedures, rather than those who face political problems as they actually are.[7] Given the limited amount of time and attention people give to public affairs, such simplification is a necessity, but it leads away from the confrontation with societal problems. Lippmann perceives the dimensions of the problem as a modern development, but he realizes, as well, that the problem is far from being entirely a new one. The viability of democracy itself is at issue.

Thus, for Lippmann, the founders of the American republic are considered as mistaken political theorists. They did not adequately take into account the limited understanding the people had of their political environment. In their classical democratic theory, it is assumed that public opinion "constitutes a moral judgement on a group of facts." Lippmann maintains, in contrast, that it is instead "a moralized and codified version of the facts," given the "present state of education" (pp. 81–2). With the general public poorly educated about public affairs, public opinion can not be the basis for the public good.

The founders also did not understand the problematic nature of leadership, according to Lippmann. He criticizes Hamilton for believing that the natural leaders were the merchants and professionals, and Jefferson for believing that leadership was to be found naturally among the planters and farmers (and even perhaps among all the people) (pp. 163–4). Theirs was a position that placed faith in specific social classes or groupings, without adequately considering the functional requirements of leadership. They based their positions more on faith than on clear political and social analysis, a position much more prevalent in Lippmann's day among those who placed their faith in the proletariat, the peasantry, or even the middle class. For Lippmann, the central problem was not being confronted: who has the knowledge to lead?

Both leadership and public opinion, then, were not properly understood or addressed by democrats. They substituted democratic dogmas for proper analysis. Lippmann radically questions these dogmas (p. 158). Public opinion, in his judgment, is not the fountain of informed common sense, but a polluted reservoir of popular prejudice. Leadership is not the automatic attribute of the common man or of a natural aristocracy, but requires knowledge and skills. In the tension that exists between the hierarchies of intellectual life and the egalitarianism of democracy, Lippmann comes down strongly on the side of intellectual hierarchy.

This is the framework for Lippmann's critical analysis of the cultural and political practices of his day. It leads him to a critique of the manipulation of interests in mass society, and to an understanding that the presentation of common interests is always an articulation of enlightened leadership. It leads him, further, to criticize

Fabian socialist alternatives (his own youthful political faith), because they conflate the problem of selfishness with problems of leadership and misinformed opinion, and do not take into account the funda-mental problems of public opinion and the necessary distance between the leaders and the led (pp. 185–94). He is convinced that no popular institution, no institution that is distinctively democratic, is capable of resolving the dual problem of misinformed public opinion and manipulative unenlightened leadership, not even the press, his own avenue of public action. He clearly doubts the press' capacity to help organize and inform public opinion, asserting that the press reflects and intensifies "the defective organization of public opinion ... Public opinion must be organized for the press for it to be sound," not by the press (p.19).

For an answer to the problems of democratic public life, he consciously goes beyond the democratic arena, turning to the sphere of scientific expertise. His, in the final analysis, is a technocratic faith – "the key inventions have been made to bring the unseen world into the field of judgment" (p. 165). He hopes that the present state of knowledge can be brought to the amateur for his or her judgment (p. 166). For Lippmann, like the later critics of ideology, there is a stark alternative: tyranny or expertise (p. 184). He invests hope in what he calls (for us at the end of the century quite ironically) "intelligence work." It is disinterested expertise which will save democracy from its fundamental problems.

In the tension that exists between democracy and intellectual expertise, Lippmann comes down strongly on the side of expertise. His faith in science may seem quaint to us. He hopes that by "interposing some form of expertness between the private citizen and the vast environment in which he is entangled" the problems of democracy can be overcome (p. 238). He wants the social scientist to be in the middle of all policy decisions, at every point minimizing the negative consequences of public opinion. He proposes that experts be connected to each branch of government to control the negative consequences of democracy, both those deriving from poor political leadership and those deriving from poorly informed public opinion. Only in this way will the complicated realities of the social world, and not just the simplified stereotypes of public discourse, be central to political decisions. As with Alexander Hamilton, his classical American hero, Lippmann is primarily concerned with the ineffectiveness of government. Unlike Hamilton and the other founders of the American republic, he views the ignorance of both the political elite and the political mass, of the leaders and the led, to be the chief threat to a good political order. This is his equivalent of the classical American enemies of liberty: "love of luxury" or "the rule of the rabble." His answer to the problems of democracy is, then, to be found in the authority of science.

DEWEY'S PUBLIC AND ITS PROBLEMS

Dewey also turns to this authority, but he does so in support of democracy, not as a protection against it. Dewey does recognize that there is a problem; however he investigates it not by considering how the public has been compromised, but by trying to investigate what a public actually is, how it is formed and informed, and how it may be reformed. He starts with a pragmatic social psychology, in direct opposition to Lippmann's political psychology.

Dewey opens his book on an anti-metaphysical and anti-foundationalist note. He maintains that political facts do not exist outside the minds of citizens, and that ideas about public philosophy are not properly understood outside of the facts. His explicit task in the opening passages is to lay the groundwork for a careful interactive understanding of the public that avoids the conventional wisdoms of political philosophy. "We must in any case start from acts which are performed, not by hypothetical causes for those acts" (p. 12). Thus, he does not examine competing theories of the state and its functions, but instead observes what it is that people do together in making a public life. He observes:

The public consists of all those who are affected by the indirect consequences of transactions to such an extent that it is deemed necessary to have those consequences systematically cared for. Officials are those who look out for and take care of the interests thus affected. Since those who are affected are not direct participants in the transactions in question, it is necessary that certain persons be set apart to represent them, and see to it that their interests are conserved and protected. The sources involved in the performance of this office are *res publica*, the common-wealth. (pp. 15–16)

He presents this set of definitions to underscore that the public and the state are made up of concrete persons (interacting in specific ways) not a separate "collective impersonal will" (p. 19).

While Lippmann starts with the individual's incapacity to understand the complexities of the greater political world from his

or her parochial position, Dewey tries to demonstrate that there
are only parochial positions. They constitute, and reconstitute in
interaction, the greater social world. That human beings associate
is his starting proposition (p. 23). Large-scale social institutions,
such as the state, are but instances of human interaction. From
Lippmann's assumption that the problem of the public is a
consequence of individual incapacity, it follows that the solution to
the problem will be found in overcoming the incapacity. He
proposes the intervention of the expert. Dewey, in contrast, sees
the problem in the breakdown in the relationship among associational activities, between primary group activities and those of the
large scale democratic state.

Dewey understands that the democratic state is a modern development. It is an outgrowth of industrial society, which makes it
possible for the public to be conscious of its existence as a public and
organizes itself to secure and protect its interests (pp. 76–7). The
democratic state emerges as the "great society" (the large-scale
industrial society) and strengthens the state and the individual at the
expense of the intermediate associations (p. 98). Yet, large-scale
industrial regimes are still dependent upon associations in myriad
ways for "wants, tools, materials, purposes, techniques and abilities"
(p. 105). He presents a kind of dialectic of industrial development
(pp. 106–9), which leads to "the eclipse of the public."

He tells the story of the eclipse of the public in America.
Technology plus community equals democracy, but the technological
side of things, linked with the concentration of wealth, overwhelms
the associational base of American democracy (pp. 110–42). Public
institutions both are based on local practices and exist in a functional
continental system (p.113). The demands of the functional system
undermine the associational grounds of the institutions, thus weak-
ening the system. Citing Lippmann, Dewey observes that the public
is therefore lost and bewildered (pp. 116–17). But Dewey's explanation for the situation is a strikingly different one. While Lippmann
takes public ignorance to be the natural course of events, seeing the
extreme manifestation of public ignorance in his own times as
indicating that such a problem represents a major challenge to
democratic theory and practice, Dewey argues forcefully that a
concerted effort to bridge the gap between the associational public
and its governing institutions and officials can and should be
attempted.

Dewey observes that there is cynicism about the role of the public in elite and popular forms, among capitalists and socialists (p.118). His fear is that political bosses will fill the gap between the state and the public (p. 120).[8] His hope is that education can fill the gap in a fashion which will support democracy.[9] As it was in his times, he is deeply concerned that people find talking about public issues boring (p. 139). There is, he maintains, a cultural lag. The changes in the Great Society's economy and technology are not being matched by appropriate cultural changes. "Till the Great Society is converted into the Great Community, the Public will remain in eclipse. Communication alone can create a great community" (p. 142). This leads to his "search for the great community," as the answer to the problem of the public.

Dewey agrees with Lippmann that knowledge and inquiry are the answer to the problems of the public. While Lippmann's solution is elitist, Dewey's is fundamentally democratic. Dewey maintains: "The prime condition for a democratically organized public is the kind of knowledge and insight which does not yet exist" (p. 166). "There can be no public without full publicity in respect to all the consequences which concern it" (p. 167).

Here Dewey's disagreement with Lippmann is most evident. Lippmann argues that the check on oligarchy is an intellectual aristocracy, according to Dewey (pp. 204–5). The industrial revolution freed individuals, but this does not mean that they are most able to rule. This revival of the "Platonic notion," of which Lippmann is the major public advocate, is more appealing because the philosophers are replaced by experts, given that philosophy is subjected to almost universal practical ridicule. Yet, despite the appeal, Dewey finds the argument unconvincing for three reasons: 1. because the very ignorance, frivolity, and jealousy of the masses which weaken their capacity for sharing in political affairs also make them even more unlikely to submit to the authority of the experts, 2. because experts are shut off from the knowledge they need to serve to the degree they make up a distinct class, and 3. because democratic procedures uncover social needs and problems which expert philosopher kings cannot perceive on their own (see pp. 205–6). The rule of the experts is both politically impossible (reason 1) and not likely to be effective (reasons 2 and 3).

Having shown the inadequacies of the elitist response to the problems of the democratic public, Dewey concludes that there is only one solution to the problems of democracy, more and improved democratic debate. "The essential need, in other words, is the improvement of the methods and conditions of debate, discussion, and persuasion. That is *the* problem of the public" (p. 208). "Until secrecy, prejudice, bias, misrepresentation, and propaganda, as well as sheer ignorance are replaced by inquiry and publicity, we have no way of telling how apt for judgment of social policies the existing intelligence of the masses may be" (p. 209). Along with Lippmann, Dewey realizes that the American public in its contemporary condition is not able to take part in the complexities of democratic governance. But this does not mean that the public is incapable of self-rule, that democracy is an impossibility. Rather, it suggests that the public must be freed of ignorance and manipulation. It must develop a capacity to inquire critically into its situation and act more wisely. Lippmann assumed that publics were incapable of this, but Dewey shows how Lippmann's conclusion is more a matter of sensibility than evidence. With the opposing sensibility, Dewey reveals the weaknesses in the elitist position.

Dewey's critique of Lippmann suggests that the intellectual's relationship with democracy is even more complicated than we have considered thus far. Not only are democracy and the intellectuals in conflict because of their opposing principles of egalitarianism, on the one hand, and hierarchy, on the other, while they are mutually supportive because democracy needs the intellectual judgment of the intellectuals. Intellectuals, further, need democracy once they enter the public realm. Public intelligence of the sort Lippmann was after requires democratic inputs. Intellectuals who know best on the grounds of their special knowledge, be they experts or political vanguards, tend not to be particularly wise in the public policies they advocate. Dewey's understanding of the associational groundings of public life shows us why this is theoretically. The failures of technocracy and of totalitarian intellectual and political movements empirically demonstrate the soundness of his theoretical insights.

ELITISM VERSUS THE PUBLIC; THE PUBLIC VERSUS ELITISM

The debate between Dewey and Lippmann is filled with irony. The men, themselves, in their forms of public action, apparently belied their own intellectual positions. Dewey was a populist of sorts, but he spent most of his working life in the philosophy departments of elite universities. Lippmann was an elitist who wrote for the popular press. The cultural complexity of their vocations made these apparent paradoxes less severe. Dewey's philosophy of pragmatism was America's democratic contribution to modern academic philosophy, with its roots in the transcendentalism of Emerson and Thoreau, the politics of Frederick Douglas, and the poetry of Walt Whitman.[10] Lippmann's journalism was of a special establishment school, of access journalism, in which the journalist and the public figures he or she covers form public policy in tandem and inform the public as they deem it to be necessary and in the public's interest.[11] Dewey and Lippmann practiced as they preached. Dewey developed a special way of doing philosophy in public which informed public opinion, particularly in and through public education, and Lippmann did "intelligence work" in his close interaction with high government officials. They each contributed to our understanding of the life of the intellectual in democratic society and the life of democracy in intellectuals.

Beyond the two personalities, Lippmann's elitist approach and Dewey's public orientation are intellectual archetypes in modern democratic society. These are kinds of connected critics (in the sense of Michael Walzer),[12] who forge their connections with society in entirely different ways. Lippmann's work points to the necessary connections between political and intellectual elites, and he sought such connection in his life. His practical affairs and his theoretical positions were mutually supportive. He lived in concord with his philosophy, and his philosophy was a reflection upon the life which he lived. The same was very much the case for Dewey, although the life and the philosophy were in opposition to Lippmann's. Dewey was the public intellectual who addressed the general public. His task was to inform the public from the bottom up, and he tried to do this in his work on education and in his many books written for the general public on broad social and political themes. At the beginning of his career, he even took part in a utopian attempt to publish a newspaper, *Thought News*, which had as its defined goal breaking the privileged class' monopoly over science and knowledge. The positions of Lippmann and Dewey also then have another sociological dimension. What is the public the intellectual should address? Lippmann points to the powers, while the general public quietly observes their deliberations. Dewey points to the people, not differentiated in his formulation. Most intellectuals operate somewhere between these two positions. They address themselves to each other, as they hope, or at least pretend, that they are addressing the powers or the people. It is the truly successful intellectuals, such as Dewey or Lippmann, who break through this pretense.

Both Lippmann and Dewey recognized that there were gaps between the intellectual, the political elite, and the general public. In complex industrial societies, the Great Society as they both understood this term, there was no natural connection between leaders and led, and between both and intellectuals. Lippmann primarily concerned himself with the gap between intellectuals and political leaders, while for Dewey the primary problem was between the general public and its political and intellectual leadership, to the detriment of both the leadership and the public. The difference between the two thinkers is one of sensibility. Elitists, such as Lippmann, can no more be convinced that the general public can be educated about the broader social world, than Dewey, and other radical democrats, can be convinced that the public cannot be so educated. Thus, while Lippmann addresses himself to the political elite and explains his and their discussions to the general public, as spectators of real politics, Dewey addresses himself to the general public and its leadership as fellow citizens, in the voice of the intellectual as an equal.

In Lippmann and Dewey, we observe, then, two distinct kinds of intellectuals in modern democracy, arising from the way they view the relationship between the intellectual and the political elite and the general public. There are those intellectuals who view their public as being the political and cultural elite, who "realistically" realize the limitations of public opinion and address themselves to the powers and their elite opponents, and there are those who view their public as being constituted by their fellow citizens, who realize that political leadership and decision are only as good as they are empowered by the common sense of the citizenry. Common sense has a telling critique of realism; and realism has a way of challenging common sense.

From the point of view of common sense, Dewey realized, and the history of the twentieth century has underscored, that the enlightened leadership of experts, be they paternalistic advocates of social justice, or hard-nosed social and political technocrats, or political vanguards of the left or the right, has all too often ended in failure.

When the tension between democracy and intellectuals is decided decisively on the side of intellectuals, grand intellectual aspirations have not been achieved, and politics have become a disaster, or at least a failure, from the great experiment of the Bolsheviks to the attempts in the United States to resolve political problems with the tools of social science.

On the other hand, Lippmann's realism included an understanding of structural constraints on democratic association that Dewey in his naïvete did not recognize. The tension between the masses of people, and the intellectuals and the powers that be, which Lippmann perceived much more accurately than Dewey, does exist, and Dewey's response to the tension between the elite and the bulk of the population seems rather weak. It seems highly doubtful that the gap between the state and corporate powers and ordinary people can be overcome by talk and education alone, as Dewey seems to suggest. Lippmann, with a world-weary conservative sensibility, viewed the gap as inevitable and tried to overcome the democratic prejudice which ignored the existing structures of authority. For those, such as Dewey, who question this authority, there should be a recognition that his means of addressing its injustices are not adequate. Sometimes action and not only words must be used in the constitution of public life. Civilized discussion alone will not eliminate the structures of power and interest that separate the powers from the general public; discourse when confronting such power sometimes must turn to shouts.

For all their differences and with their opposite successes, both Dewey and Lippmann suggest that the intellectual's role is one of quiet and sober investigation, deliberation and discussion. They held this position, no doubt, as a matter of personal and cultural disposition, along with a theoretical tendency to overlook the importance of class conflict in the formation of public opinion and the constitution of democracy. We now turn to some more contemporary thinkers who have been neither so polite nor insensitive to the problems of structured group conflict. Besides the elitists and the talkative democrats, such as Lippmann and Dewey, there are also shouting intellectuals, such as C. Wright Mills and Edward Said. Such intellectuals cannot accept the prevailing power structure, as the conservative elitist intellectual can. They do attempt to address the limits of elitism and civilized discursive intellectuals.

CHAPTER 4

The subversive intellectual and the public

Walter Lippmann and John Dewey both knew that there was something fundamentally wrong with public life in their day. They faced
the fundamental dilemmas of intellectuals in modern democratic
society, and they were early critics of the effects of mass media on
American public life. They proposed radically different explanations
for how the "eclipse of the public" came about, and considered
radically different solutions to the problem. Lippmann turned to a
scientistic elitism for the solution, while Dewey turned to radical
democracy. Yet, despite these opposing positions, these men shared a
lot. They were gentlemen. They imagined social and political life to
be a gentlemanly affair, bounded by norms of civility. Lippmann was
a contented realist; Dewey a contented idealist. Missing from
Lippmann's and Dewey's analysis is a critique of power; also missing
is a sense that sometimes disagreements in democracies are articulated in a rude fashion. We now turn, then, to the question of power
and the appreciation of the limits of civility, and consider how these
shape the life of the intellectual in democratic society. A logical
starting point is the work of C. Wright Mills, a man who was a
student of pragmatism, Dewey's philosophic orientation, and a
harsh critic of conservatism, Lippmann's political orientation and
personal disposition.

C. WRIGHT MILLS'S POWER ELITE

C. Wright Mills, in contrast to Lippmann and Dewey, was a
discontented realist, a cynical idealist. He understood and was
outraged by the vulgarity of power in political life. This led to a very
different approach to the problems of the public and its eclipse.
Writing in the post-war period, during the anti-communist reaction
and before the radical changes in the American universities, Mills

shouted about the problems of the intellectual in a mass society. His professional jeremiad, *The Sociological Imagination,* is a classic intellectual critique of narrow-minded professionalism.[1] Sparing no prisoners, he attacked the leading luminaries of his profession: Talcott Parsons, for his overly grand theories, and Paul Lazarsfeld, for his narrow-minded empiricism. There was no moderation in these attacks. Mills went after Lazarsfeld even though he was a colleague at Columbia with whom Mills worked closely, who was primarily responsible for bringing Mills to the Columbia sociology department, then one of the most prestigious in the country. Mills used the same sort of directness in all his sociological endeavors.

Like Lippmann and Dewey, there were fundamental tensions in Mills's intellectual and personal profile.[2] Given the nature of his critical intellect, he had an estranged relationship with his social world. He proclaimed that sociology was constituted by a blend of history and biography, but he disdained all conversations about personalities as gossip. He was a fundamental critic of American politics, but he prided himself in his disengagement from political activity, not only of the Democratic and Republican parties, but of more marginal political organizations as well. He was a radical critic of the power elites and their institutional bases of power, while he was a professor at one of the leading elite academic institutions in the nation. His was a politics of populism, while his depiction of American society had a decidedly elitist outsider's view of the lives of ordinary people.

Mills was a forceful, but ambivalent social critic. His position emanates from his understanding of the relationship between the power structure of American society and the general population. While Lippmann and Dewey analyze the public and its problems, respectively, through a political and a pragmatic psychology, Mills seeks to address these problems through a sociology of power structures. In the opening of his masterpiece, *The Power Elite,* Mills presents his starting point:

The powers of ordinary men are circumscribed by the everyday worlds in which they live, yet even in these rounds of job, family, and neighborhood they often seem in these driven by forces they can neither understand nor govern. "Great changes" are beyond their control, but from every side, such changes now press upon the men and women of the mass society, who accordingly feel that they are without purpose in an epoch in which they are without power.[3]

His is a concern with how the structures of power in mass society and its well-developed power elites define the lives of ordinary people.

Mills is deeply troubled that the relationship between intellectuals and the public no longer exists, because the public no longer exists. The power elite presides over a mass society which replaces the democratic public. This is crucial because of the special importance of intellectuals in his overall sociological scheme. The public has become a mass and the hopes that the intellectuals will address important problems and inspire political action are diminished.

Mills analyzes the formation of the elites who control the dominating institutions of American society, and attempts to show how the elites and their institutions interconnect. With obvious political commitments and considerable passion, he analyzes the injustices of American society. He is a committed social critic, looking for a way to take on the powers that be. The hero of his investigation, the agent who is capable of revealing the lie of American liberal democracy, is, though, not the ordinary person but the intellectual. "The independent artist and intellectual are among the few remaining personalities equipped to resist and to fight the stereotyping and consequent death of genuinely lively things."[4]

The intellectual like everyone else is a victim of the bureaucratization of the social world. He or she is distinguished, according to Mills, in that he or she still has some capacity for resistance. Thus, while Mills pays attention to the situation of ordinary people, it is the critical intellectuals who have the capacity to act in his analyses, while others are either victims or victimizers. Yet, Mills is not optimistic that intellectuals will be able to play their role adequately. The transformation of the public into a mass makes this next to impossible. Intellectuals have lost their control of the means of communication and the end result is that there is little possibility of opposing the power elite.

In contrast to Lippmann, Mills takes seriously the viewpoint of the ordinary person. In contrast to Dewey, he knows that the power structure of mass society constrains what ordinary people can possibly do on their own, even with education and improved discussion. Mills, none the less, holds a normative position quite like Dewey's, and he follows Lippmann in his critical analysis of the eclipsed public. He combines Lippmann's "political psychology" with Dewey's pragmatic interactionism to arrive at a radical and structural critique of American liberal democracy. While Lippmann observes the limits of personal observation in the complex society and how the limits lead to an inaccurate picture of the problems facing the greater society, Mills notes what happens when Lippmann's observation becomes a common wisdom. He observes that most of the images we have "in our heads" come from the mass media and that we have come to distrust what we observe, believing that what is true is what the media stereotypes have defined as being true. "We often do not really believe what we see before us until we read about it in the paper or hear about it on the radio" (p. 311). This leads, in Mills's judgment, to the transformation of a potential democratic public, of the sort that Dewey describes and the makers of the American republic assumed, into a mass society (pp. 298–324).

Because Mills understands that this mass society is a new sort of social structure enforced by the prevailing social institutions and their elites, the problem of the public cannot be overcome simply with the improvement of the citizenry through education or with improvements in public communication. Unlike Dewey, he thus does not propose possible solutions. He only highlights the nature of the problem. Mills, as an intellectual with a "sociological imagination," keeps a critical attitude alive and calls for participation, but, given the findings of his analysis, it is quite unclear to him, and to us his readers, how that participation is to be realized. If he is right about the workings of the power elite and mass society, there does not seem to be much room for political action, and this is not only a theoretical issue; it is a practical one as well. This had direct impact on the politics of the New Left in the sixties and on the politics of identity in the eighties and nineties.

Just as the elite politics of access journalism and the functioning of the elite powers follow from Lippmann's approach to the public and its problems, and the educational reform movement and conventional electoral politics against the established powers follow from Dewey's position, the radical politics of the New Left, which discounts conventional institutions of education and conventional politics as viable forms of opposition to domination, follows from the position of Mills. The American New Left, indeed, was deeply influenced by Mills's writings.[5] Tom Hayden, the primary author of the "Port Huron Statement," was a careful student of Mills's works. The founding document of the Students for a Democratic Society is directly informed by Mills's analyses of American society in *The*

Power Elite and *White Collar*. Both the students' critique of American society and their sense of what was to be done drew heavily upon Mills's position. They spoke in their own names, as students (young intellectuals), criticizing the problems of mass society from the point of view of independent intellectuals. Their challenge was to make connections with the greater society which they never accomplished, either in the days of their grass roots community action programs or in the ideological excesses of the anti-war movement. They may have affected the way Americans have come to see themselves and their authoritative institutions, casting into doubt the legitimacy of authoritative claims and contributing to the general societal cynicism.[6] They did disrupt the complacency of mass society and its culture for a while. They may even have had an impact on the general culture, but they never did develop and disseminate a meaningful radical politics for the average American, as they intended and as is consistent with Mills's position.

The theoretical and practical failures of the radical position, as we will observe below, are a prelude to the conception of the public role of the intellectual today.

THE PUBLIC AND POST-MODERN PROBLEMS

The debate between Dewey and Lippmann occurred before the rise and fall of Nazi totalitarianism and full-scale Soviet totalitarianism (Stalinism), before the second world war, the end of colonialism, the cold war and the post-cold war period. It is a modern debate, concerned as it is with the problems of modern industrialized societies, ignorant of the problems of post-industrial societies and post-modern politics and culture. It is, from certain points of view, a white, patriarchal, eurocentric debate, distanced from the concerns of multiculturalism and feminism. The work of Mills is also so distanced. Yet, it seems rather clear that these authors still address issues central to cultural and political problems of our times, and this is discernible no matter where one stands on the question of post-modernism. This is because the problematic relationship between the intellectual and the democratic public remains as a pressing issue, animating much of our political and cultural controversies. The Dewey–Lippmann–Mills debate is ongoing.

Indeed, while the debate between Dewey and Lippmann, and Mills's response to it, is a modern one, post-modern contestations are imbedded in the alternative positions presented. Dewey is distrustful of traditional distinctions between high and low culture. He knows that the ways of the societal elite and its high art of governance are intimately connected with popular associations and the low art of face-to-face interactions. He, with his philosophy based on experience and his polemics against metaphysics, is as suspicious of grand narratives as Lyotard and the post-modernists. Knowing the other is as important to Dewey and the pragmatists as it is to Derrida and his followers.[7] Lippmann, on the other hand, who can hardly be compared to the post-modernists, nonetheless, also questions the enlightenment prejudice that reason and democracy are necessarily compatible. He understands the power of knowledge and that liberal democratic governance must be deconstructed. He is well aware of the power of the media and the challenges they present to inherited political philosophies.

Yet, despite the similarities between the concerns of the first part of the century and the prevailing concerns of our day, our problems are not simply a repeat of earlier problems. The relationship between the intellectual and the democratic public has become increasingly complicated since Dewey and Lippmann's time. This is because of radical changes in intellectual life and in the life of democracy, what has been famously called the post-modern condition.[8] Of central importance are: the impact of social diversity and multicultural perspectives on the relationship between the intellectuals and the public, and the fissure in political tradition at the end of the century. Mills also worked before these impacts. The discussions of diversity have been particularly prominent among academics, while the discussion of our political fissure, the break in our political traditions, has been left relatively unexamined.

The challenge of diversity

Lippmann, Dewey, and Mills assumed a certain common ground for public action, both political and cultural. They tried to transform the ground to their own liking, recognizing and valuing its existence. Indeed, they never doubted its inevitability. They could not conceive of a society without a common ground, without a center.[9] This is how they conceived of the problem of the public and the formation of public opinion. The inevitability of such a centralized public formation is now in question. While Dewey and Lippmann wondered whether public opinion was well informed and whether it could be reformed, some contemporary critics worry about its very existence, along with Mills, and others celebrate its demise.[10] Some question whether there ever has been a truly common ground, maintaining that it was an ideology for special interests masking as common ideals and principles. Others go even further and question the desirability of a public domain and the pursuit of a common or public good, apart from class, gender, racial, or ethnic interests.[11]

Diversity both as an empirical reality and as a normative ideal challenges previously prevailing notions of a common ground, a public good, and public opinion. A public opinion that has been formed with the systematic exclusion of the marginalized, of people of color and of women, for example, cannot simply be solidified by the inclusion of the previously excluded. Its associational grounding must be transformed for a successful inclusive process to be achieved, and success is difficult to attain. This much can be understood by following Dewey's own approach to the formation of the public, although he himself never considered such issues.

Once the Democratic party in the south, for example, moved beyond its segregationist base and included blacks, the associational grounds of opinion within the party had to be changed for a true transformation of the Democratic party. This was a long time coming. The fact that blacks and whites came to be included was a significant change in itself, but the group life that informed the opinion of the party had to change well beyond that simple fact for the integration of the party to have its full effects. Put simply, the Klu Klux Klan no longer could be the social world which significantly informed opinion, while black Churches had to become ever more important for party life. The associational base of public opinion had to be transformed.

But such transformation does not come easily. There are often very severe constraints upon fundamental change, as is indicated by the resiliency of the conservative hegemony among southern Democrats. While the previously excluded may be granted participation in public activity, the old interactive ways for the formation of public life do not then just disappear. "Old boy networks" are persistent parts of public life.

The inclusion of the previously excluded into public activities, of women and African Americans, for example, into positions of authority in corporations, political offices, the universities and so forth, then, present recurring political problems. On the one hand, when the subordinated are first included, the terms of inclusion involve a distinct disadvantage; on the other hand, with time, the included group may transform the public in which it comes to take part, as the associational world of the public expands. Paradoxes and recurrent dilemmas result. In the example of the Democrats, the racist southern party over a long period of time became its opposite, the non-racist party (or at least the less explicitly racist party), leaving racism for the Republicans. Given the persistence of racism, the solid Democratic south is being transformed into the solid Republican south. Was that change?

There are always competing judgments and conflicting interests concerning the associational transformation of a public life and the generation of opinion within the public. Should an oppressed group enter into association with its oppressors in a common public? Or should it maintain an independent public existence? If it does enter into a common public activity or set of activities, how long will it accept subordinated status, if at all? Can the dominant group accept the changes in public life that come with the changes in the composition of the public? Will the rules of the game be enforced in such a way that old privileges will be maintained? If not, will the changes in public life and opinion be acceptable to the old guard? When people with significant differences are part of the same public, will they attempt to ignore their differences or highlight them? The confrontation with the "other," as this set of problems has come to be called, presents an almost infinite set of resolutions to these questions, both formal and informal. Intellectuals define their relationship with publics, and indeed define and help to constitute publics socially, as they raise and attempt to answer such questions. The elitist and the radical democratic approaches, the approaches of Lippmann and Dewey, still are followed, but these are complicated by the problems of diversity and plurality. Are the elites to be addressed the elites of the dominant or of the subordinate? Is the public to be addressed the general public, or the public of a distinct group? Which addresses serve the interests of democracy? Which serve the interests of efficiency and political saliency?

Lippmann, as a critic of Dewey, realizes that ordinary people lack the resources to understand critically the complexities of social, economic, and political life. As a conservative, he views this as inevitable. He opts for informed discussion among the political and intellectual elite. Mills and after him the "post-modernists," usually as cultural radicals, extend Lippmann's position, while they usually reject his politics. Mills, along with the post-modernists, maintains that the very constitution of a general public is a structured form of inequality. Something they, as opposed to Lippmann, do not like. They observe that some take part in public discussion and others are excluded, because of class, gender, or racial discriminations; some have the resources to dominate public discussion and others are destined to be dominated, because of the unequal distribution of cultural resources. The general publics of the past have been the privileged domains of dominant groups: the whites, the males, the Europeans, the propertied, and so forth. New perspectives and people brought into the public domain are necessarily subordinated to the rules of those who have previously excluded them. A general public is not the ideal from a multicultural point of view; rather, the development of publics, or at least of fields of discourse and move-ments of social action for the excluded, is considered a more just and desirable situation.[12] The role of the intellectual from this point of view, then, is to deconstruct the oppressive general public and its common sense, and to help constitute alternative publics, discourses, and social movements.

Edward Said, in his now classic book, *Orientalism,* presents an argument about the relationship of the East and the West with such a project in mind. He exemplifies the move of the "subaltern intellectual," the intellectual from the marginalized position. His is a concern with how the world of Islam and the Middle East has been depicted by the imperial powers of Europe and North America. The cultural discourse of Orientalism is shown to be an extension of the political practices of imperialism. Knowledge and power are shown to be intimately connected. He reveals how the broad range of European writing on the "Orient," in fiction and in the scholarly writing of area specialists, invokes a superior position toward a universal other. He explains his position:

My objection to what I have called Orientalism is not that it is just the antiquarian study of Oriental languages, societies and peoples, but that as a system of thought Orientalism approaches a heterogeneous, dynamic, and complex human reality from an uncritically essentialist standpoint; this suggests both an enduring Oriental reality and an opposing but no less enduring Western essence, which observes the Orient from afar and from, so to speak, above. This false position hides historical change. Even more important, from my standpoint, it hides the *interest* of the Orientalists.[13]

He contends that his argument is not against the West, but against the universal contrast between West and East. The contrast, even as it is sustained by those Westerners who are quite sympathetic to their Oriental experiences, ultimately defends these interests and is written from the position of superiority.

Said's work, as the reader should be able to imagine even if she or he is unfamiliar with the Middle East, is controversial. He attacks a broad range of Western experts on Islam and the Arab world with broad strokes, labeling as apologists those who think of themselves as scholars, identifying those who have had clear imperialist designs on the region, such as Arthur James Balfour, with those who seem to be their opposites, sympathetic literary and scientific observers of a different world, such as Gustave Flaubert and H. A. R. Gibb. Said's position is not simply that there have been literary and factual distortions in Western accounts of the "East," and that this has served the interests of Western powers. This could be the grounds for scholarly debate and resolution. Rather, Said's thesis is that the tradition of "Occidentals" thinking about "Orientals" is itself a mode of domination. Public and informed discussion about the other is built upon the other's distance and subordination. The discussion is politically performative. Orientalism is a system of domination.

This leaves the "Orientalist" little room for rebuttal. There is only denial, which is believed or disbelieved, depending on which side one is on. Thus, in his polemics with Bernard Lewis, Said asserts that Lewis, renowned as a distinguished expert on Islam and the Middle East, hates his object of investigation and is a tool of American foreign policy, while Lewis responds that Said is the ideologist, not properly respectful of scholarship.[14] Debate is re-placed by the assertion of conflicting irreconcilable positions. In such a confrontation, the pursuit of truth seems to be impossible. The assertion of political position, and its defense, become the intellectual task. Ideology is all there is. General public discourse is eclipsed.

At the same time that Said's work has been controversial, though, it also has been highly influential: an early study in post-colonial inquiry, a prelude to post-modernism, a highly effective critique of Western hegemony. For post-modern and post-colonial intellectuals,

Orientalism has had a significance reaching beyond its substantive subject matter.[15] Said debunks a grand narrative of western rationalism and its growth, as it confronts the myth of universal Oriental backwardness. He shows how the myth of this narrative is incorporated into scholarly and literary studies, and he reveals how its completeness undermines both the specificity and the value of the differences among cultures. He demonstrates how deeply ingrained the myth of backwardness is, and how it is linked first with European and then with American colonial and neo-colonial domination of the Arab and Islamic worlds. Key Western cultural achievements are shown to be implicated in the support of colonialism, from the literary achievements of Austen, Flaubert, and Conrad to political ideals of democracy and freedom.[16]

Through these critical judgments, Said seeks to empower the powerless. He seeks to level the playing field of political culture. Showing the inaccuracies of the representations of the Orient, he hopes to open the terrain for the insights of the political constituencies of the Near, and not so near, East, for the Egyptians and the Syrians, the Algerians and the Muslim Indians, and especially for the people of Palestine, his native ground. He is the intellectual spokesman of social movement of the subaltern. For appreciative readers of *Orientalism* and his other works, Said exemplifies how one can be an intellectual in our times. He provides an answer to the Mills dilemma of the intellectual in mass society. Said speaks to the problem of public life in a mass atomized society. He is the exemplary politically connected social movement intellectual.

In his *Representations of the Intellectual*, Said turns to Mills as providing compelling answers to the problem of what intellectuals should do and represent today. He admires Mills as "a fiercely independent intellectual with an impassioned social vision and a remarkable capacity for communicating his ideas in a straightforward and compelling prose."[17] He seems to agree with Mills's heroic understanding of the intellectual, as the last social agent with the ability to resist the forces of mass society, with its propensity to force standardization and dehumanization. But Said adds a more contemporary twist. Mills focuses on the fate of the individual as he or she is manipulated and restricted by the powers of large societal institutions. The imagery of the fifties and early sixties is in clear view. Said shifts the focus and the political imagery. Building on Mills's position, Said declares:

There is an inherent discrepancy between the powers of large organizations from governments to corporations, and the relative weakness not just of the individuals but of human beings considered to have subaltern status, minorities, small peoples and states, inferior or lesser cultures and races. There is no question in my mind that the intellectual belongs on the side with the weak and unrepresented.[18]

Mills's image of mass society is that of a large collection of atomized individuals not understanding the nature of the social forces that define their lives, unable to act politically. He believes that the critical intellectual can do little more than attempt to illuminate the nature of this situation, but there is an uncertainty as to what then can be done politically. The political failures of the New Left, as I have suggested above, can be understood as a manifestation of this uncertainty. It had little understanding of its relationship with the public. This ultimately led to a politics of spectacle and despair, which was directed not only against the power elite, but also against the general public. Mills's prose reveals a hope for general public deliberations and decision making, even though his analysis suggested that such deliberations were no longer a possibility. As the New Left turned to the politics of provocation in a language of revolutionism, it abandoned the public. Mills's diagnosis stood. The individual was alone. Action was beyond her or his capacity.

Said escapes this predicament by underscoring that domination is not just of the isolated individual. He does not accept the notion of loneliness and has a much clearer sense about what the intellectual should do politically. Individuals, Said realizes, are group members. While they are exploited as they are members of these groups, they also can respond to exploitation as group members in social and political movements. People are subordinated not just as atomized cogs in the wheels of mass society, but as members of identifiable groups: as women, as blacks, as workers, as Arabs, as Palestinians, and so forth. While this does point to the thoroughness of domi-nation, it also involves an appreciation of the possibility of resistance and a defined role of the intellectual, i.e. to be on the side of the weak and the unrepresented groups, to articulate the logic of their position. The partisans of the New Left, would, no doubt, approve of this sort of stance, but something new is being added. Attention is focused inward, to the constitution of specific groups of identifica-tion. Group empowerment, not the public or common good, is the political concern. A delimited public good, that of the subaltern, is understood as the consequence of empowerment. Said typifies the relationship of the intellectual to this task.

Said functions as a critical intellectual of a new sort. In the name of the other, he works as a cultural and political critic and activist. He believes that his otherness, his experience as an exile, exemplifies the position of the intellectual. The exile's sensibility sheds critical light on the claims of the host culture. His or her engagement in the politics of another world, in Said's case of Palestine, is the basis of critique. The condition of exile, as either an actual or a metaphorical experience, provides the intellectual with a critical perspective:

Exile for the intellectual ... is restlessness, movement, constantly being unsettled, and unsettling others. You cannot go back to some earlier and perhaps more stable condition of being at home; and, alas, you can never fully arrive, be at one with your new home or situation.[19]

Even if one is not an actual immigrant or expatriate, it is still possible to think as one, to imagine and investigate in spite of barriers, and always to move away from the centralizing authorities towards the margins, where you see things that are usually lost on minds that have never traveled beyond the conventional and the comfortable. [20]

The goal of intellectual engagement is not to inform common sense, as was the end for Dewey, Lippmann, and even Mills. It is rather to unsettle common understandings in the name of the marginalized, to be subversive, not in the name of truth, but of an identity position. The common view worth nurturing is that of the marginalized, to help empower the oppressed, to fortify their resistance. Said seeks to confirm that "the subaltern *can* speak, as the history of liberation movements in the twentieth century eloquently attests."[21] The role of the intellectual is to facilitate such speech and such movement.

As talk provokers, as intellectuals, Lippmann's primary concern is with the elite; Dewey's primary concern is with all the public associations of a society, and Mills generally agrees,[22] whereas Said's concern is with the formation of a public opinion among the marginalized, with the formation of a subaltern public opinion and capacity for political action. He debunks his discursive opponents, be they Orientalists, Zionists, or any other group that he deems to be against "the side of the weak and the unrepresented." He declares himself to be always against those in authority, and he believes that this is the natural position of the true critical intellectual. His political sentiment, thus, resembles that not only of Mills, but also of Sartre and many others who have romanticized the intellectuals of the left.[23]

Said's identification of the intellectual with the marginalized and their politics represents a challenge to democratic practice, which he leaves unaddressed. He appreciates the role of the intellectual as she or he supports the subaltern, but he does not seem to appreciate the potential contribution of the intellectual to society-wide deliberations that exist between individuals and across group categories. If common deliberations are deconstructed, democracy is undermined. Said is deeply committed to the strategy of deconstruction (specifically of Orientalism, but also in his approach to the task of the less than totally critical intellectual in public life as well). When he states with absolute assurance that "Orientalism expresses antipathy to Islam, Hellenism sympathy for classical Greece,"[24] one wonders if this could possibly be true of all Western scholars who have chosen to study Islam and the Arab world, and even if it is true of all of them as individuals, one must be uncertain whether this is all there is to their works. An entire arena of deliberations is condemned without qualification. Is it not the case that work that is shaped by questionable political attitudes, Aristotle's commitment to slavery for example, may have a value that reaches beyond the questioned attitudes? Should not the arguments of others, even of opponents, be considered on their own terms and not simply dismissed? Even if we recognize the cogency of Said's critique of the Western confrontation with the other of the Near East through centuries, and even if we know all too well that similar critiques of subaltern studies, of studies of women, blacks, Jews, and so forth, would yield similar results, it does not seem possible that all Western studies of Islam and the subaltern are so clearly and completely negative.

Said no doubt would concede the point (as is clearly indicated in his writings on Conrad), but he proceeds as if the concession were not made in his study of the intellectual. He categorizes intellectuals as being either critics or apologists. The intellectual functions as an ideologist. His is a radical vision. The intellectual is either part of the problem or part of the solution, either the exiled critic, such as, archetypically, Theodor Adorno and Max Horkheimer, or the exiled servant of the adopted state, such as Henry Kissinger and Zbigniew Brzezinski.[25] He fails to realize that on both sides of the barricades these intellectuals have a tendency to function as philosopher kings.

Said ascertains the side of the righteous and is absolute in his commitment to their cause. This is most evident in his appraisal of the situation in Palestine/Israel, an understandable situation given his biography and his political engagement,[26] but it is also apparent in how he discerns the role of the intellectual. The intellectual is not an agent for public deliberation, but of political assertion. He or she may empower in Said's account, but contributing to a common sense and informing a general public opinion are not featured. The democratic public is endangered.

Here is the dilemma of multiculturalism. The commitment to the subaltern, to the marginalized and the oppressed groups in any specific society or in the globalized international order, serves to bring new critical perspectives into the public arena. Said clearly has accomplished this in his literary and political writings. But when the commitment is not constituted within some framework for the perspectives to interact, some constituted cultural space where those holding diverse perspectives can, in the words of Hannah Arendt, "speak and act in the presence of others," multiculturalism threatens to become a form of multitribalism. Diversity as a principle threatens to make diverse social practices incommensurable. Even if the idea of plurality yielding unity is understood as having an ideological dimension (in the United States it is an official slogan), it does not mean that all attempts at mutual understanding and informed public opinion are futile. A fundamental dilemma of democratic culture is at issue here, and the intellectual has a responsibility in addressing it. The public deliberations that democracy requires must be open to the expression of the full range of public opinion and judgment of the populace, but it also must be presented in a form and in a place where the exchange of opinions and judgments is a possibility. The way intellectuals address their audiences expands or diminishes the possibility of realizing these sometimes conflicting requirements. The controversies over the issues of political correctness and multi-culturalism in the American universities are manifestations of this.

Discussions about these issues, as they appear in debates about multiculturalism, post-modernism, and the various cultural and theoretical positions of identity politics, are all too often presented in strong categorical terms, conducive to academic discourses and a confrontational politics, but not democratic deliberation.[27] Cultural observers and political activists decide *a priori* what the resolution of the problems is or ought to be. In the following chapters, I will attempt to avoid such categorical resolutions, by examining how intellectuals facilitate discussion about the other and the impact this has on public life and its constitution. The issues involved require detailed examination, not broad theoretical resolutions. We will examine how intellectuals help constitute and subvert public domains for the discussion of pressing social problems. We will observe the strengths and the weaknesses of the domains, their openness and degrees of oppression. It will become clear that the relationship between civility and subversion, as intellectuals confront the societal problems of the margins and the general public, is situationally problematic. The task of subversion is pressingly needed when the problems of race and gender cannot be addressed through the prevailing common sense. But subversion unbounded by civility yields dogmatism and worse. There is no pre-existing formula for knowing when the civil or the subversive should end and its opposite should begin. This is a matter of political judgment. The balance, nonetheless, is something that is achieved through time by a multiplicity of agents, intellectual and otherwise. Intellectuals like Said and Mills disrupt and others respond taking the implications seriously and attempt to revitalize difference so that something other than the confrontation between Said and Lewis can be constituted. We will examine this as the common sense of race in the United States and of gender in Central Europe are subverted. But before proceeding to this examination, we must consider how the large-scale geopolitical changes and the break in the fundamental structure of our political culture also have challenged the relationship between intellectuals and their publics worldwide.

The fissured traditions of public life

Diversity presents itself today as a pressing problem because of the explosion of global economics, politics, communications, and culture.[28] We, with all the differences that define the human condition, live closely together. It is no longer possible to imagine societies or cultures that live totally apart from each other. It has been the convention in sociology and in everyday life to use the word "society" as a synonym for the nation state. This notion of society, as a self-contained unit, which is based on nineteenth-century understandings of the world, no longer makes much sense.[29] International politics, culture, and economics are becoming the

defining realities of daily life: from sporting events to other branches
of the entertainment industry, from banking to scientific inquiry,
from televised warfare and diplomacy to international conventions
on human rights. An international world stage is a, if not the, (post-
modern) fact of our times. In the past, different sorts of people
tended to remain separated from each other. Because this can no
longer be maintained, diversity presses upon us. Yet, it would be a
mistake to believe that the problems of diversity are something
entirely new. The topic of Said's inquiry, Orientalism, emerged as
Europe, centuries ago, attempted to come to terms with the civilizational other, the "Orient." Said's critique of a long-term pattern of
international hegemony appears when the confrontation with the
other has come home, when it is, in fact, a normal part of societal
life. Said writes about the long duration of Orientalism, and we
think about domestic racism, sexism, and the problems of inter-
ethnic relations and nationalism in their short duration, as they have
become pressing political concerns. His life is archetypical of the
intellectual, of the subaltern *provocateur*, one who inspires the questioning of established positions, one who is never comfortable with
authority, and he has been very successful in his chosen task. Said
understands himself as being against consensus.[30] There has repeatedly been a need for such a stance, and there always will be a need
for political disruption. But Said's position is disturbing when we
realize that disruption of political traditions has become a major
problem, contributing to the crisis of our times. The senselessness of
the post-cold war political world requires coherence as much as an
unsettling of an unjust centralized common sense.

There is, at the end of the twentieth century, a fundamental
confusion of political perspective, a general uncertainty about what's
left and what's right.[31] Intellectuals in democratic societies attempt
to face this changed situation, at the same time that they face the
problems of diversity. The great modern political traditions of
liberalism, conservatism, and socialism, the bread and butter of
political intellectuals in the modern era, have been undermined by
the collapse of communism and anti-communism, and by the crises
of the welfare states of Europe and North America. This does
provide the opportunity to avoid the stale ideological clichés of the
recent past, to rediscover the discursive responsibilities of intellectuals, avoiding ideological temptations, but it does, as well, lead to
political confusions. Making sense in public has become extremely

difficult, not only because it is always difficult to be an intellectual, especially in a democracy, and these difficulties have become even more pronounced with the confrontation of the other, but also because the repertoire of political ideas which we have inherited has become strikingly stale.

Staleness is especially a problem for the political left. My specific concern about Said's position on the role of the intellectual and his self-understanding of his role as an intellectual, his reflexive support of the oppressed, his simple-minded leftism, is that it does not take into account the fact that it is the left in the former free world, in the former anti-communist domain, that has been most weakened by the political confusions of our fissured political traditions. Said, and others of his critical disposition, proceed as if these changes have not occurred. Post-modernists, post-structuralists, radical feminists, and queer theorists, among others of the academic cultural left, proceed ignoring the dimensions of the change in the global political culture after the fall of communism. On the global stage and in the arena of domestic politics of Europe and North America, and probably beyond these regions as well, the right makes sense, while the left engages in cultural controversies and a cultural status hierarchy that function apart from the fields of consequential political and societal life. Many may not like the right-wing packages being presented by neo – and not so neo – conservatives, but the projects of privatization, global markets, fundamentalist religious positions, and nationalism are understandable to significant portions of the world's citizenries. Intellectuals of the left have thought their way into an apparently permanent marginality.

Said is an intellectual celebrity on the American left. He shares this status with such figures as Noam Chomsky, bell hooks, and Cornell West. They all have a tendency to preach to the convinced: to declare the rightness of their position, to exhort the righteous to act well, to denounce those who act poorly, to be "for all the good things and against all the bad ones," as Saul Bellow once satirically put it,[32] without presenting an argument to the unconvinced, the non-partisan. The common sense of their positions, as they have influenced the life of academe, has come to be labeled political correctness. Right-wing critics of the so-called academic left caricaturize concerns about sexism, racism, Western hegemony, and the injustices of free market economies, and these criticisms are not countered in ways that make sense beyond academic left enclaves.

Thus, the right prevails in the broader public arena, as the left celebrates the marginal and denounces the central for its oppression. But because the center is not being challenged directly from the left, and it continues to function in and through the mass media, it is dominated by the positions of the right. Balanced budgets, prayer in schools, the privatization of public concerns, from social security to schooling, are the central items on the post-cold war political agenda, not the injustices of race, class, and gender, and the problems of de-industrialization and the devastation of the environment.

I, therefore, am not persuaded by much of the argument against a public life by the doyens of political correctness: the post-modernists, multiculturalists, and advocates of identity politics, even as I am quite aware that their concerns for the problems of diversity are pressing. I think they often substitute ideology for principled politics. Marginalized philosopher kings imagine that, through a magical intellectual slight of hand, they solve real political problems by withdrawing from ongoing political life. Academic politics have become more real to some post-modern critics than the consequential democratic politics of the general society.

Yet, I do not want to suggest that there is nothing to post-modern, multicultural and identity-based criticism. On the contrary, because the politics of our times are fundamentally different from those of the times of Lippmann, Dewey, and Mills, these forms of criticism have a great deal to say about our public culture. This is because of the problems raised by diversity and the impact of the other, to be sure, as the cogency of Said's position indicates, but it is no less a result of our radically changed geopolitical and geocultural situation. The politics of culture on the world stage lends cogency to post-modern deliberations.

I will attempt to show in the remainder of this inquiry that no simple post-modern master narratives will replace those of the modern era, but that minor narratives, dealing with concrete pressing problems, are being written and read by intellectuals, and they may be related to the old political traditions. These can and should be coordinated in and through discussion in public, not through a theoretical slight of hand. In fact, the minor narratives can help form the public sphere beyond the control of the state and the direct influence of economic logic. This is a key, perhaps the key, critical intellectual role of our times. Intellectuals sometimes inspire informed deliberations about the minor narratives and their relationships. Yet, all too often, they are silenced or are overwhelmed by the shouts of ideology, professionalism, and media manipulation. We will consider how intellectuals try to make sense of our fundamentally transformed political world, aiding or undermining the democratic capacity to deliberate in public about pressing social problems.

A word or two more about the implications of the fissure in the major political traditions of democratic polities: in the immediate aftermath of the fall of communism, and anti-communism, there has been much speculation about the changes in the political world. Some have heralded the end of history; others see the reassertion of history in a replay of nineteenth-century nationalist furies, still others see the outbreak of post-modern savagery, and others see the reassertion of civilizational conflicts formed on the boundaries of old empires.[33] I have thought that the key political problem was that the categories of both the left and the right were equally challenged by the dramatic changes in our political world, as the notion of a systemic socialist alternative disappeared, and that the task was to reinvent the political traditions of the left and the right in a non-ideological manner.[34] I still think in the long run that this is the major political task for intellectuals. Probably in the long run the rightist project will be understood as being as fundamentally challenged by its internal inconsistencies as has been the traditional project of the left. Yet, despite the inconsistencies on the right – the tensions between a concern for tradition and national fate, commitments to traditional religions and old-fashioned sexual moralities, especially concerning the place of women in public life, and the commitment to unfettered development of a market economy – it is not reaching the point of crisis because the left is decimated, incapable of seriously challenging the right. While the left has disintegrated, the right prevails, remaining unchallenged. In the short term, then, in order to lend coherence to political deliberations, it is essential that the left not deconstruct, but reconstruct its political narrative of enlightenment and freedom, not as a grand narrative of absolute truth, but as a rallying point around which the minor narratives of a pluralistic world can be centered.[35] In the long run, a sensible conservative approach to our times is no less needed.

Hannah Arendt, an intellectual who directly confronted the horrors of the twentieth century, was on to this. Her distinctive political theory addressed the problem of the end of the inherited political tradition and authority.[36] She started with the simple, but often ignored, fact that the experience of twentieth-century barbarism cast into doubt common-sense political understanding. The striking similarities of the various forms of modern tyranny, of National Socialism, Fascism, and Soviet Socialism, to her mind, made the conventional ways of thinking about politics obsolete. The mass murder and official terrorism, the grandiose aesthetics and scientistic ideology, the militarism and the totalism of domestic policies, the conflation of truth and political coercion, were shared by the tyrannies of the left and the right, suggesting that leftness and rightness were not any longer significant ways to make the most crucial political discriminations. Today, with the collapse of the major totalitarianism of the left and the right, it is the left and right in the democratic domain that now are challenged, with conservatives speaking of themselves as revolutionaries and those on the left looking for lost ideals. The democratic left and right are in a state of confusion, challenging intellectuals to help make sense of political order and contestation.

CONCLUDING REMARKS

Let's review the progress of our inquiry into the situation of intellectuals in democratic society.

There is a deliberation deficit in contemporary societies, and intellectuals seem to be uniquely equipped to address this. They can encourage talk about difficult problems societies face, but doing this is no easy matter. Not only do all democratic citizenries inherently distrust the elitism that is involved in the intellectual's position, but the mass media challenge the possibility of reaching the public, and the confusion of ideology with political principle, and of intellectual commitment with the demands of professionalism, makes the contribution of intellectuals to democratic deliberation difficult. In order to avoid these difficulties, it is necessary to understand exactly who the democratic intellectual is, to appreciate that he or she is a stranger who pays special attention to his or her critical faculties, an autonomous agent fostering informed discussion in public. But democratic public life itself is a problem. In the twentieth century, it is in eclipse, and it is unclear whether this is because of too much democracy or not enough, or because the powers work against the public, democracy, and intellectuals, or because the public is a manifestation of power of the center against the subaltern, or because the tradition of political common sense has been broken.

As I have already suggested, I do not believe that these uncertainties can be addressed with a theoretical gesture. They only can be addressed concretely by acting citizens. We thus turn to a consideration of how intellectuals and their fellow citizens address the problems of the deliberation deficit and the problematic constitution of public life.

CHAPTER 5

The civil society ideal

Walter Lippmann, John Dewey, C. Wright Mills, and Edward Said, two civil intellectuals and two subversives; a conservative and two radical democrats in the American tradition, and one radical critic of the Western tradition: they all helped their societies to deliberate. They all in their own ways provoked their compatriots to talk. As there are limitations to their individual accounts of the intellectual and the public, the type of talk they provoked each has limits. Lippmann sought to interject intelligence into elite discussion, but was silent about the intelligence gleaned from popular experience. Dewey built upon such popular wisdom, but did not consider the way power works to structure public deliberations. Mills took into account this power and tried to subvert the prevailing common sense that served the power elite, but he was quite unclear about who it was he hoped to address and what might be the venues of their deliberations and actions. About this Said has been quite clear, but as he has attempted to speak in the voice of the subaltern, he has left out of his account the possibility of civilized discussion with those who disagree with him. The intellectuals serve their societies well when they provoke talk in this variety.

The relative importance of civility and subversion must be determined situationally, considering the challenges and problems a society faces at a given time, in a given place. Sometimes civility seems to be a key to the very existence of democratic society, as in this chapter we will observe was the case of the democratic opposition to totalitarianism in East and Central Europe, and sometimes subversion is the only way that the claims to democratic association can be realized, as the difficult (at least for me) case of Malcolm X in the United States reveals (see chapter 8). To the subversive, the civil intellectual appears to be the apologist, the servant of power, the ideologist. To the civil intellectual, the rudeness of the subversive suggests a lack of seriousness, a disruption of a reasonable order, a utopian ignorance of the possible, ideology. Yet, we will observe not only how both the civil and the subversive are necessary, but also that the quest of the civil can subvert a perceived unjust social order (in the case of Central Europe) and the subversively rude can civilize democratic practice (in the case of race relations in the United States). The subversive and the civil projects of intellectuals are intimately related and together they contribute to the constitution of a democratic society. This was most apparent in the former Soviet bloc.

My conviction that intellectuals matter, I must confess, ultimately is derived from personal experience: my close observations of the emergence and the victory of the democratic opposition in East Central Europe, from the early seventies through the early nineties. I have had the good fortune to have observed personally how a small group of intellectuals fundamentally transformed the geopolitical world. They did so not by winning the favorable ear of those who were in power, nor by representing directly the dispossessed, as Said might imagine it would have happened, nor by engaging in brave acts of military valor, nor through exercising political leadership. Rather, they accomplished the apparently impossible by simply pursuing a free public life as an end in itself, within their own limited social circles. They "acted as if they lived in a free society" and in the process they created one.[1] They paid especially close attention to what Said ignores.

They faced incredible repressive powers, and they often paid dearly for their humble acts of self-expression and self-determination. They formed informal seminars and published modest journals of cultural and political opinion, and for this they faced long jail terms and charges of treason. At a time when they were at most shadowy names for their compatriots, the political authorities treated them as a significant political threat. Their movements were carefully monitored. Their friends and family paid for their associations with those who dared to act outside officially prescribed patterns of behavior. From a conventional point of view, all this seemed to be rather excessive. Even in Poland, where oppositional activity was most advanced, only a few thousand people were involved until the Solidarity period. Yet, both the opposition and the authorities seemed, at least instinctively, to understand the seriousness of the apparently marginal intellectual activities. The oppositionists realized that if they acted as if they were free, and they could sustain and extend this pretense, real freedom would be constituted. The authorities, on the other hand, knew that continued totalitarian control, based on and justified by an official ideology, depended on the appearance of the absolute authority of the Party-state apparatus, which was significantly undermined by the continued existence of a politically principled intellectual opposition. Alternatives were then open to a population which might be acted on, and, as we know now, they were. Oppositional intellectual activity constituted a limited free public domain in an otherwise totalitarian context, and first in Poland with the Solidarity labor movement and then in the whole region with the various citizen movements, this public opening was used to overthrow the communist powers.

The exact sequence of this history, its causes and its interpretations, will be debated for many years.[2] In this inquiry, I will explore one meaningful proposition drawn from the East and Central European experience of recent years: intellectuals who act as if they live in a free society, who engage in free and open discussion, and in the process open up space for public deliberation, significantly contribute to the capacity of a society to deliberate and act democratically. It is my contention that the creation of autonomous public space for people to speak and act in the presence of others was a key to the transformation of previously existing socialism, that it is also a key to the possibility of successful democratic constitution in the nations of the former Soviet bloc and to the vibrancy of democracy in the former "free world." Intellectuals are often tempted to engage in other activities. Real power is tantalizing; moral authority is enticing, strong ideological commitments seem more decisive, expertise more practical, but these can lead away from the pressing task of informed deliberation.

The experience of East and Central European intellectuals of the old bloc begs to be considered from every political and theoretical angle. This was a high point of intellectual intervention in public affairs. The initial strength and subsequent weakness of the Central and East European intellectuals must be understood if we are to understand the role of intellectuals in democratic society. All prevailing political positions have been challenged by the consequences of the intellectuals' actions in that part of the world. Conservative distrust of intellectuals for their impracticality and their immorality, the position, for example, of Paul Johnson, is significantly undermined by the high moral principles of the East European secular left and by its respectful relationship with religious sensibilities and religious institutions, and by the practicality of its oppositional stance. Elitist realism, such as that of Walter Lippmann and contemporary Lippmannians from Ronald Steele to Henry Kissinger, is challenged by the acuity of the oppositions' understanding of the strengths and weaknesses of the communist state. Intellectuals with broader understandings of history and political, economic, and social theory did not lead the workers of Solidarity. They advised and learned from their compatriots. The idealists, such as Vaclav Havel, proved to be the genuine realists in their oppositional stance. Old Leftists are confronted by the fact that the vanguard of the workers' state, not the privileged intellectuals, became the object of the workers' wrath. Indeed, the intellectuals proved to be allies of the toiling masses in their opposition to actually existing socialism. New Leftists are challenged by the commitment of the intellectuals and workers to "bourgeois" freedom, their respectful relationship with their elders and cultural traditions, and their conviction that capitalism is not the root of all evil, but a desirable inevitability. The conservative, the liberal, and the radical are forced to reconsider their positions in light of the developments in Eastern and Central Europe: with the fall of communism and the intellectuals' contribution to the fall.

This reconsideration is indeed observable. It is summarized by the reintroduction of an old-fashioned concept in contemporary political discourse. Intellectuals did not only change the political world by engaging in practical actions, such as joining the workers in Gdansk and producing unofficial publications, they also made it possible to rethink the available political alternatives.

Intellectuals provide democracies with their political vocabularies. They have done this in the past and they are still doing it today. They are not the only people who do this, particularly in contemporary democracies, but the way they do it provides opportunities to be true to democratic principles. The alternative word smiths include political handlers, propagandists, and advertisers of various sorts, and political and social scientists. They move from one extreme, that of mass manipulation, to the other, that of scholarly objectivity, distanced from public life. Intellectuals exist between these extremes; they conceive of the words which name alternative ways of thinking and acting in concert, ways that are understandable for the general public. Thus, when we think about economic life, for example, whether we are of the left or of the right, we ponder the nature of capitalism, a word coined by Marx. When we consider competing judgments concerning the viability and desirability of this named system, we think of conservatism, liberalism, and socialism, as they have been given meaning by such historical figures as Edmund Burke, John Stuart Mill, and Karl Marx himself. The inherited political alternatives of our world, the alternatives that have been weakened in the recent past, have been made sensible largely through the work of such intellectuals.

And this is not only something of the past. As the opposition to communism took a radical reformist turn in the late seventies and eighties in Eastern Europe and the Soviet Union, as the limits of the welfare state became evident to those on the left and right in Western Europe and in North America, as the notion of a systemic alternative to capitalism, called socialism, was cast into doubt for many of critical disposition, a new way of considering the relationships among the state, the economy, and cultural life was presented by intellectuals, and it has spread like wild fire. In recent years, the idea of *civil society* has been reborn in the opposition to Soviet power, and the revived concept has been used throughout the world by a diverse set of political actors.

Naming and exploring the meaning of political projects have given such projects viability, although it is clearly not the case that intellectuals, in a magical way reminiscent of mythology, have brought modern political life into being by providing the proper words. Political positions do not automatically arise from the intellectual's pen, but they also are not simply reflections of objective conditions. They are formulated and communicated in response to common experiences, with successes and failures. This is central to the everyday life of democracies and to their long-term futures. It is a main reason why intellectuals are key actors in the democratic arena, even when they seem to be marginal. The support of the capacity to talk about societal problems includes the formulation and introduction of political vocabulary. Here, we consider how the reintroduction of an ancient concept helped millions to come to terms with the fundamental changes in their political world.

CIVIL SOCIETY IN TRANSITION

The notion of civil society is an old and distinguished one, in use at least since the seventeenth century, central to the ideas of the Scottish enlightenment social philosopher Adam Ferguson, and to the political theory of Hegel and through him Marx. On American grounds, it was the strength of American civil society that led de Tocqueville to have hope for "democracy in America." Yet, despite this distinguished history, it is only quite recently that the term has re-entered political discourse. For the casual observer of political affairs, the term appeared in public life as intellectuals attempted to describe and name the political strategy of the democratic oppositions in Czechoslovakia, Hungary, and Poland, and of Solidarity in Poland in the late seventies and early eighties. Now an ironic turn of events can be observed. After the successes of 1989 in the very places where the idea of a civil society experienced its rebirth, there is a serious question whether it can be properly applied as a model of political development. Both the reemergence of the term and the present controversies surrounding it illuminate the complexity of the relationship between the intellectual and political life not only in the former Soviet bloc, but in the former free world as well.

The adjective "civil" rarely appeared before the term "society" in political discourses before the 1980s.[3] And then, "suddenly," not only were a wide array of social scientist using the antique term, but it rapidly passed into broad political discourse: fluidly passing through the lips of members of Congress, State Department officials and even Presidents of the United States. There are now three distinguished scholarly volumes that attempt to clarify the meaning of the ancient concept: the highly critical, *The Idea of Civil Society* by Adam Seligman, the anthropological and contextual *Conditions of Liberty: Civil Society and Its Rivals* by Ernest Gellner, and the reconstructive, historical, and theoretical *Civil Society and Political Theory* by Jean Cohen and Andrew Arato.[4] They do free the term from the easy confusions of rhetorical fashion, and, particularly Cohen and Arato, illuminate how the concept can be used for a non-totalistic critique of actually existing capitalist societies, i.e. liberal democracies, without giving up on democracy as an ideal. Yet, while there is much to learn from these analyses, they do not directly explain how it came to be that a new concept has been put on the agenda of everyday political life. The odd position of certain political intellectuals in Eastern Europe does this. It helps us understand both the revival of the ancient concept, and what the consequences of the revival are likely to be for the life of democracy in the political East and the West, and perhaps in the South as well as the North.

THE INTELLECTUAL OF ACTUALLY EXISTING SOCIALISM

The position of intellectuals in actually existing socialist societies was a very odd one. Now that the regimes have disappeared from the face of Europe and now that the positive progressive hopes for the new socialist order have faded even among those who support the few remaining actually existing socialist systems, it is hard to remember how complicated the situation was for intellectuals working within communist orders. The lives of intellectuals were filled with ironies: characterized by honor and shame, grand hopes and illusions, petty opportunism and unacknowledged acts of bravery. The intellectuals were on the road to class power under socialism, and they were socialism's most resolute opponents.

The privileged status of intellectuals was a consequence of two distinct facts of the ideological life of the old regime: the ideological support of the political elite and the ideological role of the cultural elite. Lenin's innovative Marxism, which valorized the role of the professional revolutionaries, was a rationalization for a leading political role of at least some intellectuals. Despite the disparaging sentiments directed by Party apparatchiks against the intellectuals, for their irresoluteness, their privilege, their disconnectedness from the proletariat (the real force of history), intellectuals in large numbers became the party bureaucrats who ran the Party-state. And those who did not, those who maintained their commitment to a distinct intellectual or cultural endeavor, set apart from official politics, were generously supported by the socialist regime to promote its legitimacy. Cultural works favorable to the socialist order were used as a substitute for actual popular support expressed through free elections. The claims that the socialist order was the order of the future were affirmed by the imaginative and "scientific" works of supportive intellectuals. The socialist order, more than liberal democracies, needed intellectuals for operation and legitimacy, and, as a consequence, intellectuals (Party and state officials along with creative artists, scholars, and scientists) enjoyed privileges unknown to the general population.

These privileges are especially evident after the fact, after the fall of the communist system. For those who were part of the party apparatus, old privileges have proven to be transferable. The administrative skills and the access to assets and information explain why a large portion of the new capitalist elite was in the past part of the old communist elite. But for the old cultural elite, serious problems have developed. Well-subsidized publishing houses, theaters, centers of research, newspapers and magazines, art galleries and museums, and the like, are no longer needed for ideological purposes, and the people whose lives depend on these institutions are experiencing rapid downward social mobility.

Yet, despite the advantageous position of the old political and cultural elites, when we think about the experience of the intellectual in previously existing socialist societies, privilege is usually not the first condition that comes to mind. Rather, political repression of culture and the struggle for cultural freedom seem to have been the definitive characteristic of "socialist" intellectual life. Aleksander Solzhenitsyn, Andrei Sakharov, Vaclav Havel, Adam Michnik, George Konrad et al. . . . against the repressive Party-state. Along with the recruitment of "cultural workers" for the building of socialism came severe restrictions on cultural life. The intellectual struggle for autonomy came to be at the center of resistance to the communist system. It was indeed the worst of times, as well as the best of times, for intellectuals.

The privilege and the repression together defined the situation of intellectuals in the previously existing socialist societies. The problems of the economics of intellectual life today are more like our own, so they are more understandable. But the politics of intellectual opposition was more at the center of the functioning of the failed system; its legitimacy and stability were on the line. The intellectual oppositionists, the so-called dissidents, engaged in a long struggle against the communist orders. The evolution of that struggle and its final outcome gave us civil society as a new ideal of political life.

ON THE ROAD TO CIVIL SOCIETY

To begin with, the oppositionists, the dissidents, were a kind of loyal opposition. Those who were not loyal, those who did not accept the legitimacy of the socialist order, were brutally repressed. Dissidents, when they were successful, used the rhetoric of the new order to question the details of its implementation. Over time and in different settings, a broad array of work followed this pattern: from the various avant-garde art and literary movements of the twenties in the Soviet Union to explorations of Marxist Humanism in Poland, Yugoslavia, and Hungary in the sixties and seventies. The politics connected with such cultural works also varied over time, strikingly represented by the major crises of East Central Europe, from the Hungarian revolt of 1956, to the Czechoslovak reforms of 1968, to the Polish reforms, uprisings and protests of 1956, 1968, and 1970.

In each crisis, the political struggle was centered around the attempt to make the socialist order more humane: to include in its daily life the concerns of ordinary people as they had to confront their problems. Demands ranged from insistence on fair food prices to pleas for the freedom of the press and of the university. The rhetoric of socialism was utilized in the pressing of the demands. When economic planning failed to deliver a decent standard of living, striking workers demanded the creation of workers' councils in Poland and Hungary in 1956. This innovation was presented as a truer form of socialism. When an attempt was made to include liberal guarantees of freedom of the press and competitive elections in the prevailing order in Czechoslovakia and Poland in 1968, this was called socialism with a human face. Despite the fact that the Hungarian revolt was violent and was clearly pushed by a grass roots social movement, while the Prague Spring developed through elite-inspired reform, in both the break with the ideals of socialism was only suggested by the course of events, but never occurred.

After the failures of 1968, in Czechoslovakia and in Poland, the opposition broke with the socialist ideal. This involved a practical adaptation to the course of political events and a real theoretical break. As a practical matter, the possibility of the humane trans-formation of the socialist system seemed to be unattainable. Revolution from below, in Hungary in 1956, did not work. Reform from above, in Czechoslovakia in 1968, did not work. And in Poland, reform from above in 1956, and from below, through the actions of intellectuals and students in 1968 and the actions of workers in 1970, also did not work. Given Poland's long and frustrated experience, it should not be surprising that it was the place where an alternative political strategy developed most prominently.

The starting point of the new approach combined the realization that the system could not be changed from within with an appreciation that traditional anti-communism, which rejected any collaboration with the "reds," had few prospects. There was an understanding that the system was too strong to be overthrown head on, but it was too rigid to accommodate real social change. This led to the abandonment of Marxism, as a language of criticism, by intellectuals, and to what came to be a self limiting movement of reform from below on the part of opposition activists. Socialism and Marxism came to be totally discredited. They came to be viewed as so intimately linked with the existing repressive system that intellectuals and their fellow citizens could only think about change in the most pragmatic of terms. There was a desire to say no to various sorts of indignities, to increase as much as possible areas of self-determination, without presenting a radical immanent critique of socialism and without presenting a systemic alternative to the existing system of domination.

After the strikes of 1970-1, the workers of Poland were determined to resist unexplained steep increases in food prices. This was clear to even the most casual outside observer in the early seventies.[5] When the increases were announced in 1976 to the surprise of no one, apparently apart from the leadership of the Polish United Workers' Party (the CP), there were spontaneous protests throughout Poland, which led to the rescinding of the increases within a day of their announcement. The Polish economy was in a shambles, and it continued to decline when the price increases were not instituted, but more important from the point of view of the fundamental changes of the coming decades was the strategy intellectuals developed in response to the workers' revolt and its repression.

Some of the worker activists were severely repressed as a result of their actions, after the unrest was quieted. Poland's leading critical intellectuals formed a defense committee to support the workers and their families, and to publicize their situation to the nation as a whole. They formed KOR (the Polish abbreviation for the Committee to Defend Workers), an organization which later became renowned world-wide[6].

There was an apparently humble quality to the activities of KOR, which would be replicated on a much larger scale by the activities of *Solidarnosc* four years later. It did not demand the resignation of the government which so unwisely and undemocratically instituted food price increases, nor were there demands for the government's resignation on the grounds of its unjust repression of worker activists. Rather, attempts were made to press for a fair trial for the workers facing socialist justice, with demands that the socialist legal standards, i.e. the laws of the communist regime, be respected by the authorities.

An illegal newsletter, *The Bulletin of Information,* was published by the group to inform its limited audience about the progress of the workers' cases, the efforts to support them and, later, the situation of workers throughout the country. This proved to be the beginning of an extensive alternative cultural system, which by the eighties included alternative university courses (the *Flying University*), literary and arts magazines, publishing houses, newspapers, and even alternative (clandestinely broadcast) radio and television. When the authorities did not repress the limited illegal publishing, it grew into a large-scale alternative cultural system which developed to a degree that officialdom could no longer repress it, not even with the imposition of martial law. An alternative system of public life, a free public life, formed. Although the independent trade unions of the seventies, which were a small part of this activity, were rather modest affairs, their development into *Solidarnosc*, the nation-wide, independent, self-governing trade union, was the fruition of the democratic opposition's activities. These activities were not directed against the prevailing communist order. They did not have as their explicit aim challenging the legitimacy of the Party-state. Rather, they sought to create a domain independent of Party control and direction.

There was something odd about this strategy. It did not seem real or, at least, usual. It seemed to be outside of the normal understanding of the goals of political action. Conventionally, political orientations and tendencies were directed toward the state, increasing or decreasing its power, changing its directions, even abolishing it (the position of the anarchists). Yet, there was Lech Walesa declaring that this labor movement, which clearly challenged communist dominance of Polish society, was not a political organization and did recognize "the leading role of the communist Party." He seemed not to be interested in the state at all. The image he used was the one of the opposition: of society versus the authorities, where the end of social agitation was for society to be left alone, at least a little more than it had been.

When this was the strategy of the small democratic opposition, of relatively isolated urban elite intellectuals, it seemed to many, thinking in conventional terms, to be one destined for failure. The authorities would use a sort of "socialist repressive tolerance," allowing intellectuals to play their games of invisible independence, publishing little dissident sheets and the like, while the Party-state used its repressive apparatus and the mass media to define the situation of the great bulk of the population, maintaining its monopolistic grip on power and privilege in society. Following this strategy, the Party would both maintain its dominance and gain some increased legitimacy (especially for foreign consumption) as being liberal.[7] But this interpretation failed to recognize how the "civil society" strategy, on the basis of principle, linked past experience with future possibilities in a cogent fashion.

In the socialist system, an alternative social life had been built into the very structure of the socialist order. On ideological grounds, the Party had attempted to direct and control all aspects of social life. Agriculture, industry, education, housing policy and urban planning, philosophy and the arts, genetics and physics were all subjected to official inspection, interpretation, and control. Censorship, political repression, and, in the end, economic failure were the direct, most well-known, consequences of this. But there was as well an unanticipated consequence: the systemic resistance of the competent against the incompetent.

Experts in farming, industrial technologies, housing and cities, along with cultivated scientists and artists, sought with success to maximize their autonomy from those who would define their fields according to the official ideology and not according to the demands of their specific fields. A systematic alternative to the official order was built into the social structure of politically controlled practices. It, of course, existed more as a potential than as an ongoing reality, but it is this potential the oppositionists acted upon. They brought forth the implicit civil society that existed within the communist-dominated social structure. Society in its apolitical and even anti-political form opposed the state.

The activists themselves did not at first see the relationship between their anti-political actions and the old concept of civil society. The developing idea of acting freely in a repressive context, of acting "as if one lived in a free society," creating zones of increasing freedom and viewing these as the proper end of oppositional action, was presented by Adam Michnik, one of the leading intellectual activists in the Polish opposition, in his major piece, "The New Evolutionism."[8] He and his active compatriots used the imagery of society versus the state. Although the term civil society was not being used at first, the idea had been used as a way to describe the nature of totalitarianism in the intellectual circle to which Michnik addressed himself. The by-then-exiled Polish philosopher Leszek Kolakowski, had characterized the uniqueness of totalitarianism as its systematic attack upon civil society a few years before Michnik's famous article.[9] Kolakowski argued that the destruction of the autonomy of independent social life, of a civil society, was the major characteristic of communist totalitarianism. With Michnik's practical argument circulating around the same national and international circles as Kolakowski's, the application of the one to the other was soon made by observers of Polish political events. Among an international group of intellectuals connected to the democratic movements in Eastern and Central Europe, the idea of civil society applied to the situation of actually existing socialism gained currency. In Hungary, Mihaly Vajda used the concept to explain theoretically the fantastic Polish development of Solidarity. In the United States, Andrew Arato did the same, as he interpreted the Polish events for his American audience. And in Poland, the theoretical application became a part of opposition political discourse.

A new concept was born, or more precisely an old one was given new life.[10] In a sense, this was of little significance. Lech Walesa and his fellow workers in *Solidarnosc* did not change the course of their actions because a small group of intellectuals around the world started using an old-fashioned term to describe them. The logic of acting as if one lived in a free society had its own momentum; it did not need refined intellectual support. The workers established their own authority as a consequence of their independent political actions.

Yet, the discussions about civil society did point to connections between the actions of these workers and the rest of Polish society, freed from the ruling ideologies. For the communists, the workers were of special importance not only because they had potential economic clout. They also were supposed to be the agents of history: the revolutionary socialist class. That the workers were in revolt against the purported workers' state presented a deep ideological crisis for the communists. As long as the ruling ideology was accepted, the central importance of the workers' revolt for the whole society was clear. With the delegitimization of the ruling ideology, though, it was not. The idea of civil society proposed by dissident intellectuals made it clear that there still was such a link between diverse social classes, between people who lived quite differently. This became especially important when a state of war was declared by the Polish authorities in December 1981. The mode of resistance took full advantage of the insights of a civil society theory. Underground Solidarity concentrated on maintaining an alternative cultural and social world independent of Party control. Most of these activities did not directly benefit the workers of the trade union. Yet, their understanding of the importance of an independent social force free of the Party-state assured their support. The renewed concept informed the strategy of one of the most extraordinary political struggles of our time, contributing in a significant way to the collapse of the Soviet empire.

CIVIL SOCIETY AND THE INTELLECTUALS AFTER THE FALL OF COMMUNISM

From the practical context of Eastern and Central Europe, interest in the concept spread beyond the confines of the old Soviet bloc. Liberals (in the European sense) were interested because it suggested that their critique of the bureaucratic state, that of both actually existing socialism and the welfare state, seemed to be confirmed by interest in the subject. Their cheers went to and for the market. Conservatives were interested because the primordial units of the family, community, and religion could be included in a concern for civility. And even social democrats and American liberals could be interested in the idea of civil society because the limitations of industrialized visions of social democracy could be confronted, and the strengths of the so-called new social movements could be included in the concern for civil society. This was an old concept for new times.

It is important to bear in mind the transformations of the concept. In the hands of contemporary thinkers, civil society has come to be problematically related to the system of economic practices, while it is generally agreed that civil society is clearly apart from the state. Whereas liberals and neo-liberals (in the European sense of these

positions) are glad to identify civil society with the free workings of
the market, as was the case for Ferguson, Hegel, and Marx, many
contemporary analysts and political actors join de Tocqueville in
seeing a more problematic relationship between civil society and the
economy. Thus, for example, both the conservative sociologist
Edward Shils and the social democratic political theorist Michael
Walzer view the distance from pure economic calculation as being a
definitive attribute of civil society.[11] For Shils, civility cannot be
reduced to economic calculation; patterns of respect and deference
are a key to a civil order. For Walzer, a civil society is one in which a
level of decency is accorded all citizens; economic degradation is
understood as being unacceptable. On both (American) liberal and
conservative grounds, civil society has its intellectual advocates. The
ideal of civil society has become a carrier of opposing values and
conflicting interpretations. It has become a way to consider alternative notions of the good society and the common good in the
West. Ironically, in the former Soviet bloc, it has been challenged in
a significant way.

AROUND THE OLD BLOC

In the former communist world, the recent fate of the ideal of civil
society is directly linked to the fate of the independent critical
intellectuals and their role in the emerging democracies. The
intellectuals were identified with the ideal of a civil society. As we
have observed, strategic necessity inspired theoretical innovation.
Dreams of an officially sanctioned "Humanistic Marxism" and a
"Socialism with a Human Face" ended in nightmares, and a group
of intellectuals, initially small in number, began to develop a unique
strategy, a reform from below, one which involved ignoring the
politics of the Party-state. They advocated a societal secession from
the Party-state in delimited spheres of cultural and social life. At
first, the strategy in the hands of the intellectuals was confined to
symbolic acts supporting human rights activities and some independent publishing. The aforementioned activities of KOR, and the
activities of Charter 77 in Czechoslovakia, and journals such as
Beszelo in Hungary and *Zapis* in Poland, typified this strategy of
opposition. The societal strategy revealed its full potential when it
developed popular support. Solidarity in Poland expressed its
strength.

After the fall of communism, the strategy and the theoretical inquiry led to new problems and questions in the former Soviet bloc. Opposition was not enough; the social constitution of a modern order was the primary task. Discussion about civil society moved in two contrasting directions. In the post-communist orders which had experienced a significant democratic opposition, in Hungary, Czechoslovakia, and Poland, talk about civil society began to look suspiciously utopian, and it looked like an ideology for the centrality of intellectuals in public life. It seemed to some that people like Adam Michnik in Poland and Vaclav Havel in Czechoslovakia were using the civil society strategy to maintain their leading political roles. Theirs seemed to be the position of the impractical and self-serving intellectuals. Both the danger of intellectuals and their impracticality have been a concern of civil society's critics.

People and particularly the new political and cultural elites were tired of the intellectuals' impractical dreams. Civil society seemed to be a contemporary version of the old promises of socialist society. This was a time of hard geopolitical realities. The pressing tasks were state building and the construction of a sound market economy. The ideal of civil society seemed to come from the world of dissent: at best fuzzy-headed, at worst, a leftist subversion of the free market, a disguised neo-communism. Here was the Czech battle of the Vaclavs: Prime Minister Klaus versus President Havel, the power of the market and the promise of consumerism vs. the power of the powerless and civic ideals, the businessmen versus the intellectuals. Variations on the Vaclav themes were observable elsewhere.

But at the same time, the theme of civil society was playing itself out in a strikingly different way. Places like Bulgaria, Romania, Slovakia, the former Yugoslavia, and the former Soviet Union seemed to lead the way in adopting fundamental questions. Can a civil society be built in the newly independent nation-states? Has a civil society ever been a part of their experience? Will it be a part of their future? Even in the nation that experienced oppositional civil society activity to the greatest extent, Poland, the capacity to sustain a civil society as a normal component of societal life, and not as part of a conspiratorial subversive structure, seemed to be far from certain.

Civil society in these inquiries was understood in two distinct but related senses, as Gellner has explained more generally. On the one hand, civil society was understood as being the distinct location in a

social order where free associational activity, apart from the imperatives of the state, tempers the state's capacity to dominate. (Some,
such as Cohen and Arato, would add the same qualification of
market and corporate domination.) On the other hand, civil society
is a society as a whole in which such social qualification functions as
a regular and primary part of social life. The prime examples are the
nation-states of Western Europe and North America, according to
Gellner, not as typifications of modernization, as a universal necessity,[12] but as special and difficult cases of social organization.

The attacks upon civil society tended to function in what might be
called the magical domain. Some, such as Klaus, purported to
answer all political and economic problems with the magical wound
of the market. Shock therapy and privatization would solve all the
problems of the so-called transition. He seemed to be counselling, to
paraphrase the old union slogan of Joe Hill: "don't mourn, priva-
tize." Don't become consumed by the problems of ethics and
memory, build a sound economy. Western transitionologists presented similar formulas for the making of proper constitutions and
the building of adequate civil service and policy apparatuses.
Concern for civil society seemed to be hopelessly out of date when
compared with the pressing practical needs of state building and the
construction of a sound economy.

The problem with these apprehensions is that the differentiated
structures of modern societies were considered as alternative keys to
the non-defined transition, purportedly the transition to democracy.
Some argued that the economy is the key to the successful transition;
others that it is state building, and still others that it is civil society.
Here we have an empty contestation. It is the stuff of which good
academic debate is made. Advocates of each position can marshall
the evidence in their favor and publish in the pursuit of tenure and
professional advancement. The notions that needs of the state or the
market must take priority over the concerns with civil society are
also material that can help fuel partisan debate. Ideologists on each
side of the question can man the barricades with their axiomatic
certainties. Blend the academic foolishness with the partisanship,
and ideological struggle may be forthcoming. It is sometimes
observed by critics that absolute commitment to civil society model
is a rationalization for critical intellectuals,[13] but it is no less true
that absolute commitment to the market is the ideological commitment of the businessman, and absolute commitment to the state is

the commitment of the politician or the bureaucrat. Beyond such dogmas, recognition of the interconnections among the economy, state, and civil society make the exclusive concern with one without the others incomplete.[14]

Yet, the tendency toward ideological formulation is very real. There has been a tendency for the intellectual innovation, the perception of civil society as a part of contemporary life, to get carried away with itself. The advocacy of civil society can take on an ideological appearance when the term takes on a misplaced concreteness. Another consequence of the misplaced concreteness is that the civil society position can seem to be strikingly weak relative to the institutions and political forces it is up against.

People acting freely in public had great effect in and against the communist orders. People spoke and acted together as if they lived in a free society and in the process they created an alternative political power. This brought to mind the importance of civil society as it had been explored in the history of ideas and led to fuller considerations and descriptions of civil society in modernity. In East Central Europe, though, it led to the idea that civil society may be *the* appropriate model of transition, especially important as nationalism appeared as the alternative form of mobilization. It came to appear to some that the alternative normative grounds for transition was nationalism or civil society. Thus, Gellner chooses civil society over democracy as the way toward an open as opposed to an authoritarian society. Note the echo of Popper in the subtitle of his *Conditions of Liberty*, "civil society and its rivals."

This for obvious reasons led to considerable consternation. On the one hand, if civil society is in fact the alternative to authoritarian systems, if we think about civil society systemically and structurally, it is strikingly weak in the societies of the former Soviet bloc. Civil society is a West European and North American exception, not a part of the past or the present of Eastern and Central Europe. On the other hand, as a systemic alternative in this unusual part of the world, it seems to be the creation of intellectuals under the guardianship of intellectuals. It is civil society by command of the intellectuals, not as the development of the natural course of events. It seems to be a rationalization of class power.

These negative aspects of the civil society "model" are not the necessary result of intellectual innovation, but are, rather, in large measure a consequence of a misunderstanding of the role of the intellectual in democratic society. The innovation should help the intellectuals and their fellow citizens to consider and talk about the problems they face. They do not provide easy or complete answers to political problems. Civil society is not the answer to the transition, but a way of perceiving its complexity. It helps observers and political actors come to appreciate a significant dimension of the societal changes which have occurred with the fall of communism, and can inform deliberation and action based on this appreciation.

Important aspects of civil society, particularly a free press, exist to a much greater extent after the fall of communism than before. Before the great changes of 1989, the alternative systems of publication in Poland, Czechoslovakia, and Hungary helped facilitate the formation of an independent public opinion that the authorities had to confront. Foreign broadcasting, such as Radio Free Europe, amplified the impact of the alternative system. Yet in comparison to the role of the free press today, not only in these countries, but also in Russia, Bulgaria and Romania as well, the previous system of free public communications was minuscule. In each of these countries, newspapers expressing a broad range of political opinions flourish; radio and television are not absolutely free of government influence, but in comparison to the communist control of the past, they are remarkably independent. Russia has even managed to tolerate a free critical press in the time of war. This does not mean, of course, that all is going well in these countries, but it does mean that the state does operate in a way that is fundamentally constrained by an independent public opinion. The ideal of a fully developed independent civil society may be a long way off. A civil society in the Anglo-American sense never did exist, but the societies are significantly "civilized," extending the sort of action that marked the beginning of the changes in the eighties. This is an important part of the changes these societies have experienced, every bit as important as the changes in the political and economic systems.

There is a wide array of citizens' initiatives around the old bloc which are now a part of the political realities along with the free press: from women's protection groups in the former Yugoslavia, to human rights groups in Slovakia, to the trade unions of Poland. These groups are not always appreciated by the new political elites, and the groups' battles for their continued existence are far from assured, but that they exist is testimony to the persistent viability of civil society in post-communist societies.

The proponents of civil society may have been the critical intellectuals in the previously existing socialist society, and among the chief proponents of civil society in the post-communist orders are again the critical intellectuals, but unless they maintain that civil society is *the* key to democracy, they are advocating a position that cannot be construed as being a rationalization for their access to power. Like reasonable advocates of market reforms and state building, they are responsible defenders of important independent institutions of complex society. One institutional sector – the economy, the polity, or civil society – cannot be substituted for any other.

The practical question about civil society is, though, not whether civil society exists or not, but how broadly does it function, how does it relate with other components of society, and what are its effects? The free market critics of civil society are concerned that a focus upon citizen initiatives will frustrate the formation of a sound economy. The proponents of sound state-building and statecraft are concerned that the immediate functioning of popular sovereignty will make the constitution of the rules of the political game impossible. The advocates of civil society also have their special concerns, related to the workings of the state and the economy: the threat of a politically manipulated populism and nationalism drawing on the economic frustrations of those who are suffering from the economic changes and do not understand them.

Populism, of nationalist and other varieties, is a real threat in the post-communist situation. Yet, the proponents of civil society point out that the economic changes are unlikely to be successful without popular support for and understanding of them, and constitutions that do not address the concerns of organized society are merely pieces of paper. Civil society is a way of making economic change effective within a democratic political environment, of increasing understanding and support through public discussion, and of making constitutions and the rule of law legitimate. The balance between the threats and supports of the independent public action within a civil society for economic construction and state-building is a matter of political judgment and action.

The viability of civil society is especially important in Eastern Europe because of its apparent social alternative, authoritarianism and xenophobic nationalism. Nationalism of the worst sort has become a significant part of the post-communist situation, not only in the former Yugoslavia, where the television cameras and the world press have focused our attention, but also in the former Soviet Union. Dangers of nationalist repression very much exist in Slovakia, and potential tensions exist between Hungary, and Slovakia and Romania, and between Poland and Ukraine, and Russia and the Baltic Republics. Authoritarian xenophobic nationalism is very much a part of the political landscape, and the way to avoid nationalism is not at all clear since it still has a remarkable capacity to mobilize populations.

If we think of civil society as a well-developed type of social organization, it will appear to be too weak in the post-communist situation to address adequately the problems of manipulated xeno-phobia. It will seem that another way of resisting waves of collective hysteria must be formulated. Some believe the discipline of the market will do the trick, others that corporatism is the answer. They hope that the power of the market or of a rational state will stem the tide of primordial irrationalities. Others are more fatalistic. They see the realization of a more humane social order to be a matter of collective fate: limited to those who are more European, are truly a part of Central Europe, have a Habsburg and not an Ottoman past, and so forth. Technocratic responses and resignation to civilizational fate seem to be inevitable alternatives to primordial hatreds when civil society is reified.

But when civil society is understood in a more concrete, and less ideological, fashion, the search for magical solutions is abandoned, as is lazy reference to civilizational fate. Instead attention is focused on the expansion of the concrete actions of free public activity as the actualization of a civil society, and the effects of these actions can be charted. The story of civil society is not a new grand narrative, replacing the narratives of the state and the economy, but a minor narrative to be considered along with others by the democratic public.

For the involved political actors this presents a possibility that an alternative to the failure of democracy exists. For outside observers, it suggests how to make sense of the failures in the Balkans, along with the relative successes of Central Europe. We observe, with dismay, how the state-controlled media manipulated public opinion in the Balkans, inflaming a far from inevitable genocidal conflict. We observe how civil responses to the slaughter, such as the organization Women in Black, in Croatia, Serbia, and Bosnia work to inform opinion in other ways. Beyond the Balkans, we can analyze carefully the struggle for free media in Russia and observe its effects on the ability of the state to execute an unpopular war in Chechnya. And in detail, we can observe the formation of networks of voluntary associations and independent social institutions, as they develop around the old Soviet bloc, and help redefine societal life, interacting with the development of a democratic state and a sound economy.

The actions of self-declared independent intellectuals and citizens helped revive the concept of civil society, as it contributed to the demise of communism. The same type of action can contribute and has contributed to a more humane post-communism. It is of crucial importance that the practices of intellectuals, as political actors and as observers, do not make such civility seem unattainable.

IN THE FORMER FREE WORLD: IN THE WEST

In "actually existing democracies," such as the United States, the intellectual's task concerning the ideal of civil society is in many respects the opposite of the one in the former Soviet bloc. In the East, there is a need to avoid overly reified terms, to realize that the narrative of civil society is not grand, but minor. The tyranny of theory is a recent memory. It is sown into the fabric of societal and political life. Intellectuals as philosopher kings are held in deep suspicion. The tyrannies of anti-Marxism threaten to replace smoothly the tyrannies of Marxism: markets for anti-markets, and nationalism for Leninism. The idea of a civil society in this context must not appear to have a misplaced concreteness. As an alternative to communism and anti-communism, it is too weak. And when it does not appear to be too weak, it appears as an ideology for the continued ascendancy of intellectuals. The societal referents of the term in their concreteness need to be appreciated; if they are not, they may be overlooked. The role of theory and ideas in the West is very different. A strong dose of theory injected into the body politic would not be a bad thing. The cry for theoretical reflection can be heard. The narrative of civil society might be minor, but at least it is a narrative that can inject sense into public deliberations. Public theoretical reflection seems to have become a monopoly of the right. Ideas that may provide an alternative to the right's overrationalized conception of men and women and oversacralized conception of the public good are much needed.[15] One can almost hear the people's cry for civil society.

The "civil society strategy," born of the apparent weakness of the opposition in the context of a totalitarian power, said a great deal about politics in the modern era, and the nature of social movements of the political East and the West. Thus the writings of such anti-political authors as George Konrad, Vaclav Havel, and Adam Michnik gained wide Western readership, and not only among close observers of the old bloc. The imagery of the oppositionists of society set apart from the authorities looked a great deal like the ideal of a civil society articulated independently of the state. Civil society became an international hot topic of theoretical inquiry. But the translation of the concept into the political world of the Western democracies is a difficult endeavor.

The term civil society, as we have observed, is heard in political discourse of everyday life in the former Soviet bloc in two different negative rhetorical contexts. Either politicians and citizens wonder whether they ever had one and whether they are capable of having one under present conditions, or those who use the concept or ideas related to it are critically appraised as propagating a new ideology to sustain the hegemony of the intellectuals. In the political West, in the United States specifically, the term appears in a more confused fashion. It is used in ways that fit a wide assortment of alternative political orientations, ranging from George Bush's "thousand points of light," to feminist attempts to sustain an independent social movement, to conservative attempts to de-statize social welfare programs and reinterject conservative religious morality into public life. It is simultaneously under- and over-theorized. The modifier, civil, appears in political discourse before the noun, society, as a way of expressing little more than the idea of good or peaceful society. As I write this text, I notice that with the conclusion of the successful negotiation of a peace agreement in Bosnia, a spokesman for the State Department hoped for the sustaining of a civil society as the alternative to continued war. There is not much specific understanding about the nature of civil society in such a declaration. The spokesman was not thinking about any particular set of social and political arrangements reminiscent of the order that began to emerge in the struggle against communism or in the history of ideas. He was just hoping for a peaceful resolution of the wars in the former Yugoslavia. In the academic world, in contrast, the topic has great specificity and is the subject of serious and sustained theoretical reflection. This apparently explains the reemergence of the term in political discourse, but does not in a serious way inform meaningful political action.

The usual separation of public life and academic life is exaggerated in the case of the civil society idea. It is a new term which serves both academic and public purposes, but the latter does not inform the former because the idea of civil society moves against the academic current. While it is connected to the greatest accomplishments of the political intellectuals, the definitive defeat of twentieth-century totalitarianism, it moves in opposite directions from dominant academic fashions: deconstructivism, post-modernism, and multiculturalism.[16] Said's concern for the subaltern, as we have observed, involves a turning away from the nurturing of an autonomous non-partisan public space. There are some bases of commonality: both academic fashion and the civil society thinkers are usually skeptical about grand narratives of progress and liberation; both the fashion and these thinkers are aware of the limitations of enlightenment dreams of the rule of reason, and critical of the conflation of power and truth; both the "post-modernists" and the "post-totalitarians" are aware of epochal changes in the way we think and the way we act. But there are striking differences as well, centered around the evaluation of liberal traditions of democracy and freedom; academic fashion assumes and radically questions them, while civil society thinkers are aware of their historicity and fragility, attempting to substantiate them further.

It is on the political left that the idea of civil society would seem to be of the greatest practical interest. After the fall of communism, the right makes sense, both its market and moral logics make sense; to a large portion of the general public (even though these two logics have inherent contradictions), while it is notable world-wide that the left no longer speaks a sensible language for the general public. Yet, despite the need for a new way of understanding and organizing public action, civil society is subjected to sustained theoretical critique from the left. It purportedly privileges those who are hegemonic and the system that sustains the hegemony of males, whites, and privileged classes. A clear disjuncture exists between the practical implications of the academic left cultural critique of the injustices implicit in the liberal political and cultural order, and a civil society critique of the order of things. The cultural left focuses on identity politics, the possibility of knowing and its cultural framing, and the subversion of hierarchies of cultural judgment; the advocates of civil society (and a related group of intellectuals often identified with communitarianism) want to transcend identity politics, establish a consensual grounding for truth, and maintain that cultural judgment must be sustained. The advocates of civility in the West do not only face the resistance of those who argue for the logic of the state and the market; they face as well the criticism of those who view them as apologists for the ongoing workings of the liberal state and the market and their injustices. The alternative to the right is fractured; intellectuals disunite. The way to overcome this fate is in the actual politics of culture in society, to which we now turn. We will observe the struggle within the institutions of civil society in post-communist Europe and consider the transformed role of the artist-intellectual in this struggle. Then, we will apply insights of this observation to an understanding of the lives of intellectuals in actually existing democracies.

CHAPTER 6

The intellectuals and the politics of culture after communism

My research experience in Central Europe, from a marginal cultural movement, Polish Student Theater of the post-war era, to a marginal but articulate political movement, the Polish democratic movement of the seventies, to a broad and profound societal movement, *Solidarnosc* of 1980 and 1981, to an underground oppositional cultural movement, Underground Solidarity of the eighties, to the major transformations of 1989 world-wide, testifies to the potential power of the intellectual in democratic society.[1] It points to the importance of the ideal of civility and the intellectual's relationship to it. This experience suggests that when we reflect on the significance of the intellectual in democratic society, we should keep in mind that the consequences of intellectual actions may seem relatively isolated with fleeting duration, but can become wide ranging with long-term consequences.

My experience further suggests that the intellectual may be not only a public scholar or scientist, or a scholarly or scientific political actor, but also an artist with public concerns. The Central European intellectuals, who acted as if they lived in a free society, constituting freedom and revitalizing the idea of civil society, often were artists, poets, painters, musicians, the makers of film and theater. Their experiences, and the relationship between these and the experiences of others, provide us with an opportunity to consider more closely the changing role of artists as intellectuals in the making and substantiation of democratic society, and to consider the connection between the artists' struggle for cultural independence and the task of constituting the institutional supports of civility.

In this chapter, we will take advantage of both of these opportunities. I will show how the practical experience of artists in totalitarian situations informed an anti-ideological and anti-political orientation to intellectual life. I will examine this orientation as it clarified in the critical theory of Milan Kundera and the social actions of artists and intellectuals both before and after the fall of communism. We will then consider the broad general implications of these experiences, orientations, and reflections for intellectuals beyond the old bloc.

The distinction between the role of the scientist and that of the intellectual is much more easily drawn than the one to be made between the role of the artist and of the intellectual. Following Sartre, we may understand that a physicist is acting as an intellectual when he signs a letter of protest against nuclear armaments and not as an intellectual when he works in his lab. We may further realize, contrary to Said, but following the insights of Mannheim, that both Oppenheimer against the bomb and Teller for the bomb acted as intellectuals. Using one's expertise as the grounds for addressing a general public is a key to such distinctions. Yet, this simple distinction is not as easily made in the case of artists and artist-intellectuals. We may be able to assert such a distinction when we contrast the painting of Picasso in "Three Musicians" and his design of the dove of peace, but does the distinction hold in the case of "Guernica"? Sometimes the work of an artist is an intellectual act, a public, even a political, intervention, and sometimes a purely artistic act, as it is interpreted, is transformed into an intellectual intervention, and sometimes a deeply political art is depoliticized. The difficulty in making such distinctions is an important part of the intellectual power of art, but it does not mean that all art is political or intellectual. The situation of the artist in the old regimes of East and Central Europe reveals wonderfully the complexities involved.

The situation of the artist in previously existing socialism was unique. In a world with little space for free deliberation and political action, it often was left to the artist to provide the opportunity for citizens to consider alternative views of existing political realities. There were no alternative political movements in Poland in the early fifties, for example.[2] All political alternatives were repressed by the Stalinist regime. But in the basements of university dormitories, in rudimentary cafés, a satirical theater movement started to develop. The works of student theaters were theatrically simple. They did little more than mock the official order in a charged social context.

When the performers read from the Party press, all they had to do was read the headlines with an eyebrow raised to turn official propaganda into a parody of itself. Indeed, even without the eyebrow, the context of the theater setting of like-minded critical performers and audience assured the satirical effect. Theater presented a space, when none other existed, for sharing discontent with the official order of things.

From these modest beginnings, student theater developed significant artistic ambitions and complexity. The great works of the interwar *avant-garde*, of Stanislaw Witkiewicz and Witold Gombrowicz, first found a Polish audience in these theaters. Polish and international classics were performed as alternatives to socialist realism. As the aggressive political expression of these theaters became less possible during the early sixties, with the increasing rigidification of official politics, student theaters enriched the Polish cultural scene, making significant contributions to a theater which was becoming renowned internationally as one of the most accomplished and challenging. Despite official censorship, this theater world was far more experimental than, for example, American theater. Among the great representatives of the Polish theater scene were: the "Poor Theater" of Jerzy Grotowski, the "Plastic Theater" of Jozef Szajner, the dance theater of Henryk Tomaszewski, and the numerous innovative productions of classic and modern drama at such centers as the National Theater in Warsaw and the Teatr Stary of Cracow.

In 1968, one of these theaters dramatically connected the cultural and the political, highlighting how art contributes to public deliberations and to free civil actions, how artists and their audiences come to act as intellectuals. A production of a Polish classic, *Dziady* (Forefathers Eve), at the National Theater led to a major student revolt and then to an anti-liberal, anti-semitic crackdown by the Polish regime. The play, a great dramatic epic poem by Adam Mickiewicz, included portions with anti-czarist lines. The audience reacted strongly to these, turning the production into an anti-Russian demonstration. While it was not at all clear whether the demonstration was a result of a particularly provocative production or the provocation lay with the audience, in January of 1968, the performance was forced to close. Apparently, those in power in Poland and in the Soviet Embassy deemed the production and the audience's response to it an anti-Soviet manifestation. The final performances were packed, including famous cultural figures who returned from abroad to support the production and to be seen by the public. The disturbance then went beyond the theater walls to a demonstration at the statue of Mickiewicz near the university. Protests were held at the university. Demands were made for artistic, cultural, and academic freedom. The protesters were brutally attacked by workers sent by the police. An infamous nationwide "anti-Zionist" campaign was launched. The Party used the traditional method of anti-semitism to repress a movement for cultural and political reform.

The exact circumstances of the protests and their repression are still mired in controversy. It is unclear whether the whole affair was a provocation of one faction of the Party or another, looking to gain ascendancy against its ideological opponents, or if it were, as it appeared to be, an open confrontation between forces of reform and forces of reaction, which were manipulating the anti-semitic card. For the present purposes, it is sufficient to observe the complicated nature of the connections between the artistic and the political, without examining their direct relationship with the configuration of social and political forces then operating in Poland. A work, which by all accounts was not explicitly tendentious, became a public statement, an occasion for a public forum. A fine piece of literature became a political expression.

Yet, extensive interviews with Polish and East European independent and critical artists, in and out of theater, have revealed that they strongly resist an explicitly political art.[3] In a cultural context in which official art had been used as an instrument of the Party-state, independent artists and critics have understood art as a separate domain, not reducible to politics. Paradoxically, writers and other artists who have played a major role in the politics of previously existing socialism have been most vociferous in their disdain for political art. A subtle distinction was made in the artistic realm which anticipated the strategy of civil society as it later developed in Central Europe.

The performance of *Dziady* was understood as not being a political act, just like the performances of the student theater movement I studied were understood both by the regime and its creators as not being political. They were permitted and created as artistic endeavors. The creators of the theater, literature, poetry, and the plastic arts agreed that the task of the artist is to create an independent world of aesthetic expression, not engage in politics. This approach to the politics of culture was common throughout the old bloc. An explanation of this position has been clearly articulated by one of the most famous and controversial writers of Central Europe, Milan Kundera.

Kundera is another intellectual whose biography is filled with paradox. He is well known for his political pronouncements and for his opposition to totalitarianism, but he is, as well, a forceful opponent of political art. Famous outside of Czechoslovakia as a representative figure of the opposition to communism, the author of novels such as *The Joke, A Book on Laughter and Forgetting*, and *The Unbearable Lightness of Being*, which are filled with attacks on the stupidities of totalitarianism, he was seen to be a sellout by a broad spectrum of the dissident circles in his native land in the eighties.[4] While he has been an articulate dissident from the official order of things, both in previously existing socialism and actually existing capitalism, a strong opponent of ideological politics and culture, and of commercialized culture and political life, he has somehow managed to flourish as a leading cultural figure on both sides of the old iron curtain. Kundera's novels are saturated with political and philosophical reflections. Yet, he is not an anti-communist author, and he never confuses literature with philosophy.

It is within these paradoxes that Kundera summarizes the role of the artist as an intellectual supporter of democratic society. Kundera is a partisan of the "art of the novel," the title of a collection of his critical essays. In these essays, taken together with his volume *Testaments Betrayed*, Kundera presents an account of the artist as a contributor to democratic and free society.[5] A key to his account is the non- (even anti-) ideological nature of good art. Kundera describes the broad theoretical and political significance of his position in *The Art of the Novel*, and he develops a non-tendentious understanding of art in *Testaments Betrayed*.

His art is that of the novel. About its independent value, Kundera is unambiguous. He traces the history of the novel to Cervantes and asserts that "The novelist needs to answer no one but Cervantes."[6] In answering Cervantes, Kundera maintains, the novelist is giving definition to great European ideals, presenting an alternative to the negative vision of modernity elaborated by philosophical pessimists such as Edmund Husserl and Martin Heidegger. They express dismay over the crisis of technological civilization, and Kundera observes that the novel presents the alternative.

If it is true that philosophy and science have forgotten about man's being, it emerges all the more plainly that with Cervantes a great European art took shape that is nothing other than the investigation of this forgotten being... All the great existential themes Heidegger analyzes in *Being and Time* – considering them to have been neglected by all earlier philosophy – had been unveiled, displayed, illuminated by four centuries of the novel...[7]

For Kundera, this form of remarkable cultural achievement must be understood as a revolt against the claims of rationalism and science. He observes:

the spirit of an age cannot be judged exclusively by its ideas, its theoretical concepts, without considering its art, and particularly the novel. The nineteenth century invented the locomotive, and Hegel was convinced he had grasped the very spirit of universal history. But Flaubert discovered stupidity. I daresay that is the greatest discovery of a century so proud of its scientific thought.[8]

Distanced from science and rationality, the art of the novel, and indeed all art, ought to be distanced from the realms of morality and politics as well. In *Testaments Betrayed*, Kundera considers the consequences of mistaking art for politics and ethics. The testaments of art are betrayed by the sentimentalities and manipulations of ethics and politics. Kundera reflects on the damage done to the art of Kafka and Janacek by Max Brod, Kafka's great friend and advocate. They wrote and composed playful works of ambiguity, while he promoted them as serious moral advocates. His moralism, his commitment to the serious moral reflections on the tragedies of modernity and to the national significance of a Czech composer, turn his readers away from their artistic accomplishments. And in doing so, they are turning away from life toward kitsch.

Kitsch is "the translation of the stupidities of received ideas into the language of beauty and feeling,"[9] It is:

a seduction that comes out of the collective unconscious; a command from the metaphysical prompter; a perennial social imperative; a force. That force is aimed not at art alone but primarily at reality itself. It does the opposite of what Flaubert, Janacek, Joyce, and Hemingway did. It throws a veil of commonplaces over the present moment, in order that the face of the real will disappear.[10]

Kundera favors art in the battle against kitsch. European civiliza-tion, as he understands it, is at stake. Confusing this project with that of politics is to diminish human capacity. The point is not that politics, philosophy, or art is a more fundamental enterprise; it is that they are different and must be distinguished.

Even the politics of culture, as a positive intellectual project, would be compromised if they are not so distinguished, Kundera suggests. He tells the story of a concert by Glenn Gould.

Glenn Gould gives a concert in Moscow for the students of the conservatory; after playing Webern, Schoenberg, and Krenek, he gives his audience a short commentary saying: "The greatest compliment I can give this music is to say that the principles to be found in it are not new, that they are at least five hundred years old"; then he goes on to play three Bach fugues. It was a carefully considered provocation: socialist realism, then the official doctrine in Russia, was battling modernism in the name of traditional music; Glenn Gould meant to show that the roots of modern music (forbidden in communist Russia) go much deeper than those of the official music of socialist realism (which actually was nothing but an artificial preservation of romanticism in music).[11]

This is the sense in which the performance of *Dziady* in 1968 was political, and it is the sense in which the youth theater of Poland in the post-war period engaged in a political project as it maintained its cultural independence, and it is the sense in which the deeply apolitical Kundera came to be known as a political intellectual. Theirs is a political engagement which emerges from within the cultural autonomy and traditions of an independent artistic culture. It is a politics for the independence of civilization against the stupidity of totalitarianism and repression, the independence of a free public life against the ideological intervention into the cultural sphere.

There was a kind of natural history to the politics of this independence. In the darkest days of Stalinism simple acts, such as those of Polish Student Theater, were involved. Managing to say forbidden words, publicly sharing doubts about the official order of things, were significant accomplishments. Some space was opened for the independence of aesthetics and for political critique with the protection of these simple acts, but not much. With limited liberalization of the repressive system, in the post-Stalinist period, more aesthetic innovation was possible, and there was more sustained, if often subtle, room for political criticism. Gould's performance and comments on his performance, as reported by Kundera, indicate the nature of this development. There was acceptance by the regime that the official aesthetics should include the accumulated accomplishments of cultural traditions. The official claim was that these accomplishments reached their zenith with the achievements of socialist realism, but Gould the performer and his audience, and the critic Kundera, could contrast the official claim with interpretations of their own. They could, in public, share a refutation of official claims in performance and discussions about performance.

It is within such space that the performance of *Dziady* and its audience's reaction occurred. Its broad political implications developed because there was the opportunity to explore the world of Mickiewicz within the political context of the Polish People's Republic. Mickiewicz's work was banned during the Stalinist era, seen as being a remnant of a reactionary past. After political changes in 1956, which brought into power a regime that used as its official ideology the notion of a Polish road to socialism, the availability of works such as *Dziady* legitimated the official politics. Kazimierz Dejmek, the director of the play, used this in 1968 to produce a new rendering of a national classic, a centerpiece of Polish literature, and it passed censorship on these terms. In interaction between audience and performer, including the audience from the Soviet Embassy, the cultural work became a political provocation, a way of questioning the existing, as well as the historic, relationship between Russia and Poland. The intellectual intervention included the active presence in the public of intellectuals and artists, i.e. in the audience, once the play was banned. The mass demonstrations were a continuation of this intellectual intervention.

This sort of half-visible, half-hidden, intellectual intervention was predicated upon the actions of the authorities, on the existence of an official truth and censorship. Intellectual action was anti-ideological in the sense that it was based upon the avoidance and subversion of official ideology. Later, in the aftermath of the repressions of 1968 in Poland and in Czechoslovakia, the official ideology was turned off, in two stages: first in the early and mid-seventies, as an act of subversion, then in the late eighties, as a result of the collapse of the official truth, culminating in a struggle for a new civility, the constitution of a normal civil society. The nature of the intellectual intervention by artists changed with the turning off of the censor, the frontal denial of the legitimacy of the official truth.

In the first stage, in relative isolation, artists and intellectuals started to do their work as if there were no official censorship, a process we have observed in the previous chapter. They worked to subvert the official socialist order. They started to create their work without considering what the potential reaction of the censor would be, and without considering official justification for their works' acceptance. Political theorists and activists interested in human rights no longer went through mental gymnastics to account for a marxist humanism, a national road to socialism, or socialism with a human face, and poets and novelists stopped attempting to demonstrate the progressive projects of their works to themselves, their audience, and the authorities.[12] These works were directed against ideology in general and not only pitted against a specific ideology. They revealed an appreciation of the distinction that should be made between ideology and culture. Kundera's account of the novel neatly summarizes the aesthetic and critical disposition of this cultural movement.

Later, the cultural sensibility came to animate political activism of intellectuals and of a broad public in the Solidarity movement in Poland, reflected in the theoretical discussions in and about civil society, as we have already seen. The struggle for establishing an independent world for cultural expression and reception, which had in a sense its beginnings in the raised eyebrow in student satirical theater, developed with the cultural space revealed in the work of performers like Glenn Gould and of commentators, writers like Kundera, and flourished with the establishment of Solidarity. With Solidarity, and the developing oppositions in Eastern and Central Europe, and the collapse of the Soviet Union and bloc, the task was transformed from the cultural project of dissent and subversion of the official ideological order, to the sociological project of turning the symbolic public space established by cultural work to the institutionalization of this space, to the constitution of autonomous cultural institutions. Intellectuals and artists had to transform a sort of Socratic gadfly status into a more permanent and normal modern form of existence.

THE POLITICAL PROJECT OF CULTURAL AUTONOMY

The problems intellectuals and artists in the old bloc face after the fall of communism are both substantively political and cultural, and, more formally, structural and institutional. The move toward the institutionalization of cultural autonomy follows the pattern we observed in chapter 2. There is an establishment of a normal zone of intellectual action, regularizing the condition of the modern intellectual. Following a modern pattern, the problems intellectuals and artists in the old bloc face, in some ways, are becoming quite like those of the more established democratic societies, but in others they are still strikingly different. There are also increasingly important differences among the intellectuals of the previously existing socialist societies.

Intellectuals, as political actors and not cultural creators, find themselves in extreme situations. They are at the forefront of diametrically opposed political and cultural tendencies. Some, such as Mihajlo Markovic, a social theorist from Serbia, view the recent past as a repressed nightmare and the distant past as a primordial reality, becoming ideologists for nationalism and xenophobia. Others, such as Vaclav Havel, a playwright from Czechoslovakia, attempt to take responsibility for the recent past, avoiding idealizations of the distant past, and attempting to act democratically and liberally in the present. Both of these particular men were activists of the left opposition to actually existing socialism: Markovic a leading member of the Yugoslav Praxis Group, and Havel a leading member of the Czechoslovak Charter 77. They, along with many others, are now on opposite sides of political divides, separating a variety of nationalisms from each other and from liberal democracy. And both Markovic and Havel, and many other intellectuals like them, have profoundly disappointed their previous comrades. They are judged to be failed politicians: Markovic, as a chief ideologist of the Milosovic regime, because of his effective support of the insupportable, Serbian hegemony and the pursuit of ethnic cleansing, and Havel, as the last President of Czechoslovakia, because of his ineffective support of the highly supportable, the preservation of the federation of the Czech and Slovak republics and the pursuit of a liberal democracy. Indeed, because of extremism on the one hand, and ineffectiveness on the other, intellectuals have very rapidly left the political arena, sometimes provoking horror, and sometimes in bewilderment.

The collapse of the communist left opened up the political arena to anti-communist intellectuals, many of whom had past associations with communism and were, at least in their backgrounds, of the left. For decades, there were no legal opposition parties, people of the right lived in obscurity if not in jail, and all governmental and even economic positions were controlled by the Communist Party. Thus, relatively independent critical intellectuals, those who functioned in the embedded civil society, artists, writers, and professors, were among the few people capable of engaging and leading the public. Havel, as the playwright President of the Czech Republic, epitomizes this phenomenon.

The political leadership of such intellectuals immediately after the fall of communism, which was relatively short lived, exhibited some of the classical problems of intellectuals in power, typified by nationalists such as Markovic and democrats such as Havel. On the one hand, intellectuals were apt to commit themselves to a politics of ultimate ends, as Max Weber once put it. On the other hand, they were prone to moralisms and a tendency to propose theoretical solutions to problems demanding immediate practical solutions. They became guilty of the treason of the intellectuals that Julian Benda denounced over sixty years ago. Nationalists maintained that they were defending the interests and the honor of their compatriots, while their society fell apart and ordinary people suffered. Their concern for the good of the nation was focused upon some idealized version of the past, a sort of primordial utopia. The actual predicament of the nation, let alone of other nations, was not considered. Intellectuals self- identified as democrats also often have not understood the situation of the people in whose name they acted. They have thought too much about the processes of democratization and not enough about the condition of the demos. As we observed in the previous chapter, democratic intellectuals have imagined an idealized future, a "normal" civil society, which is in fact their notion of West European society. They have realized how far they are from such a society and have sought to enact the necessary reforms to foster its achievement. International institutions such as the World Bank and the IMF even have encouraged them to do this. Some politically engaged democratic intellectuals have become obsessed with the problems most observable to their own theoretically overdetermined experience. In the name of democracy, they have too often ignored, or viewed as obstacles, the concerns of their fellow citizens. Intellectuals who became politicians tended to become enamored with their own ideas and to lose sight of the concerns of their constituents. They viewed politics abstractly, missing its concreteness. In my view, this was what possessed the intellectuals who became enamored with shock therapy at any cost.

In the normal course of events, in established democracies, the danger of intellectuals in politics is relatively minor. They are politically marginalized through normal democratic procedures and democratic prejudices. As should be apparent, I am not at all alarmed by this tendency. It is now becoming evident in Central Europe. The intellectuals' abstractness, their lack of understanding of the concerns and views of their compatriots, has led to their defeat in free elections. In the Czech Republic, Hungary, and Poland, this has been the fate of both nationalist and democratic intellectuals. As in the United States and in Western Europe, the intellectuals probably will not play a direct political role.

We observe yet again the separation of culture from politics, which characterizes the historical entrance of intellectuals on the modern social stage. Some of the differentiation follows the path of public rejection just described; intellectuals are rejected by their fellow citizens, the voters. But even more commonly, intellectuals themselves have sought to avoid direct political engagement. This is an institutionalization of the cultural sensibility of artists such as Kundera.

Immediately after the fall of communism, there was a vacuum of political leadership which independent minded intellectuals filled, some quite reluctantly. When that period ended, their vocation had to be considered anew, along with their relationship to the general public. Many, of even the most politically engaged, sought a non-political existence, or at most the political role of the critic and commentator, rather than the role of the direct political actor. They built upon their past experience of an anti-ideological political existence, even naming their political orientation "anti-politics".[13] The problems of intellectuals in post-communist Europe, then, became more like the problems of intellectuals in the post-anti-communist west, with the major differences being that communist ideology penetrated the societies of the old bloc much more thoroughly than did anti-communism penetrate the societies of the "free world," and the institutional supports for an independent intellectual life were in disarray in the societies of previously existing socialism. At the same time that the sensibility of a differentiated culture was central to the creative practice of leading intellectual artists in the region, the actual differentiation was quite under-developed. Intellectuals developed a sensibility which was a reaction to the inadequacies of their everyday existence.

A primary aspect of cultural politics in the region, thus, includes significant struggles to maintain or establish the autonomy of cultural life. There are struggles to maintain and establish intellectual and academic status, and there are struggles to reach the public. There are attempts to understand the changed circumstances of political, social, and cultural life, and there are attempts to avoid or deny the necessity of seeking such understanding. It is on the political margins that significant intellectual action can be found, not only, or even primarily, in the heroic leadership of society in the fashion of Havel and Markovic.

In order to understand the way the challenges of the post-communist period are being met, it is necessary to examine more closely the differences among the intellectuals under communism and then how they are adapting to their changed situation. At the risk of some oversimplification, I believe we can observe four different types of intellectuals in the previously existing socialist system. There were the party-ideologists, the official cultural workers, the officially accepted relatively independent intellectuals, and the oppositionist intellectuals. These types of intellectuals have responded to the post-communist challenge of establishing the conditions for an autonomous cultural life quite differently.

Those who most closely identified with the communist order, who were the prominent apologists and enforcers of Marxism-Leninism, have lost their institutionalized grounding. Their previous position was defined by the de-differentiation of cultural life by the Party-state apparatus, and with the apparatus gone so is their position. They have responded in three ways: withdrawal from the cultural field, conversion to a new orthodoxy, or recommitment to their failed ideological vision. In a strict sense, these ideologists were not intellectuals in the past and are not intellectuals in the present. They were servants of the regime, without independent critical judgment. They did not act as people who paid an unusual degree of attention to their critical faculties, but as clerks who paid an unusual amount of attention to official directives.

Yet, they have not spontaneously disappeared. They are trying to maintain their jobs sometimes by playing old political games or by adapting to the new ideological order of things. Established professors of Marxism-Leninism are suddenly proclaiming their understanding and appreciation for the virtues of liberalism. They are often pretty ignorant of the creed to which they now proclaim fealty, but this often is nothing new, since in their old incarnation as

Marxists, they often had less to do with the writings of Marx than with the commands of the Party. Theirs has been an occupation of survival, and this has not changed. On a trip to Sofia, it was reported to me that a Bulgarian survey of liberal arts academics indicates that most of those employed in the universities still refuse to discuss in interviews political problems concerning the role of the intellectual in the making of the new social order. For these academics, such questions are of private concern, not connected with their professional or public responsibilities. And when such figures face new political pressures for anti-liberal conformity, they continue to be compliant. Thus in Slovakia, there have been pressures against "Czechoslovakies" in the university. That is, the nationalists in the government of Vladimir Meciar have established a political environment which has encouraged nationalists in the university to meet the economic pressures they face by cutting costs through the firing of liberal scholars who were against the breakup of Czechoslovakia (and who were also at the forefront of the opposition to the communists). Those who have done the firing include old oppositionists of a nationalist bent and old communists who have discovered nationalism. Joining them, through their silence, have been the bulk of the academics who survived the communists' purges, the post-sixty-eight "normalization," in silence: professors of the History of Scientific Socialism who have become political scientists, who knew how to survive then and who are surviving now. As a result, the university students of Bratislava have again been kept in ignorance.

I am pointing to one of the most sensitive issues in the politics of cultural life of the post-communist period: the need to purge the university (and other cultural institutions) of the political hacks of the old order, on the one hand, and the need to go beyond the politics of purges, on the other. In Slovakia, they have had the worst of both worlds. Yet, everywhere intellectuals face these problems. In eastern Germany, they have just about completely purged the professors of the old regime, while in the rest of Eastern and Central Europe, although the most incompetent and the most compromised have been encouraged to retire, the great bulk of the professoriat remain in their positions.

As I have already suggested, this is not as bad as might be assumed. If we imagine that the communists indeed succeeded in turning the university and other cultural institutions into Party-state apparatuses, the continuity of officially tolerated intellectuals in positions of authority would indeed be dismal. Yet, in fact, built into the existing structures were conflicts between those who took seriously the independent cultural values of the university and other cultural institutions and those who were ideologically most rigorous. The tension existed everywhere, though the balance differed greatly. In Czechoslovakia, after 1968, independence was rare, but in Poland the universities were for the most part relatively independent institutions, especially after the birth of Solidarity. Such independence, which to some degree existed throughout the old bloc, was predicated upon official tolerance of some independent intellectual and cultural judgments, necessary for the ruling elite if it hoped to benefit from the fruits of such cultural activities as scholarly inquiry, and upon complicated strategies of intellectual independence by those who in the main worked within the ideological system. There were those who attempted to appear as official cultural workers to their Party-state supervisors, but who attempted in one way or another to achieve some independence as they accepted the official limits and fulfilled their official responsibilities.

Now many people remember themselves as being part of the "opposition from within." This took many forms, from Party leaders who believe they showed greater leniency in fulfilling their repressive responsibilities than someone else would have in their position, to the workers in the Party press in the basement of the Central Committee headquarters in Warsaw, who published opposition journals and books. In a certain sense, almost everyone was a hidden oppositionist in Eastern and Central Europe, since just about no one believed in the ideological scripts they were forced to recite. Yet, since the system worked through an odd legitimation process, which I have labeled and analyzed elsewhere as a legitimation through disbelief, it is hard to maintain that all those who now remember their distance from the prevailing system did not serve the functioning of the order. They may have made it momentarily more humane, but they still served the order of things, as it was.

I do not mean this judgment to be as harsh as it may sound, because I am well aware that the order of things included a great deal of cultural and even political independence. Great artistic works which had nothing to do with official ideology were created and reached a public. Educational institutions maintained standards of cultural excellence apart from official ideology. Science of international quality sometimes flourished and not only that which had direct military application. Perhaps more often cultural mediocrity was the rule, but that there were striking exceptions indicates the great importance of those who were part of the system but preserved and created anew works of independent intellectual value within official institutions. These people and their works are the starting point for normal intellectual life of the post-communist period.

The intellectuals who survived and helped autonomous culture to persist now find themselves in a changed situation. The patterns of adaptation of the past inform and misinform the present. The commitment to cultural autonomy has to be much more positively rendered than in the past. It is not enough to resist the powers that be; cultural autonomy must be positively supported. The facilities for cultural life were politically administered in the past. Educational institutions, as well as publishing houses, art galleries along with theaters, movie theaters as well as film production companies were supported by the Party-state. The struggle for autonomy was about avoiding the ideological strings that came along with the support. Reaching an audience was never a problem, because the public for culture also was politically administered.

Now the state is withdrawing its support, and the intellectuals are facing a new set of problems. Not only are they short of support, their public has become quite uncertain. The mass culture of the West, especially from the United States, competes with the innovative cultural work which used to draw such wide attention when it somehow managed to surface. The political daring of some intellectuals is now available as the normal part of competitive politics. Marginalization appears not only in the political realm, but in the cultural realm as well, and some intellectuals are clearly confused by this. Institutional subversion is not enough, now institution building is the pressing imperative.

The only independent institution builders of the past were the hardcore oppositionists. They were the ones who freed themselves from the official order and established an independent social world, a civil society in miniature. Moving from this world in miniature to broader societal projects is of course not easy. There are some striking successes, such as the transformation of the underground Solidarity newspaper in the Warsaw region to *Gazeta Wyborcza*, now Poland's leading daily, a paper known for both its high journalistic standards and its commercial innovations. There are interesting attempts to establish independent institutions of higher learning in Bulgaria, Slovakia, and Poland, and there are numerous new research, consulting, and marketing firms, along with new cultural centers and commercialized galleries and media. Nonetheless, in many cultural institutions, inertia and slow decline seem to be the order of the day. As the central governments attempt to adjust to the hard budgetary realities of the economic transformation, there are dwindling state funds for cultural enterprises, and as these funds diminish, those with positions in cultural institutions fight to maintain their position. All but the most compromised maintain their position, and as a result there is little room for innovation and institution building. I do not mean to suggest that the situation is hopeless. It is not. But, I do want to point out that institutional reform is far from easy. Among the most aware and most accomplished intellectuals, those who were steadfast in their commitment to intellectual integrity during the communist years, there is an understanding that fundamental change is both necessary and likely to be very difficult.

INTELLECTUALS AND THE PROBLEMS OF UNDERSTANDING

The necessity of change goes beyond the need to adapt to the destatized politics, economics, and culture. It involves, more profoundly, the need for the intellectuals to come to terms with the confusions of the post-communist era. Their world as they have known it for generations has been overturned.

Around the old bloc, people have a remarkable sense of having emerged from a political, economic, and cultural sleep. For a long time, membership or activity in the Communist Party was the primary referent for being political. The secondary referent was opposition to the Party. Economic activity effectively meant fulfilling or circumventing the five year plan. And the life of the arts and sciences was focused on Party-state patronage and on censorship and repression. Societal activity was so much channelled by Communist Party domination that the sudden disappearance of the domination has caused profound disorientation and confusion. Conservatives who sought to maintain order in the recent past simply supported and attempted to strengthen the Party, and those who sought change on liberal, radical, or conservative grounds withdrew support, as much as this was possible, and attempted to weaken the party. Suddenly, without the accustomed political monopoly, the orientational grounds for social action have been transformed. The past fifty to seventy years appear as a dream, the logic of lifetimes as phantom visions; even the distant past, the past of monarchs, national heroes, and imagined greatness seems more real.

Their problems of understanding is related to problems of understanding evident in more established democratic societies. In the liberal democracies everywhere, conservatives, liberals, and radicals are confused by the collapse of communism. Conservatives and liberals have lost a unifying opponent which facilitated consensus among liberals and conservatives, as well as distinguishing conservatives from liberals, i.e. related to hard versus soft approaches to communism. And radicals have had their fundamental belief that there is a systemic alternative to capitalism cast into doubt. The post-modern claim that we live in a fundamentally different order certainly does gain saliency when we consider how our basic modern political categories of the left and of the right have been confused. Yet, compared to the situation in the old bloc, elsewhere the situation is one of clarity and stasis. Their world has been fundamentally disrupted. People need to understand the most elementary logic of their new situation.

Herein lies the great promise and paradox of intellectuals in Eastern and Central Europe. The intellectuals of this region significantly contributed to the impossible, the peaceful overthrow of totalitarianism. They did this by reasserting the power of free public discourse in a repressive context. Yet now when there is a concerted attempt to institutionalize democracy in this region which has had very little democratic experience, this lesson of the intellectuals is being lost, overwhelmed by the imperatives of establishing a sound economy and an ordered and perhaps even democratic state. Thus, the need to strengthen and extend autonomous cultural institutions has not been viewed as being of primary importance. And thus, informed public deliberations about the problems in the new order are being limited. A free debate and a free press certainly do exist, but the acute analysis of opposition circles, which reached an informed public well beyond those circles in the recent past, is not being extended as much as it could be. The practices of the artist intellectuals no longer seem to be of great importance.

Intellectuals of all sorts are attempting to adjust to the new realities. They are defending their positions, and they are attempting to create new ones. They are struggling to figure out how to maintain and extend cultural autonomy, given the very new obstacles they face. They need to learn how to bring the fruits of that autonomy to a broader public, something which came almost automatically in the times of opposition. Interestingly, voices of the subaltern may help to extend the public and strengthen civil society, as is the case with the struggle to establish women's movements in the region (discussed in chapter 10). This all has broad implications because of the situation of the polities of East Central Europe. The desire to maintain a secure existence can overwhelm the struggle for cultural autonomy. Fairness toward intellectuals of the old school can lead to the miseducation of the younger generation. If creatively reflective work does not reach the general public, the confusions of the immediate post-communist situation may lead to political, economic, and even military disasters. It is likely that all of this will happen in some places and some of it will be avoided in others. Intellectuals play a pivotal role in the new democracies, and their struggle for cultural freedom continues to be at the center of their public existence.

Indeed, the struggles of the Central European intellectuals, both before and after the fall of the communist systems, have been focused on the struggle for cultural freedom. In the recent past, as with the case of Socrates, they were primarily concerned with speaking their own minds in a hostile setting. In the name of progress and working people, the authorities restricted public life, censored cultural works, rewarded those who paid tribute to the "ideological gods," and punished those who "mocked" them. The punishment, in the worst of times, even equalled that of Socrates. There was, though, a significant difference between the case of Socrates and that of the intellectual critics of the communist regimes, a difference belied by the term used to identify these critics, dissidents. The "dissidents" sought to articulate views opposed to the authorities, but not to common opinion. Quite unlike Socrates, they tended to champion positions held, or at least not opposed, by the general population. As we know quite well, this did nothing to better the conditions under which the critical intellectuals were forced to live, nor did it directly weaken the repressive force which they faced.

After the fall of the communist regimes, it is tempting to conclude that the struggle for cultural freedom represented a clear victory for freedom by the critical intellectuals over the cultural bureaucrats.

Yet, this sort of account minimizes the experience of the years of repression and cultural sterility. It then seemed that the world of "actually existing socialism" was the alternative modern social order, and that intellectual dissidents were a group of isolated impractical idealists who did not face up to prevailing realities, of little consequence in the world of practical action.

While the struggle for cultural freedom in the recent past often did seem peripheral, it now appears to have been of the highest practical importance. An understanding of the role of the intellectuals in democratic society must include both of these perceptions. Although intellectual activity, specifically as it is centered on the issues of cultural freedom, frequently seems to be superfluous, it often appears after the fact to have been of crucial importance. One can imagine how the practical movers and shakers viewed Socrates in his day. Yet, his influence is still with us. In the old Soviet bloc, the intellectual chickens came home to roost rather rapidly (if we think in large-scale comparative historical terms). From the early sixties, intellectuals created zones of critical autonomy apart from the official order, and this has proven to be highly consequential. The activities of these intellectuals created the space for more open public deliberations.

Now, as in the established democracies, the intellectual politics of cultural freedom appears within the context of the struggle for security. People who made their peace with the old order and compromised the cultural freedom of critical intellectuals are naturally trying to do the same again. Involved are: ideological compromises of the worst sort and normal human accommodations, the weighing of the relative merits of various political stances and consequential political conflicts over relatively small differences in intellectual judgment, intellectual ironies and seriousness, dogmatism and tolerance. In short, the struggles over cultural freedom in the new democracies are very much now like the struggles over cultural freedom in societies such as the United States, to which we turn in the next chapter.

CONCLUDING REFLECTIONS: THE IMPLICATIONS BEYOND THE OLD BLOC

The political experience of intellectuals in Eastern and Central Europe certainly cannot be easily generalized. The central democratic role they played was unprecedented, and will not easily be repeated. Other intellectual revolutionaries have significantly affected the politics of their day – French and Russian revolution- aries and their imitators come to mind – but their support of democracy has been highly problematic, at best. Strikingly, what distinguishes the East and Central European intellectuals is their self-limitation, their understanding that there is a strong distinction to be made between their intellectual visions and criticisms, and the world of political struggle, competition, and compromise. Thus, there is the reappreciation of civil society as an ideal, an understand- ing of the importance of a free public life independent of the mandates of the state and the economy, discussed in the previous chapter.

In this chapter, we have observed how this unusual political and theoretical orientation has been linked to the activity of and ideas about artists, developed in the communist period. Since these positions were formed in a political and cultural situation which is now over, it may seem that they do not have much to say to the post- communist and the post-anti-communist situations. Yet, in that a key to the power of the art, and the social and political practices which applied the sensibility of the art, was the opening of space for deliberation in a totalitarian context, and in that we live in societies characterized by a *deliberation deficit*, the experience of Eastern and Central Europe does speak to our concerns. It points to the desirability of an aesthetic position that involves an appreciation of the distinctive contributions the art of the novel (and of the other arts) has to make in enriching our reflections on the human condition, and it points to the necessity of constituting social supports for opening space for public deliberations. Recent experi- ence of the post-communist societies points to the imperative of establishing independent cultural institutions, and the need for intellectuals to work for such institutions. These intellectuals have been leaving the central political arena, willingly and unwillingly, and engaging in more specialized struggles in the cultural sphere. As they do this, I have argued, following the insights of Kundera, they are supporting the constitution of a more democratic society. Yet, there are limitations to this position. The institutionalization of cultural autonomy is not only supportive of democracy. Much that is of importance in the arts, for example, has little or nothing to do with politics and public life. It may be the case that the artist who contributes to an understanding of the human condition, such as Kundera's novelists, contributes to the deliberative capacity of a society, both through a confrontation with the complexities of the human condition and in the development of human capacity through the development of artistic form. But there is more to art than these contributions. Art may have little or nothing to do with deliberative capacity. It may be, and often is, a private pleasure or challenge, not a matter of public concern. It may not be critical. It may celebrate connectedness, rather than be the work of the sort of stranger who is an intellectual. A good society includes such non-political, non-public cultural endeavors. A democratic society that includes these is certainly more desirable than one that does not, although the fate of democracy does not necessarily lie in the balance.

Further, it is also the case that cultural freedom, of the artist and of others, may be antagonistic to democratic society. The life of Socrates again comes to mind. But also the life of Plato. Developed autonomous cultural institutions, including the academy (now as well as then), may become too distant from other institutions of society and less able to contribute to democratic life. They may even undermine democratic life. With this concern in mind, we now turn to a consideration of the American university and then to the confrontation with identity politics in the United States and between the old political East and political West, considering both the necessity and the limitations of cultural autonomy.

CHAPTER 7

The university

A vibrant intellectual life is not assured by the autonomy of cultural institutions. Our East and Central European colleagues are now struggling for a necessary but not a sufficient condition of their deliberative role in democratic society. This is most evident as we turn to the American scene, particularly to the American university. On the grounds of the American university, we often observe how the autonomy of a cultural institution may even work to undermine intellectual criticism and public deliberation. This is of great importance because much of America's public life is now found in the universities, overshadowing the traditional public spaces of cities. As painting, music, and theater have found their place in American universities, so has intellectual life. The strengths and weaknesses of the American university, as an independent cultural institution, therefore, have broad public implications.

When we look for intellectuals in American society, the natural starting point is the universities. It has not always been the case. Through much of American history, intellectual life was a component part of the liberal professions,[1] and even up to the post-war era intellectuals tended to center around independent journals and magazines more than in university departments and research institutes.[2] But today general interest magazines and critical political and cultural reviews no longer are profit making enterprises on the open cultural market. They are more often appendages of academic departments. And the professions are focused much more tightly on their areas of expertise than on their civic responsibilities. Universities are where the great bulk of the intellectual action is. I will attempt to show that the struggle for university autonomy has established conditions for free intellectual activity, but that the achieved autonomy, as well, has compromised that activity. Within the American university, intellectuals, scholars, and narrow-minded professionals have developed an autonomy not only from the centers of power, at least on occasion, but even from their publics, with very negative results.

The autonomy of the university in America has been a long-term elusive goal; the university's relationship with public life and the life of intellectuals has constituted a complicated cultural reality. This is not because significant autonomy has not been achieved, but because its achievement and its results, in relationship to one center of power, have been followed by its compromise in relationship to another center or set of centers of power and with the public at large. The elusiveness of the autonomy and its complicated consequences have been results of the pluralism of American society, or, more precisely, of the complex differentiation of power in American society.

Academic autonomy was an issue at the very beginning of the settlement of colonial North America. The Puritans came to the shores of Massachusetts Bay in order to practice their religion freely. Contrary to the old myths Americans have learned in primary schools, they came here not to establish the principle of religious freedom, but to be able to practice their religion, in their minds the true religion, freely.[3] This practice included training for the ministry. Thus, Harvard College was founded. The tension, between the positive freedom which the colonists sought and the negative freedom with which the old elementary school lessons confuse it, has been ever since a part of academic life in America.[4] Back then, the struggle of the new educational institution was to train the next generation of ministers, true to the religious vision of the Puritan community, free of the influence of the Church of England. Later, the issue of autonomy involved attempts to become free of the earlier task in educational life, to be free of indigenous religious orthodoxy. With increasing religious diversity in America in the eighteenth and nineteenth centuries, and the development of an enlightenment view of culture and politics, the struggle for the autonomy of higher education was waged against sectarianism.

Thus, Thomas Jefferson, after being President, became the great academic radical of his day. In the spirit of the enlightenment, he viewed religion as the enemy of free liberal education. His struggles to free his university, the University of Virginia, from dogma took the form of the founding of a state – and not a religiously backed – university. To his mind, this was the way the university could be free. Later in the nineteenth century, others tried to establish an intermediate path, endorsing the religious basis of liberal education, but seeking to make the base non-sectarian, a generic Protestantism. In the last century, Jefferson's approach to higher education seemed to involve the most radically independent position, too radical for most of the educational reformers who followed him, for those in both the public and the private sectors.

Ironically, in recent years state universities and colleges have been contrasted to "independent universities and colleges" (often institutions founded by religious orders), revealing the view that the state, and not the Church, is the most likely institution to compromise the autonomy of university life. Indeed, the independence of the American university has been carved out against considerable religious, political, and economic constraints, while the positive roles of university life have never been clearly agreed upon.

From the point of view of university professors, academic freedom is primarily constituted by their right to teach and do research freely, subject only to review by their peers. This is the sort of argument that the American Association of University Professors (the AAUP) has used since its founding in 1915. It is the professional creed of the academic. The AAUP has fought against religious, political, and economic constraints on the academic autonomy of professors since its founding, moving its vision of the university to the forefront of academic life. Academic freedom, it maintains, is the defining attribute of the university. This assumes an idealized view of the university as a community of self-governing scholars, dedicated to independent inquiry, against all dogmatic constraints. The independent authority of science justifies this approach toward university governance.

Yet, from the legal point of view, which is a manifestation of the history and economics of universities and colleges in America, private and public universities are directed by boards of trustees, more similar in their structures and functions to modern corporations than to a feudal collegia dedicated to the pursuit of scholarship. The trustees, and the administration they appoint, have a responsibility to secure funds from both private and government sources, collect tuition, hire and pay faculty, and meet other capital and operating expenses. And as in the government, with the power over the purse strings comes power over policy.[5]

All American universities, then, have built into their organizational structure a tension between the academic, professional model of self-governance and the corporate model of administrative control. To this day, for example, it is not clear whether professors in universities with Church affiliation should be subjected to the discipline of Church authority. In the nineteenth century, this was the primary concern of those seeking a university that was true to the enlightenment mission of scholarly inquiry free of dogma. Yet even today, the administrations and trustees of such institutions, and at least some of their alumni, students, and faculty, tend to argue for some special restrictions and responsibilities in such institutions, as are necessary for their particular missions. These are distinctive institutions, they maintain, which have the right to secure freely their distinctive approach to learning and research. Opponents counter that free intellectual inquiry is the hallmark of academic life. Without it, the university cannot be said to exist.[6] In turn, there are those who worry that the pluralism of academic life is being repressed by enlightenment prejudices. George M. Marsden, the leading historian of religion and the American universities, is concerned that there is no place on American universities for religiously informed inquiry and teaching.[7] The struggles against the constraints imposed by churches have been followed by a transformed situation, in which any religious inquiry or teaching is difficult to pursue in mainstream American universities. This bolsters the argument of those who want to maintain religious restrictions in church-supported universities and colleges, as a defense against the secular orthodoxy of American academic life.

Beyond the age-old conflict between the forces of enlightenment and the forces of revelation, more profane political pressures also have challenged university autonomy. During the First World War, soon after the AAUP was formed, political loyalty was assumed by the administrations of universities and by the public. The notion that dissenting positions would be protected by the ideal and practice of academic freedom was not broadly accepted, not even among professors. In an official AAUP report on "Academic Freedom in Wartime," chaired by Arthur Lovejoy, one of the organizers of the association, it was accepted that academic freedom had to be curtailed, though the report pleaded against excess in repressive practices, lest the side fighting for freedom come to resemble the forces it was fighting against. Declaring political loyalty, and using patriotic rhetoric, the report argued against patriotic excesses, but it nonetheless did condone the firings and dismissals of the disloyal.[8] Such an ambiguous approach to political constraint, coupled with academic acquiescence, has been often repeated, most notoriously during the period of McCarthyism.[9] The commitment against political constraint has been asserted, while political constraints have been accepted.

There are two consequences of this ambivalent position: on the one hand, the freedom of the university from political interference has not actually been realized; but, on the other hand, there have been repeated and escalating criticisms of this state of affairs in the name of academic freedom. Even though there have been serious challenges to academic freedom in the past one hundred years, most dramatically with the demands of patriotism during the World Wars and the demands of anti-communist loyalty during the heights of the cold war, the ideal and reality of the autonomy of scholarly life have spread and escalated during this very period. The initial timid position of the AAUP has been superseded by a situation in which even the most racist and reprehensible are accepted and regularly heard on the university.[10] The distance between the ideal of academic freedom and the reality has strengthened the ideal and in the process changed the reality: proving that there are such things as free speech and academic freedom, and, to my mind, it's a good thing.

I make this assertion with the well-known and controversial literary theorist Stanley Fish, and with the recent struggles over "political correctness," in mind. Again the autonomy of the university has become problematic. In a provocative essay entitled "There's No Such Thing as Free Speech and It's a Good Thing, Too," Fish argues from a new, anti-free speech absolutist position.[11] He has given high-level theoretical justification for political correctness. He reasonably shows that all speech takes place within a restrictive context, using Milton's classic defense for tolerance, his *Aereopagitica*, as a strategic case. Fish examines the apparent anomaly: while Milton argues for tolerance, he makes a huge exception of Catholics and others who are open to superstition. This is not a simple and single exception, Fish maintains, but a commitment to prohibit all speech that would undermine the social order to which

Milton is committed. This interaction between social restriction and public expression is universal, Fish believes. Thus, there is no such thing as free speech. It is a good thing, Fish argues, because this is the way that basic political principles are established. "Without restriction, without an in-built sense of what it would be meaningless to say or wrong to say, there could be no assertion and no reason for asserting it. The restriction or exception comes first, and the expression, *shaped* by the exception, then follows."[12]

Fish presented this argument as part of the controversies over speech codes on American campuses, which some critics take to be a fundamental attack on academic freedom. He was arguing in favor of the explicit restrictions against racist and sexist speech, because he thinks that restrictions on speech always exist, even if they are often implicit. He starts his essay with an imaginative and ironic quote "from" Samuel Johnson and Stanley Fish: "Nowadays the First Amendment is the first refuge of scoundrels."[13] He abandons the ideal because of the reality that freedom of speech is always restricted. He believes, therefore, that it should be abandoned in the struggle against racism and sexism. The autonomy of the university is being questioned by those, such as Fish, on the cultural left today, as it has been challenged by the state and the Church in the past. There is an attempt to assert that a set of moral and political principles should take precedence over the scholarly concerns of the academic community.

Before we consider the controversies over multiculturalism and political correctness and their relationship to the life of the intellectual in the university, one more sort of systemic constraint on academic freedom and intellectual freedom in the university must be recognized, that of economics. As the new ideals of secular research became ascendant, these came into conflict with other secular activities: the political needs of the state in the pursuit of a war effort, the servicing of an economy which has become more and more dependent on the knowledge industry based on universities, and the ethos of business and financial success. The latter Thorsten Veblen scathingly criticized in *The Higher Learning in America: A Memorandum on the Conduct of Universities by Business Men*.[14] The theme of Veblen's classic is that the independence of the university in America has been fundamentally compromised by the idolatry of business and its special form of success, that the forces of capitalism have replaced those of religion and politics as the chief obstacles to an independent life of the mind. Veblen implies an evolutionary progression of the constraints: from the religious to the political to the economic. He seems to have thought that with the new form of constraints, the constraints of the businessman, the problems of politics and religion were things of the past. This has proven not to be the case, as was evidenced by the impact of McCarthyism on the universities. Yet, it must be recognized that business interests do give shape to university practices, as Veblen argues. The preponderance of business leaders on boards of trustees of universities no doubt continues to have an impact on academic life in the manner that Veblen described. University concern for good public relations are the academic equivalent of advertising, as Veblen criticized, and today direct advertising of the most advanced sort is part of the standard procedure of just about all universities no matter how large and how prominent.

Yet, the constraints of politics and religion are also a regular part of university life. This is particularly evident when we realize that the politics and the religion, or at least the religiosity, can take new post-modern forms, most evident in the battles over political correctness. The moralisms of the cultural left and right are being reasserted as constraints on academic practices. This is the ground of intellectual conflicts and the grounds of conflicts against intellectuality.

POLITICAL CORRECTNESS AND THE ACADEMIC INTELLECTUALS

The "PC" debate represents an attempt by academic intellectuals to fulfill their public responsibilities. The cultural left has attempted to utilize the life of the academy as a microcosm of the injustices of the general society, righting the injustices on the immediate social grounds of the university. The cultural right has defended academic conventions as a way of defending the conventions of the society as a whole. While the controversies over political correctness have often been narrow and tendentious ways, they also have suggested significant differences of opinion about pressing problems the society faces. The positions of the cultural radicals and conservatives are presented in a field of narrow contestation, but there is something quite commendable about the debate. They appear as intellectual contestations.

From the point of view of outraged conservatives, the PC problem is centered on the politicization of the universities, the attack on free speech, the imposition of a new leftist orthodoxy. "Tenured radicals" have established an institutional base for their failed politics of the sixties and perverted the minds of the young. For those attacked by the conservatives, the cultural radicals, the so-called tenured radicals, the critique of political correctness is itself an attempt politically to silence the critical and to undermine attempts to overcome racism and sexism in American society. At issue between the cultural radicals and their opponents are competing visions of the political and moral relationship between the university and the greater society, competing definitions of the positive and negative freedoms of the university and of the good society.[15] These visions and definitions open or close the possibility of intellectual life in the university.

For the cultural conservatives, education's most central cultural role is to teach the perceived sacred values of the greater society, as was the case at Harvard in the seventeenth century. They see language codes, the advocacy of multiculturalism, and the attempts to include a broader segment of the population on the universities as politicized compromises of education. They accurately point out that there is much that is ridiculous going on in the universities today, from the odd codes on sexual harassment to the equation of the works of Shakespeare with the latest romance novels. They use the "strangeness" of the cultural consensus within the university to make their point seem most telling. They present themselves as the real intellectual critics: those who dare to question the foolish norms of academia. They play on the distance between the valuative centers of society as a whole and of the university. They are supported by the powers that be because of their societal orthodoxy. They condemn academic orthodoxy in the pages of such centers of critical inquiry as the editorial pages of *The Wall Street Journal*. They pretend to be challenging social critics because they present positions contrary to academic prejudices, as they present the positions of the dominant powers.

Conservatives depict the strangeness of academic customs as a cultural outrage, seeking to make the university more like the greater society in its cultural orientations. The principled conservative position holds that American society is held together ideally by a set of fundamental principles, tested through time, a Western inheritance, constituted from "our Judeo-Christian tradition": thus,

William Bennett's best-seller *The Book of Virtues*.[16] The core task of the university is to teach this inheritance. Notions of multiculturalism deflect from the inheritance or even suggest that "our" core values are not all for the good, equating Western civilization with Western hegemony, declaring that ideas are but masks for power and domination. From the conservative point of view, this is nothing short of barbarism. Dinesh D'Souza's *Illiberal Education: The Politics of Race and Sex on the Campus* develops the conservative position.

D'Souza takes the reader through a tour of major universities, showing how these bastions of privilege have become sites for dangerous ideological wars. He opens with an idyllic picture of the university: "There are few places as serene and as opulent as an American university campus" (p.1). He goes on to demonstrate the devastation of the idyll as a consequence of a three-pronged attack: (1) the perversion of meritocratic admission policies by lowered standards for "certified minority groups," (2) the dilution and displacement of the "core curriculum" by the inclusion of non-Western cultures in the pursuit of multiculturalism, and (3) the "Balkanization" of student life through the promotion of diversity and pluralism in separate institutions for minority groups and the protection of the sensitivities of these groups through speech codes. His is a report on the "Victims Revolution on Campus," playing on an easy dichotomy contrasting the way things are with the way they once were and ought to be again.

His ideal is liberal education, as John Henry Newman depicted it in his nineteenth-century classic *The Idea of the University*. Liberal learning is "that true enlargement of mind which is the power of viewing many things at once as one whole, of referring them severally to their true place in the universal system, of understanding their respective values, and determining their mutual dependence."[17] This integrative catholic position on liberal education, on education that distinguishes a free person from a slave, D'Souza believes, is the way that minority and all other students will achieve "true and permanent emancipation." Such a conception of education is commonly shared by the most vociferous critics of political correctness. Allan Bloom, Roger Kimball, and company believe that the gap between the cultural consensus in the universities and the consensus in the greater society must be eliminated with this ideal in mind.[18] In this way, the university should conform to the greater society.

For cultural radicals, this position is unacceptable. It is indicative of an attempt to rob the university of its fundamental positive mission. Education's crucial contribution is to provide the tools for criticism of the injustices of the social order.[19] If it does not provide such tools, it becomes nothing more than ideology.

There is, in fact, a fundamental tension within the radical position. Critical cultural theory, at least since Marx, teaches that the educational establishment propagates the dominant ideology, the ruling ideas of a time are the ideas of the ruling class. Radicals expect universities to do just what conservatives want. They, though, pit themselves against this expectation by trying to establish critical ideas and practices within the universities.

Although the conservatives are understandably concerned that the radicals have succeeded in their tasks, having politicized the university, from the radical point of view, the idealized conservative status quo ante is the truly politicized situation, where education serves the ideological function of supporting the existing social arrangements. For the conservatives, the essence of today's university problems is in the politicized humanities departments, where the great Western inheritance is under attack, while for radicals, the universities and their ideological functions are epitomized by the departments of the sciences, engineering, and business, as they serve the interests of the state and property. There is a conflict of judgment. The radicals proceed with an understanding that they are fighting against a prevailing conservative institution, which serves the greater society with its cultural justifications and with the technical expertise for its ruling elites. The conservatives see this fight and believe that it has dominated the universities to the exclusion of its proper function.

Many cultural liberals understand that there is something to be said on both sides of the PC divide.[20] For the liberal, education should provide the opportunity to mediate between these two positions. They understand that the complaints of conservatives have some basis, but that there is also a reasonable radical response to these complaints. Affirmative action does apparently challenge the ideal of meritocracy, as D'Souza complains. Yet, it does address the problem that the American university has not served the needs of the African American and the Latino populations until the most recent past. Ideas of multiculturalism and prohibitions against hate speech do contest the sacredness of the core curriculum and the ideals of academic freedom and free speech, but these ideas and prohibitions do attempt to deal with the special problems of a shrinking and more diversified cultural world. It no longer makes any sense to prepare students for an exclusively upper-middle-class white Anglo-Saxon world. Living with diversity has become a contemporary cultural imperative. And even though the promotion of diversity and pluralism in the institutional arrangements of the university can appear seriously to undermine the universal ideal of the university, it can as well be viewed as an attempt to deal with the social organizational problems of heterogeneity in a highly complex and differentiated world. The metaphor of the global village would probably be best replaced with that of the global megalopolis. Not shared values but accommodation and tolerance are what the complex international cultural world now demands, and the organizational attempts by the university to deal with difference can be understood as a rational response to this new situation.

Although there is reasonableness on both sides of the PC divide, there is also a fundamental irrationality in the debate. Conservatives, radicals, and liberals speak past each other, with little evidence that they are taking part in a singular discursive community. Intellectual gestures are made with grandeur, but the gestures are rarely exchanged across partisan divides.

THE INTELLECTUAL SCHIZOPHRENIA OF ACADEMIC LIFE

Stanley Fish's realism about free speech both fails as empirical observation and has highly negative normative consequences. He fails to understand that the existence of the ideal of free speech is an important operating part of the reality of a constrained situation, fundamentally different from the constrained situation where the ideal is not present.[21] In political orders, such as those of the former Soviet bloc, where there is no semblance of free speech, no attempt even to make the ideal appear as part of the everyday reality, cultural freedom is much more severely constrained than in social orders where the appearance of free speech is maintained, even if, as Fish suggests, it is highly restricted. He does not seem to realize that the operating ideal of free speech has the power to transform constrained situations.

This is the case with academic freedom in America. Even while the ideal of university autonomy from political, economic, and religious constraints has often been compromised, the realization that the compromise has occurred, the criticism and discussion concerning the compromised ideal, and subsequent actions based on these criticisms and discussions, work to support and even extend the ideal into actual social practice. During the McCarthy era, loyalty oaths were the order of the day, and people lost their jobs in anti-communist purges. Yet, in the aftermath of this period, the ideal of university autonomy has been significantly intensified and has come to appear as a conservative value. Those on the right, such as William Buckley Jr (and his junior associates such as Dinesh D'Souza), who now rage against political correctness and the politicization of the curriculum in support of the importance of academic freedom, forty years ago called for the realization of Christian and capitalist values on university campuses against the "superstition of academic freedom," as Buckley once infamously put it.[22] On the left, in contrast, people such as Fish seem to think that academic freedom and free speech are hypocritical supports for the prevailing social order, instruments of domination by the privileged against the "other." While there is much that is disingenuous about the debates concerning PC, the positioning of the left and the right suggest a clear social fact: academic freedom is a well-institutionalized ideal in American academic practice. Conservatives now defend and some radicals question it. Their position seems to be less a result of principled academic commitments than a reaction to political climate outside of the university. Nonetheless, it is now clear that the operation of the ideal has a significant effect on the reality, the existing social practices on the university.

Yet, there is something particularly disturbing about the debates concerning PC beyond what I have thus far presented. There is a good deal of bad faith in the PC debates that goes beyond the unsteady support of academic freedom. The debates proceed as if a McCarthyism of the left is a real danger and as if the radicalism of certain academic departments and disciplines presents a serious challenge to the operation of power in American society. Both the claims of the left concerning its critical role and the reaction of the right to these claims and to the cultural practices are highly inflated.

The power and potential tyranny of the left in the American universities is greatly exaggerated. There may be a problem with an overly zealous attempt to avoid racism, sexism, ageism, and classism (to use the jargon of the times) on American college campuses, but the cynical conservative assault on political correctness now makes it seem that any attempt to deal with the problems of race, class, gender, and age is the moral equivalent of Stalinism. There is now a new literary genre in the United States, the neo-conservative jeremiad, which takes the excesses of the youthful cultural left as its primary object of criticism. Excesses, no doubt, there are. Yet, it has become all too convenient to dismiss any attempt at addressing the problems of race and gender as they persist in the university and in the general society. To be concerned about such issues and sensitive to their complexities has become "PC," and decidedly unfashion-able. This makes it difficult to discuss major social problems, and it serves unexamined conservative interests. On the other hand, the idea that new ways of interpreting literature or new speech codes are going to have a fundamental effect on the problems of race, class, or gender is also questionable.

Although the cultural left is attempting to address major prob-lems, its attempts are failing, making it vulnerable to sensible criticisms from the right and from within its own ranks.[23] In a fundamental sense, the left's politically correct cultural politics is anti-intellectual. It attacks the role of the intellectual in democratic society. It moves students away from the free and unconstrained public deliberation. There is a fudging of difficult social questions, such as those of gender and race. Formulaic answers that do not address social and political complexity are provided.

Americans have a hard time talking about race, class, and sex.[24] The well-known politically correct way of dealing with this is to prescribe ways that they should be discussed and proscribe ways they should not be. The names of identity groups have taken on crucial meaning. Talk has been confined to "Women," not to "Ladies" or "Girls," "Native Americans," not "Indians"; "African Americans" and not "Blacks," "Afro-Americans," "Negroes," "Coloreds"; "Asians" and not "Orientals." Granted, the changes in the accepted names reveal something about the structures of deference and demeanor between the dominant and marginalized groups, and a changed name may even serve to free an oppressed group from restrictions tied to their oppression. Yet, these changes do not magically solve the difficult problems of how to deal with the inequities of race and gender. The goals of "diversity" and "multiculturalism" and the obstacles of "Western hegemony" and "dead white men" take on dogmatic dimensions when they are used as code words to promote policies and programs that are not subjected to critical review. Polite politics and policies of euphemism replace serious deliberation, political confrontation, and compromise. A left liberal consensus on dealing with difference is assumed and goes unexamined. And sometimes, in the universities, the power of the authorities, in the form of speech codes enforced by the central administration, suggests the constitution of an official truth with totalitarian echoes.[25] But this suggestion has practically nothing to do with real politics, and to pretend that it is otherwise, supports the traditional subordination of marginalized groups.

There may be some foolish things happening in the university, but it is not in the university where the political action is. The cultural wars of the university distance academics from the concerns of the larger society. They also make it appear that the only alternative to ideological madness is a super-professional apolitical academic approach to societal affairs. Academic debate, which is often quite vigorous, then, does not articulate with general political concerns. This is most apparent, as we shall see in the following chapters, in the stark contrast between the way pressing social and cultural conflicts are addressed in academic debates about such issues as race and gender, and how these same concerns are addressed in the broader society.

Such academic cultural politics are also rather convenient. One can engage in them without ever leaving one's study, by simply reading and writing for a circumscribed number of appropriate journals, and, if one is lucky, one may even get tenure along the way. One can declare a strong ideological position and imagine that the political work has been accomplished without having engaged in the difficult tasks of politics, i.e. reaching out to a constituency and acting in a responsible public fashion. One can attend a university committee meeting or stage a protest about some event on the university grounds, and imagine that the problems of our times are being addressed. In this way, the problems of racism are addressed with new theories of Afrocentrism, post-colonialism and multiculturalism, and the problems of sexism are addressed with feminist and post-feminist theories, and their competing notions of patriarchy and its implications.

PROFESSIONALISM

The controversies around political correctness in their full complexity emerge from a fundamental sociological fact of American cultural life: the gap between the valuative center of the universities and of the general society. The autonomy of the university from the centers of political, economic, and religious powers have been so complete that the relationship between the university and the public has become quite tenuous. The political center of gravity within the universities is far to the left of the general society. The universities are far more secular than other American social institutions. What is considered conservative by university professors often looks quite liberal to almost anyone else. What seems ridiculously old-fashioned and superstitious in the university is the common wisdom for the bulk of the population.[26] The conservative critics hope to center the university around what they imagine to be the valuative consensus of the society at large. The academic radicals want to use the university to attack what they understand to be the society's oppressive practices. But neither the conservative hopes nor the radical understandings take seriously the distance between the university and the rest of society. They instead engage in predictable polemics, written for the convinced, avoiding the perplexing.

A natural response to this situation is to withdraw from intellectual aspiration, finding solace in the vocations of scholar, scientist, and professional. Indeed, professionalism has been the dominant norm in the American university before, after, and during the debates about political correctness and multiculturalism.

The falseness, or at least the lack of centrality, of the PC debate in the American university is best realized by remembering what most people in the universities are doing. Both the radicals and the conservatives imagine rather idealized situations, competing versions of the liberal arts ideal. For the conservative, students and faculty should center their attention on the wisdom of our cultural inheritance. For the radicals, they should cultivate their capacities for criticism. Careers and economic aspirations play little role in either account. Yet, these are the major concerns of faculty and students alike. Students and their parents, especially in the present economic environment, view undergraduate and graduate schooling as educational means to material ends. Professors also center their attention on careers, apparently before most else. This is a time of great insecurity within the American universities, and the pursuit of tenure and professional standing has become extremely competitive. PC is a side-show. This does not mean, though, that academic freedom and intellectuality flourish. Quite the contrary, revolving around the PC debates are important intellectual problems, while professionalism within the universities silences intellectual pursuits.

Consider the discipline of sociology as a strategic case in point. Not too long ago, sociology was where the intellectual action was. Many of the most interesting American intellectual critics were sociologists by profession, prominently C. Wright Mills and David Riesman, and the discipline itself played a dominant theoretical role in the life of the social sciences, through the work of Talcott Parsons and his colleagues. In the immediate post-war period, sociology may not have been the queen of the sciences as imagined by Auguste Comte, the early nineteenth-century founder of the discipline, but it did play a central role in intellectual and scholarly life. In recent years, though, the discipline has arrived on hard times. Economic paradigms have been generalized across the disciplines as socio-logical ones once were, and the discipline has been strikingly limited in its intellectual reach. Departments of literature and new programs in cultural studies seem to be where the critical intellectual action is to be found. Between economics and cultural studies, sociology seems to have lost its way. To say the least, this dismays the movers and shakers in the profession.

It is outside the purview of this investigation to attempt a thorough explanation for the academic decline of the discipline. It must suffice to note that the celebration of the market and the ascendency of highly individualistic worldviews play a role, as do the unfulfilled promises of past policy studies executed by sociologists. Poverty, the problems of the cities, racism, and other social problems that sociologists have investigated have proven to be more intractable than past studies suggested. Sociology has been linked throughout its history with the diagnosis of the major problems and prospects of the modern social order, and as we lose our sense that these problems are addressable the discipline's popularity suffers.[27] Yet, the relative popularity of a particular scholarly discipline is not our concern. More interesting is the fate of intellectuality among sociologists and for this I will draw briefly upon personal experience.

As a sociologist, my major interests fit within the subdiscipline of the sociology of culture. Until quite recently, this subfield was considered to be quite marginal among American sociologists. More practical fields were more popular, from the sociology of minority relations, to studies of crime and delinquency, stratification, and social mobility, to social psychology, and, as these were open to quantitative analysis, their legitimacy was assured. Theory of a grand sort always had its place, legitimated by the work of Talcott Parsons and his critics, and theorists did pay attention to cultural problems, but the main activities of sociologists lay elsewhere. In the mid-seventies, a change was discernible. Quite a few sociologists of the younger generation were turning to the analysis of cultural problems, and understood this as a distinct endeavor, first in the sociology of the arts, then in cultural sociology more generally. The move into the sociology of the arts was part of the general development of sociology into all institutions and occupations. The occupations and the organizations of the arts were analyzed like all others. The ascendent development of cultural sociology was a critical response to more materialist, often Marxist inspired, moves in historical sociology. Self-described structuralist historical sociologies underplayed the significance of ideas and values, and, predictably, cultural approaches were presented to correct their one-sidedness.

For many different reasons people turned to culture, to the point that this in turn became a fashion of sorts, a hot field. In the eighties, people interested in the field organized a special section of the American Sociological Association. When they first tried, they were unable to gather the two hundred signatures necessary to become an officially recognized subdiscipline. By the nineties, the culture section became one of the largest in the Association.

The professional success of the practitioners of the sociology of culture was not matched by intellectual success. An observable anti-intellectual pattern was discernible, as the subfield advanced in the profession. Students and scholars turn to cultural sociology for a variety of intellectual, scholarly, and professional reasons. These include, among others, interest in one art form or variety of art forms, conviction that ideas about the good, the beautiful, and the true should play a role in a sociological understanding of the human condition (contrary to more materialist approaches to sociological understanding), and an interest in organizational, institutional and political cultures. These reasons may or may not be mutually exclusive. Indeed, the interest in the problem of culture has been so wide that it has not been clear exactly what culture is, and whether or not there is a general reason for it to be studied. This clearly needs clarification, but the organizers of the section systematically turned away from such clarification.

This was something that I found particularly galling. I became involved. It seemed to me that much of the sociology of culture was mediocre, having little theoretical or practical interest. It aped the research forms of more accepted work in sociology, as it turned away from what makes the study of cultural problems particularly interesting. I felt the stakes were high. A proper approach to the problems of cultural life, I thought, would serve important scholarly and intellectual purposes. It would keep alive the critical tradition in contemporary sociological study, and it would support the intellectual mission of sociological study (particularly my sociological study).

I judged that the object of study of the sociology of culture should be best conceived as the institution and practices of the arts and sciences, broadly understood. I realized that this is not the only way that the object of cultural investigation could be conceptualized, but I saw important advantages for considering it this way. This understanding provides a means for sociologists to investigate the problems of modernity and post-modernity, and opens the investigation to critical inquiry. In fact, this approach is the basis of the present study into the role of the intellectual in democratic society. The development of a relatively independent culture is understood as being one of the great accomplishments of the modern era, along with the development of the modern state and economy. The distinctiveness of the relatively independent cultural sphere is that it provides the possibility to question the commands of the state and the logic of the market, providing the opportunity for critical reflection. As we observed in chapter 2, the autonomy of cultural institutions is the modern ground of the critical intellectual, and as we observed in chapter 6 it is worth fighting for in post-communist Europe. I therefore felt that it was important to discuss with my colleagues what we mean exactly by culture; both scholarly clarity and an understanding of the importance of the works and activities of intellectuals lies in the balance.

Some colleagues agreed and the beginnings of a debate were published in the section newsletter, yet, in the main, the section organizers resisted. Not because they thought I was mistaken in my approach, nor because they felt that there was any other approach which was likely to be the more fruitful, but because they did not want to clarify the central concept for fear of discouraging potential members of the newly formed section. My intention was not to maintain that there should be an exclusive official definition of culture, but that the alternative understandings should be presented, and their relationships considered. Professional wisdom suggested that this might discourage section membership. The more members the section had, the more power the section members and leadership would have in the profession as a whole. There was little incentive for the exclusively professionally minded sociologists to fulfill scholarly responsibilities.

Indeed, a series of decisions were made that led the section on culture away from scholarly seriousness and openness to intellectuality, toward narrow-minded professionalism.[28] All attempts were made to insure that the paper sessions of the section at the annual meetings were open to the widest possible range of contributors. The thematics of the sessions were formulated in such a way that they would be open to all approaches to the subject matter. They were also chosen so that they would be viewed as legitimate by sociologists concerned with more conventional subject matter. These decisions, which I am summarizing in simplified fashion, were not reached for pernicious reasons. Quite the contrary, an attempt was being made to give all section members a chance to participate, both those with established reputations and those who were new to the field. This meant that the career benefits of the section's activities were being shared fairly, and that they were being maximized. Although the sociology of culture was becoming a recognized part of the profession, each sociologist of culture usually worked in a department as the one local marginal specialist. In order to be promoted and receive tenure, it has been necessary to show colleagues that one has done legitimate work. Thus, it has been most beneficial for cultural sociologists to show their colleagues that their work is quite similar to the work done in other areas of specialization. Not interpretive work with cultural judgments at the center of investigation, but standard sorts of organizational analysis, preferably using quantitative data, most benefits a career in sociology departments, and this is the direction the section has followed. Critical normative theory had little place in supporting professional interests.

Perhaps I am being too cynical, writing from a privileged position, a member of a department which has always rewarded the uncon-

ventional, in which the study of culture and normative investigation
are central? I recognize this as a possibility. But my point is not to
criticize my colleagues for acting in ways that are narrowly self-
interested or professionally advantageous. It is, rather, to highlight
the tension that exists between the scholarly and the intellectual, on
the one hand, and the professional, on the other, and to point out
that the professional orientation of those in the university can be in
tension with the life of the intellectual in the academy.

The results of this tension were evident at the 1995 meeting of the
professional association in Washington DC. The meeting was held at
a time when culture, almost by any definition of the term, was under
attack in Washington. The National Endowment for the Arts and
the National Endowment for the Humanities, the Corporation for
Public Broadcasting and National Public Radio were being de-
funded by an aggressively market-oriented Congress. The aestheti-
cally fine and the intellectually serious were being identified with
that which sells; no independent basis for cultural judgment was
recognized. The professional sociologists of culture, meeting in the
capital, had not a word to say about the developments. Instead, they
centered their discussion on such issues as meaning and measure-
ment (i.e. how to measure cultural variables quantitatively). The
experts in the sociology of culture played their normal professional
game of ignoring the condition of culture in society, exactly when a
broad range of cultural activities were under attack.

These complaints can, of course, be dismissed. The primary role
of the scholar is not to respond directly to political events, but to
develop an independent discipline. Yet, a discipline's independence
from public life to the point that it has little to say to the public in
crisis indicates a loss of intellectual credibility. And I should make
myself clear, I do not think this is unusually a problem with the
sociology of culture or sociology in general. It is a problem
intellectuals face in universities organized as they are around the
prevailing academic disciplines. Writing directed at the general
public is not the basis of academic promotion. Esoteric journal
publishing directed at narrow specialists is the key to academic
success. Publications in journals that rarely are read are the bread
and butter of an academic career, and accessibility is viewed as a
mark against an author. And when things get political, academics
continue to publish for themselves in their semi-private academic
jargons with an aura of scientific authority supported by the obtuse.

Ironically, this includes PC authors writing for PC academics, anti-PC authors writing for anti-PC academics, and all of them seeking promotion and tenure for their output. Ideological fashions and academic customs combine to wash out the possibility of serious intellectual exchange.

Nonetheless, the American university is in some ways a political miracle, as Said has described it. What is a distant dream in most academic settings, such as those of Eastern and Central Europe, is a reality on the American university. A wide range of intellectual and political points of view are protected by its autonomy from the sources of political, economic, religious, and cultural constraints emanating from the general society. But the achieved independence, the autonomy itself involves restrictions. Engagement with the public is not rewarded. Professionalism prevails over critical independence. Is there room, then, for that special sort of stranger who pays close attention to his or her critical capacity in the university? In the main, I would agree with Russell Jacoby that the notion of an academic intellectual has become an oxymoron, yet the question should not be answered in general. It should be answered with reference to the pressing problems the society faces. In the age of political correctness and anti-political correctness, do intellectuals, many of them in the universities, help us, as citizens, discuss the central problems of race and gender? Do ideological formulas and professionalism get in the way? These are strategic questions which will help us understand the role of the intellectual in America as a democratic society, as we turn to the problems of race.

CHAPTER 8

Race and discursive disruption

When it comes to race, America's is the very opposite of a Habermasian ideal speech situation. No problem in American society is more in need of intellectual intervention. This topic is so systemically distorted that it is sometimes hard to imagine how any honest discussion occurs across racial divides. If the role of the intellectual is to help promote informed discussion about difficult social problems, then it is in the arena of racial affairs that intellectuals are most needed in America.

Consider how we speak about the issue in the political arena. When David Duke, the former Nazi and Ku Klux Klan leader, ran as the Republican candidate for Governor of the State of Louisiana, he campaigned in codes. He did not propagate explicit anti-black or anti-semitic ideas, but instead celebrated our Christian heritage and our right to sustain it, and defended the equal civil rights of whites. In principle, the idea of equal rights for whites is, of course, a perfectly reasonable one. Yet, when the injustice of race relations still clearly involves the privilege of whites over blacks, the slogan's racist meaning is apparent. This man used the language of civil liberties and tolerance to convey his xenophobic messages. He did get perilously close to winning the election (obtaining over 40% of the total vote, including a majority of the votes of whites). Yet with his loss, racist newspeak suffered a setback.

Duke's politics was a culmination of the Republican Party's southern strategy over a twenty-year period. From Nixon and Agnew's law-and-order issue in the late sixties and early seventies to the denunciation of the Massachusetts furlough program by George Bush in 1988, the party of Lincoln utilized a race strategy to win presidential elections. The racism which was used to become the majority party was not of the old sort. Explicit racial epithets and support of official discrimination were not part of the Grand Old

Party's Southern Strategy. Rather, elliptical racist reference and withdrawal of support of official remedies against racial injustice were the key. As the Democrats became identified with the attempts to address the injustices of the racial order, however half-hearted and incomplete, the Republicans became the natural home for those against school busing for the purposes of promoting racial integration and affirmative action for the purposes of establishing a fair chance for African-American advancement in education, investment, and employment. The Republicans came to realize that painting the Democrats as the Party of the Blacks and their own Party as the Party of the Whites would lead to electoral victories. The winning streak in Presidential politics was ended by Clinton in 1992, but only with an explicit effort to avoid open discussion of racial inequalities during the campaign on the Democrats part.

Given the prevalence of racism, this was smart politics, and not totally without good, even liberal motives (from the Democratic point of view). Assume the best of motives as presented by America's leading black sociologist, William Julius Wilson, Jr: the amelioration of the disproportionate poverty, ill health, inferior education, and generally poor quality of life of African-Americans will only be supported by "Reagan Democrats" (i.e. white working-class Democrats who have in recent years voted for Republican candidates because of their perceived greater understanding of their everyday concerns) as part of a general social program, one which is not especially earmarked for blacks in any way. If such programs are developed and supported, so this position goes, blacks will benefit disproportionately, without instigating increased racism. Thus, the problems of race can be addressed without paying the price for the racist attitudes of the electorate.[1]

There is a refined political maturity in this position, with a clear appreciation of the distinction that must be made between a politics governed by an ethics of responsibility and an ethics of ultimate ends. Yet, there are enduring problems as well. It suggests not confronting racism directly, not considering in public the psychological effects of racial domination, and ignoring the frustration of the pluralistic ideals of the American polity. Although the strategic desirability of the "Wilson approach" may have been a necessity for the Democrats during the 1992 elections, we do have here an instance of political expediency serving an immediate cause, but leaving unattended the central dilemma of American politics.

Ignoring racism will not make it go away, as the political situation after the 1992 elections has made most clear. We observe, with systematic attacks on affirmative action, the slogan of equal rights becoming a synonym for continued acceptance of the unequal distribution of goods in American society on the basis of race. A racial newspeak prevails.

This is where the discursive role of intellectuals, most often situated in the academy, comes in. They contribute in a variety of ways, attempting to inform public discussions about race. Some try to break the silence; others, intentionally or not, enforce it. Breaking the silence, intellectuals can represent how we confront or avoid the problem of race, as Toni Morrison has done. They can depict the dimensions of our race problems, as Andrew Hacker did in his devastating book *Two Nations: Black and White, Separate, Hostile, Unequal.* Or they can challenge the public to prove through their actions that racism is not permanent, as Derrick Bell did in his poetic provocation *Faces at the Bottom of the Well.*[2] Such works open political discussion among the educated public, most often based in overly autonomous universities.

While we should not minimize the contribution of such intellectual work and we will analyze it in the next chapter, it does have its limits. Refined academically oriented discourse rarely penetrates a broad public, even when it is formulated in such a way as to be intelligible to the general reader, as are the aforementioned works. Intellectuals and scholars read one another's works, analyze them, agree or disagree on fine points, but in the end they do not appear to have a direct effect on the general public. These works apparently remain in the world of the academy, even though they are written for a broader public.

Breaking out of the relatively narrow circle of academic exchange, reaching the public and its leaders and representatives, is not a simple matter, as we have already observed. There are outlets, but they are limited. In the United States, serious magazines of political opinion, some very well known, like *The National Review, The New Republic,* and *The Nation,* appeal to informed audiences and are sometimes consequential. Discussion programs on television like "Face the Nation" and "The MacNeil-Lehrer News Hour," and on radio like National Public Radio's "All Things Considered," do occasionally provide opportunities for the intellectuals' contributions and provocations on race matters. An informal system, connecting book and journal publishing with major daily and weekly news-papers and magazines and select broadcasting media, sustains public debate. Yet, the normal operating procedures of this system make some topics more easily discussed than others. Political gossip and speculation, most often following a horse-racing metaphor, are easily processed. The discussion of difficult issues, complex political prin-ciples and theoretically informed intellectual judgments are not, and race talk is particularly difficult. In this chapter, we consider how the processing has been frontally challenged. In the next chapter, we will observe how the process can be civilized and enriched, involving strategic interventions of academics into the discourse of the world of the mass media.

RACE CONVENTIONS

Race tends to be presented to the public in standardized ways that obscure rather than illuminate. Discussion tends to be stereotypical, not critical. Open, frank, responsible discussion is rare. In recent times, it sometimes seems that race has become the invisible social problem: invisible because many liberals assume that the cause of past racial inequities have been overcome, or soon will be, and because most conservatives believe that the persistence of the problem is inevitable, an American fate.

From a principled liberal position, the outrage of the African-American experience is rooted in the denial of individual liberties. Slavery and Jim Crow, along with the official tolerance of social discrimination, explain the sorry condition of Black America. Address these limits on liberty by supporting legal equality, and social injustice will diminish.[3]

Conservatives in the past had their doubts about this position. They believed, and some still do believe, that an overemphasis on individual rights may overwhelm the values of traditional patterns of living. The good of a traditional community, including its brutal racism, was seen as being a greater good than that of civil rights. But now that civil rights legislation has been established, and injustice persists, it is accepted.

Conservatives and liberals, then, support the present state of affairs, with the liberals expecting, or at least hoping, that in the long term social change will occur, and the conservatives expecting, or perhaps hoping, that it will not. Thus, both liberals and conserva-

tives turn their eyes away from the persistence of racism. At the
same time, there is no denying the existence of immense social
problems which are racially correlated, from crime to illiteracy, from
drugs to poverty, from psychological terror to moral collapse. The
reality of the problem cannot be ignored, although the dominant
worldviews of liberals and conservatives turn us away from the
difficult facts.

The mass media, following the conventional wisdom of the liberals
and conservatives, tend to avoid serious portrayal of enduring racial
conflicts. The logic of "news" in a way assures this. (There is
nothing new about racial injustice in America.) The exception is the
news of sensation: the spectacle of individual inter-racial trans-
gression (inter-racial crime), broad collective racial conflict (urban
riots), and innovative media politics (as practiced, for example, by Al
Sharpton in New York). There are, to be sure, periodic reports of a
more normal sort: the internal politics of major civil rights organizations and the discussion of the racial implications of legislation and
judicial decisions. But these assume the existing racial order, very
infrequently questioning the racial ordering of things. Academic and
scholarly investigations like the ones previously mentioned do offer
alternatives, but they rarely reach a broad public, a weakness in
itself. Moreover, in isolation from real public concern and interaction, they have a tendency to become esoteric or tendentiously
ideological. Sectarian radical publications and activist groups tend
in the same direction.

There is, then, a political vacuum in our culture. It is, of course,
not complete, although it takes talent and strength to work within it.
This is the task of the engaged political intellectual.[4] It is often an
occasion where discursive disruption is more important than maintaining ongoing conversation, given that racism is embedded in the
conventions of polite conversation and in the organization of social
life. The strange and significant case of Malcolm X is a central case
in point, an intellectual disrupting embedded racism.

MALCOLM X AND LIBERAL INTOLERANCE

Let me start my analysis of Malcolm with the authoritative judgment
of Thurgood Marshall, the late distinguished civil rights lawyer and
Supreme Court Justice. Marshall had his doubts about Martin
Luther King, Jr – but he felt contempt for Malcolm X. The great

jurist believed that the primary means for progressive change in race relations was the law, and so he had considerable skepticism about King's use of civil disobedience. To him, the deliberate breaking of laws seemed, at times, a sideshow. But when he was asked about Malcolm X, Marshall responded with a question: What did he ever accomplish?[5]

Marshall's is a challenging question. Objectively reviewing Malcolm X's career, one is struck by the lack of any concrete political achievement. He was a public figure in the late fifties and early and mid-sixties whose life and reputation have attracted renewed popular attention in the nineties since the release of a film by Spike Lee about his life. Malcolm achieved national fame as the chief and most effective spokesman for the Nation of Islam, the "Black Muslims." He was a forceful exponent of black separatism, pride, self-determination, and self-defense. He presented his controversial worldview using a vivid vocabulary. He spoke of whites as "blue-eyed devils." He ridiculed those who spoke about goodwill among races. For him, race relations was a struggle between good and evil. His vivid rhetoric makes his position concerning race relations unmistakable:

Every white man in America when he looks into a black man's eyes, should fall to his knees and say "I'm sorry, I'm sorry – my kind has committed history's greatest crime against your kind; will you give me the chance to atone?" But do you brothers and sisters expect any white man to do that? *No*, you *know* better! And why won't he do it? Because he *can't* do it. The white man was *created* a devil, to bring chaos upon this earth...

Every time you see a white man, think about the devil you're seeing! Think of how it was on *your* slave foreparents' bloody, sweaty backs that he *built* this empire that's today the richest of all nations – where his evil and his greed cause him to be hated around the world!

A journalist once asked, were there whites who contributed to the black man in America? And Malcolm answered, "Yes, I can think of two. Hitler and Stalin. The black man couldn't get a decent factory job until Hitler put so much pressure on the white man. And then Stalin kept up the pressure."

About civil rights leaders like Martin Luther King, Jr, who sought integration and social justice through non-violent means, Malcolm X was equally sarcastic. Utilizing Harriet Beecher Stowe's black character Uncle Tom as an archetype, he declared:

Today's Uncle Tom doesn't wear a handkerchief on his head. This modern, twentieth- century Uncle Thomas now often wears a top hat. He's usually well-dressed and well-educated. He's often the personification of culture and refinement. The twentieth-century Uncle Thomas sometimes speaks with a Yale or Harvard accent. Sometimes he is known as Professor, Doctor, Judge and Reverend, even Right Reverend Doctor. This twentieth-century Uncle Thomas is a *professional* Negro...by that I mean his profession is being a Negro for the white man.

And for those who presented Christian love as salvation, he retorted:

Christianity is the white man's religion. The Holy Bible in the white man's hands and his interpretations of it have been the greatest ideological weapon for enslaving millions of non-white human beings. Every country the white man has conquered with his guns, he has always paved the way, and salved his conscience, by carrying the Bible and interpreting it to call the people "heathens" and "pagans"; then he sends his guns, then his missionaries behind the guns to mop up.

These quotations, taken from *The Autobiography of Malcolm X*, exemplify Malcolm X's discursive mode.[6] He is assertive and dogmatic, articulate and narrow-minded, challenging the prevailing racial order, but using the racist rhetorical forms of the prevailing order.

In countries where democratic practices are not well established, the consequences of such talk, if it prevails in public life, may very well undermine democratic prospects, for example in the new democracies of Eastern and Central Europe. If the xenophobic nationalist Zhirinovsky should prevail in Russia, the prospects for democracy there would be very slim. But within a democratic framework, with basic norms of civil deliberations and actions, with a strong, well-institutionalized civil society, the results can be quite different. Such intolerant speech, so long as it does not ultimately define the political situation, ironically can contribute to democratic exchange. There is a kind of liberal intolerance, the very opposite of Herbert Marcuse's notion of repressive tolerance.[7]

Marcuse argued that the existence of free speech, when it appears within the context of capitalist domination, can be repressive, because it reinforces the structures of domination. When someone argues for a socialist politics in America, it is assured that the argument for this political position will be marginalized and rendered ineffective. This is an indication of a higher form of societal constraint, not tolerance but repressive tolerance. Tolerance, for Marcuse, appears as an advanced form of repression. Likewise, at the time of revolution, repression may be called for because the structures of repressive tolerance must be broken. Revolutionary intolerance is desirable so that the truth will prevail. This argument, which informs the position of those post-modernists who conflate truth and power, such as Stanley Fish, is not open to the ideal that tolerance, like the freedom it supports, especially in a pluralistic world, is a significant end in itself. It also does not recognize the subversive potential of the ideal of freedom, such as we observed in the case of academic freedom. Indeed, within the context of the formal tolerance that Marcuse minimizes and dismisses, dogmatism, or at least dogmatic utterances of the sort that Malcolm expressed, can have the ironic consequence of opening up political life. This indicates the subversive potential of freedom and highlights the subversive role of the intellectual. Intolerance, to a limited degree, may even be required for democracy to function. It may force serious discussion about proscribed issues when political and cultural "good taste" suggests silence. With this in mind, the life of Malcolm X needs to be examined more closely.

THE LIFE RECONSIDERED

Malcolm's adult life divides into three periods: a period as a hustler; a period as a sort of fundamentalist religious convert and black nationalist; and a period as a more conventional religious seeker and humanist. He continually attracted a lot of attention to himself and his causes. With Alex Haley's assistance, he told his life story in terms of his coming of political age. Eventually he was martyred, and now his name has become a mass cultural icon. But speaking concretely, Thurgood Marshall was right. Malcolm X changed no laws; he established no political movement; he created no new theory of race relations or racial assertion of pride. Nonetheless, contrary to Marshall's judgment, along with Marshall and King, he left an enduring political legacy.

This is because Malcolm was an intellectual provocateur, filling the aforementioned vacuum in our political culture. Through the power of his words, he forced Americans, both black and white, to confront deep dimensions of the American dilemma, and he did it more effectively than any other public figure of his day. He was an early master of the sound bite. He promised to fight for the black cause "by any means necessary," a call for self-defense which seemed to threaten a race war. He ridiculed Christianity and mocked Northern white liberals. For too many blacks, his talk of "white devils" appeared to be an accurate description of the facts,[8] and for whites, it seemed to be an offense beyond its rhetorical excess. After his death, his autobiography served as an ambiguous morality tale, filled with exotic descriptions of degeneration and rebirth, enlightenment and revisionism, political daring and moral discipline. With the Spike Lee movie on Malcolm's life, his appeal reached a wider audience.

Malcolm X, then and now, has forced us to talk. He did so through the powers of subversion. I do not think by any stretch of the imagination that his message was all for the good. Quite the contrary, I find that my own personal judgment is much more negative than it was in the 1960s when I first read the *Autobiography*. Some of his ideas were downright silly, and others were offensive. There are serious problems here. On the one hand, using hyperbole, Malcolm shocks Americans, black and white, into recognizing the legacies of racism. On the other hand, the recognition does not come with much reasoned guidance. He unmasks the tyranny and the hypocrisy, the manipulation and the bad faith; he dramatizes the conflicts, but his proposed resolutions are little more than rhetorical flourishes – self-defense "by any means necessary," the ceding of land to African-Americans for the establishment of an independent nation in North America. To be sure, his interim goals of education, moral discipline, and self-help and self-pride have substance. The Muslims have been famous for rehabilitating prisoners and turning drug-addicted illiterates into productive people. In this way, Malcolm Little became Malcolm X, and the telling of his story exemplifies a justly celebrated achievement. Nevertheless, his long-term achievement seems to be limited to shockingly challenging racist common sense.

Yet, since his assassination, Malcolm has become a symbol for a variety of political positions ranging from socialism to black nationalism to liberalism to even neo-conservatism. For the socialist, his attack on the racism of American capitalism, including the complicity in the slave trade and the super-exploitation of free black laborers, indicates that Malcolm was pointing down the road to socialism. Indeed, after he broke with the Nation of Islam and dropped its racist ideology, he moved in the direction of a vaguely socialist commitment.[9] But for the black nationalist, it was clear that the progressive socialist rhetoric was a sideshow. Malcolm's message was about black pride and self-determination, even black domination. "And nobody should be against the black man being the dominant man. He's been dominated. I don't think that if we allow ourselves to be dominated its wrong to pass the ball around once in a while."[10] And after his death, when he couldn't speak for himself, liberals and conservatives minimized such bravado and focused on his conservative moral commitments and his commitment to and love for education. The *New York Times* highlighted these at the time of the release of the Spike Lee film.[11] Malcolm's intellectual provocations, his often dogmatic statements, have been surrounded by ambiguities, and this has oddly increased his stature and his political importance. In the interpretations about him, a discursive democratic politics about race has been formed.

Interpreting Malcolm has become an important political exercise – first through autobiography, and then through the film based on the book. The book presents a complex interpretative challenge. All autobiographies, of course, are formed by selective memory and self-justification. They all impose on the past the rationalizations of the reflective present, yielding a distinctive text in which the subject and the object are both the same and not the same. But in the Malcolm X autobiography, things are even more complicated. It is an "as told to" book. Alex Haley, an author with a politically moderate identity quite different from Malcolm's, composed the text from the long interviews he had with Malcolm, raising questions concerning the narrative voice. Furthermore, the autobiographical interviews were conducted at a time of rapid and radical change in Malcolm's life. Throughout most of the text, he is telling a simple tale of conversion and moral improvement: "How the Honorable Elijah Mohammed changed and improved my life." But in the end that story becomes, "How the 'Honorable' Elijah Mohammed is after my life." And since Malcolm was murdered before the project was completed, it is unclear how the two stories should be related.

This is of political significance because the principled basis for the conflict between Elijah Mohammed and Malcolm X was over Elijah Mohammed's racist doctrines. Malcolm turned to more conventional Muslim practices, and seemed to turn away from his more extreme racist ideology. He spoke about universalism, while he apparently never abandoned his militancy. But which of his previous positions should be revised and which should be left unchanged is not at all clear. Is the apparently moderate universal end of Malcolm's journey in the *Autobiography* the doing of Alex Haley – a conscious undermining of a nationalist life? Or does it represent an uncompleted journey toward socialism, liberalism, or even conservatism? The heterogeneity of Malcolm's life, as a text, makes such questioning possible. The strength and bluntness of his critique of American practices make the questioning worthwhile, even, on occasion, pressing.

Malcolm X got our attention with artistry. Recent research suggests that as a hustler, he was a significantly less accomplished burglar, less degraded pimp, and less strung-out addict than he later pretended to have been. He apparently emphasized his degeneration to make his reformation appear to be more dramatic. Moreover, there is evidence that his humanistic revelation in Mecca – the basis of his doctrinal parting with the Nation of Islam – had to have developed over a long period of time, which means that for a considerable period he continued to preach separatism and hatred of whites when he no longer fully believed in such things.[12] Malcolm knew how to get his audience's attention, but it sometimes involved deceit, manipulation, and demagoguery.

And as Malcolm moved his audience in one direction, his interpreters have moved it in others: aside from the already mentioned ideological directions, his not very hidden anti-semitism. Malcolm's passing anti-semitic statements, alongside his anti-Christian and anti-white remarks, have become an overriding obsession in the life of Louis Farrakhan and his disciples, to the point that the infamous *Elders of Zion* is having a publishing rebirth supported not only by the right-wing militia movement but also by black nationalists.

Away from the xenophobic margins are those who sweeten and de-ideologize Malcolm's scripts. They juxtapose two black martyrs: Malcolm X and Martin Luther King Jr, and they draw conclusions. Quite popular, as expressed in the Spike Lee film and in the rap music scene, is a kind of sentimental choosing of Malcolm over Martin because of Malcolm's aura of toughness, his style seems to communicate more directly to the concerns and interests of the portion of the African-American community which is not making it in America. Remembering Malcolm, then, is a way to remember and even a way to seek to empower the forgotten, those who have little political clout and are rarely on the political agenda outside of their assigned role as objects of vilification.

Viewed from a distance, all the different readings of Malcolm X are incomplete. When he becomes an empowering symbol for the powerless, the uncomfortable and the often reprehensible aspects of his legacy are being glossed over. In the Spike Lee film, Malcolm is tough, but he is never as degraded in his hustling stage as he portrayed himself in his autobiography, nor is he as prone to make xenophobic and sexist statements. The bad has been made less ugly, and from the point of view of those who would have him be a black nationalist or a socialist, his radical political messages have been censored.[13] In newspapers and in more specialized journals, debates rage about such issues. Since his message was never fully clarified and since he never clarified his position on separatism vs. universalism, his life has become a broadly politicized symbol, generating discussion.

We observe, then, a hodgepodge of appropriations of Malcolm X's legacy. The most ubiquitous is no doubt the most superficial: the popularity of the "X" logo in urban America. The most refined (like the excellent scholarly biography by Bruce Perry and the ethical reflections of Cornell West in his collection *Race Matters*) is the most remote, the most academic, not readily observable or consequential.[14] The emptiness of the popular symbolism and the obscurity of the refined commentary have, in a way, been overcome, as they interact. As they make up a cultural whole, they respond to the silences in our political culture. We will observe such interaction more closely in the next chapter.

To be sure, Malcolm, for some, still exists as a sectarian demagogue. Louis Farrakhan, who, incidentally, menacingly threatened Malcolm's life one week before his assassination, sustains the legacy of black nationalism, along with a makeshift religious fundamentalism. Professor Leonard Jeffries of the City University of New York invents pseudo-scientific theories about the natural superiority of blacks over whites, as Malcolm did forty years ago. Such figures, along with their imitators and followers, invoke Malcolm's life to promote ideas that gave birth to his earliest political and religious awakening. They do not confront Malcolm in his ambiguity. But it is the ambiguity, along with the original provocations, which has opened public space for deliberation about difficult and often ignored racial problems. His life can and has moved his audience from the subversive to the civil. This goes a long way in explaining the answer to Thurgood Marshall's question about Malcolm.

Malcolm X was a political intellectual who addressed the American dilemma with originality, forcing people to talk.

I am uncomfortable with this account of Malcolm X. It seems to move against much of what I have learned about cultural politics while viewing the demise of communism, and it apparently justifies dogmatism and demagoguery.

In Eastern Europe, I learned to be allergic to totalitarian politics, politics based on utopian imaginations, linked with force, which purport to explain the connections between past, present, and future in terms of a simple formula. An official truth made in the name of those who suffer from the injustice and exploitation of capitalism, but which served the interests of a superpower and a ruling party, ordered the social world, and many of the problems with that world, I grew to understand, were as much a product of the success of official ideology, Marxism, as a product of its compromise. Malcolm's quest for a politics based on truth which served as the alternative to the lies of white racism bears an uncomfortable resemblance to those official politics. Not, of course, with reference to the content of his and their political positions, but in their similar form. He, as did the socialist ideologues, took conspiracy theory to be a high form of political understanding. Those who did not see the world in its "true" light were part of the problem, not the solution. He, as did they, had a Manichean view of the world. Those who were not with him were against him, at least until his split with Elijah Mohammed. The repressive implications of such a worldview when it comes to power is now part of the public record.

As long as his politics remained marginal, as did the politics of the New Left more generally, the similarities with the totalitarian position can be ignored, or at least understood as not being central. It may be that the horrors of Stalinism are not as remote from the Western left as many have imagined. Perhaps the assassination of Malcolm is a case in point. Nonetheless, it is clear, as we have observed, that Malcolm through his autobiography opened up the discussion of race and contributed to the democratic deliberations about race.

But do I appreciate the legacy of Malcolm X only from a safe distance, and recoil against the likes of Farrakhan because the latter's threats are directed at me and my contemporaries, while Malcolm is safely buried? Certainly from the point of view of contemporary black nationalists and from the point of view of contemporary adherents of the Nation of Islam, this must appear to be the case. Yet, I do not intend to celebrate Malcolm X as a political figure, or to justify any one of his changing political orientations and proposals, nor condemn him and them. My account is presented to yield an understanding of Malcolm as an intellectual, not as a politician. He appears as an intellectual, from a distance after his assassination, as his major work, his autobiography, contributed to American public life. He has heightened our capacity to talk about race, at the same time that he advocated, at least from my point of view, questionable political positions. Appreciating his intellectual work is not the same as approving of him as a political figure. The intellectual and the politician do not play the same roles.

It is the confusion of these two roles which marks a great deal of the discussion of the sociology of the intellectual. The image of the intellectual as the perpetual critic, the opponent of all authority, has excited the passions of those on the right and the left. Intellectuals are viewed as politicians with the weapon of ideas at their disposal. It is the political combat through the media of ideas that characterizes the life of the intellectual. In the case of Malcolm X, we see the limitations of this position. As an idea warrior, he is not very persuasive, unless we believe in blue-eyed devils or take it as being highly significant that someone who believed in such devils ceased to do so. But as someone who provokes thought and discussion, his importance still lives with us. He is a major subversive intellectual.

Yet, it should be clear that there is something troubling about Malcolm's intellectuality, emanating from the tension between his political and intellectual roles. It is not that he is poorly trained, nor is it that he is not the sole author of his major work. As we have seen, his idiosyncrasies and the ambiguities of the *Autobiography*'s authorship are keys to his intellectual power. Rather, it is that his success on his own terms, i.e. as a political actor, would undermine his success as an intellectual, as a provoker of public talk. His public rhetoric suggests that he would have been quite willing to have silenced intellectuals such as himself with whom he disagreed, like the totalitarians of our day and Socrates in antiquity. What I have called liberal intolerance may explain the intellectual power of the man and his work, but the limits of this position become evident when we consider what happens after discussion has been opened. A discursive etiquette is then necessary. The different interpretations of the legacy of Malcolm X cannot be informed by the same dogmatism as are his original utterances if they are to stimulate and inform public discussion. A way has to be found to confront the logic of the mass media and to sustain alternative public deliberation.

We now examine the way academic intellectuals have in recent years dealt with this problem. There has been a kind of natural symbiosis of refined and popular discussion in the case of Malcolm X, working to solidify his position as a consequential public intellectual. A central task of the intellectual today is self-consciously to constitute such a symbiosis, to stimulate serious public discussion about race in a society that turns away from serious deliberation almost as resolutely as it seeks to avoid addressing the problems of race.

CHAPTER 9

Race and sustained deliberation

Thurgood Marshall did all he could to remain on the Supreme Court beyond the years of the Reagan and Bush administrations. His last great battle was against his very mortality. He desperately wanted to outlast the Republican reaction, to reserve his seat for a like-minded jurist, which he hoped could be achieved with a Democratic President. When he looked at Malcolm X, he saw a political firebrand, disturbing the peace and not helping to change the shape of social justice. We have observed the limits of Marshall's view, but also the limits of the views to which he was opposed. Yet, when the great hero of the civil rights movement, the "conscience of the court," considered his likely successor if he or she were chosen by Ronald Reagan or George Bush, his fears were much greater. He feared that racism would prevail over justice. He feared that their candidate would unbalance the court, and that the civil rights achievements for which he fought so hard would be significantly undermined by a conservative appointment, insensitive to the concerns of poor and black folk. Their great defender worried that they would be left defenseless. In retrospect, from his point of view, his worst fears seem to have been realized with the appointment of Clarence Thomas.

While Marshall did understand the likely political orientation of his successor, he probably would not have understood how a new form of racism was key to Thomas's appointment. Serious deliberation about the problems of race has become ever more difficult to sustain in an era of racial newspeak. A new generation of American intellectuals has responded to the challenge of the new development, with notable successes and failures. This is observable in the interpretations of and the commentary on the Thomas confirmation hearings.

The case itself has two notable dimensions: the controversy over the appointment of Thomas, as a qualified candidate, and the subsequent controversy over Thomas when the charges of sexual harassment were raised by Anita Hill. We will review these two dimensions of the case and then consider the intellectual commentaries. The intellectual contribution to public debate about the Thomas affair demonstrates the importance of civil discourse about the problems of race.

THOMAS'S CONFIRMATION

Clarence Thomas, according to George Bush, was nominated to the Supreme Court because he was the most qualified jurist in the land. Bush maintained this despite the fact that Thomas's career was propelled by a series of political appointments apparently achieved through his conservative political correctness, combined with an unacknowledged affirmative action. His career advancement was, as Manning Marable has observed, "due less to his reputation as a legal scholar and for his judicial temperament, which was nonexistent, but for his noteworthy service as a partisan ideologue for conservative Republicanism."[1]

Thomas made a career out of strategic political positioning. At Yale Law School, he was at one with the times, an admirer of Malcolm X, signing his letters "power to the people," dressing with the flourishes of the Black Panther Party. While he gained entrance to the Law School through its active affirmative action program, in later years, when it became politically useful, he reversed his fundamental political orientation. He became a forceful critic of affirmative action. In his published articles and public addresses, he forcefully attacked civil rights organizations for fostering the dependencies of African-Americans on government programs. He even criticized the landmark decision of *Brown v. Board of Education of Topeka, Kansas*, in which racially segregated schools were abolished, a key legal victory of Thurgood Marshall, who argued the case. Because he was black, Thomas could question the unquestionable. Because he did so, he became a darling of right-wing conservatives, such as Strom Thurmond, Ronald Reagan, and George Bush.

The Thomas appointment challenged racial common sense. Civil rights organizations and African-Americans faced a dilemma: should Thomas be supported in the name of racial solidarity or should he be opposed for the content of his politics and his character? For white and black liberals the quandary included a series of unresolvable questions: could a liberal oppose the appointment of an Associate Justice merely on the grounds of his political ideology? Was there reason to hope that a black man's experience of oppression in a racist society would make him more sensitive to the problems of racial injustice than likely white conservative alternatives? Is it possible that Thomas would prove to be more open-minded once on the court when he would be freed of the ideological pressures of partisan politics? A lack of certainty on such questions led to lukewarm support and lukewarm opposition to the appointment. Strong opposition on ideological grounds seemed improper; ever since the controversies over the Robert Bork nomination, the appearance of such opposition had to be carefully formulated. The opposition, instead, focused mainly on the question of qualifications: Thomas's lack of substantial accomplishment, with no noteworthy judicial decisions and with writings which were little more than the forceful presentation of partisan positions. But a thin track record did not stand in the way of the appointment of Justice Souter, and thus, ironically, such opposition was not telling (lack of accomplishment apparently does not stand in the way to appointment to the highest judicial position in the land).

Bush's nomination of Thomas seemed to be a political master stroke. By playing the race card in a new way, he trumped the opposition to a conservative ideologue to the Supreme Court. His was an extremely cynical strategy. When he asserted that race had nothing to do with the nomination, he could pretend to be taking the color-blind high road. He could bank on the difficulty civil rights organizations and liberals would have in opposing an African-American nomination, as he could satisfy his conservative critics by appointing clearly one of their own. The opponents of the appointment would be forced to make arguments against it which would have little or no attractiveness outside the narrow halls of academia and beyond the political margins. The radical legal scholar Derrick Bell, for example, did maintain that Thomas, because he supported judicial positions that structurally undermined the interest of African-Americans, was not truly an African-American replacement for Marshall. But this seemed to suggest an officially acceptable black position on legal issues and did not hold much salience among the general public, black or white. The court would be transformed; the legacy of Marshall would be fundamentally challenged with little or no opposition.

HILL ENTERS

But then came Anita Hill. When she accused the Supreme Court Justice nominee of sexual harassment, extraordinarily explosive political and cultural issues were involved. A new feminist politics displayed its coming of age. Sexual harassment in the workplace almost brought down the President's nominee, and that it did not cost the Senators who confirmed the nomination considerable political capital. The panel of white men looked as though they were part of the problem, not the solution. They, in the slang surrounding the event, "just didn't get it."

Thomas defended himself by fighting the charges of sexism with countercharges of racism. His case was apparently won when he attacked Anita Hill and his accusers on Senate Judiciary Committee and beyond for having engaged in a "media lynching." Thomas's gambit won him the nomination, but his was a hollow victory. Hill's account of their relationship has cast a shadow over his Supreme Court tenure. Although he was forceful and convincing to most of the viewing public in denying Hill's accusations, she did not seem to be lying.

The politics of race versus the politics of gender made for very exciting melodrama. The gavel to gavel coverage of the confirmation hearings presented riveting television, more for the drama of the clashes, though, than for the illumination of the conflicting issues. The Senate functioned not as a body of deliberations, but as a body of public relations. The Republican supporters of Thomas, led by Senators Simpson, Hatch, and Specter, attacked with prosecutorial rigor. The Democratic questioners of Thomas, led by Senator Biden, timidly attempted to be balanced, sensitive as they were to the dual pitfalls of racism and sexism. Not surprisingly, given the passion of their competing performances, the Republicans won. Thomas was confirmed, to the broad approval of the viewing audience.

It was left to the so-called print media to consider the broad implications. Intellectual intervention here seemed both necessary and possible. Yet, the sensationalism of the identity issues involved in the Thomas–Hill television broadcasts carried over to newspapers, magazines and book publishing. When the immediate furor had quieted down, a book, *The Real Anita Hill: The Untold Story* by David Brock, kept the sensationalist controversy going.[2] Brock made the issue appear to be straightforward. Hill is a lying, ambitious, vindictive woman, who "did in" Thomas. Using highly questionable sources and very tendentious reasoning, he asserted Thomas's innocence. The publication of this book led to a flurry of attacks and counterattacks on the editorial pages of newspapers and in journals of opinion. Conservative Republicans found the book worthwhile, filled with valuable information. Liberal Democrats and feminists criticized the shoddy journalism and questionable findings. Throughout the controversy, though, the pressing issues of race and gender were not examined in their complexity. The controversy did provide some room for debate about race and gender issues, but it was mostly reshaped by the conventions and the publicity needs of the mass media. Slogans, sound bites, and visual opportunities flew freely, while deliberate discussion was hard to find; conventional answers or sets of answers to a difficult problem were readily available, while probing questions and creative interpretations were given little attention. There was a need to turn the debate away from cliché.

INTELLECTUALS INTERVENE

Among the more profound problems raised by the Thomas nomination proceedings are: the role of racial solidarity in the post-civil rights era; the salience of diverse opinions within the world of African-Americans politics and letters; the difficulties in discerning the proper relationship between individual and collective responsibilities, rights and accomplishments; the unanticipated political dilemmas of affirmative action; the obstacles whites and blacks face in making trans-racial judgments, and the complicated relationship between the struggles for gender and racial justice. In much of the public discussion defined by the mass media, these profound practical problems were reduced to the simple melodramatic formula of whether Thomas or Hill was telling the truth. Intellectuals have attempted to break out of the confines of this formula.

It was noted by those who were counting votes for Thomas that civil rights leaders and black and white liberals did not stand clearly on the issue of Thomas's nomination. The analysis was roughly that of a card game. Did racial solidarity trump the opposition to Thomas? Would Bush's gambit work? But more important in the long run for American political and cultural life is that the complications of the Thomas nomination represented a major sea change in African-American politics, and this went unobserved in the fast-paced media world.

More reflective intellectuals did raise their voices. Toni Morrison declared:

In matters of race and gender, it is now possible and necessary, as it seemed never to have been before, to speak about these matters without the barriers, the silences, the embarrassing gaps in discourse. It is clear to the most reductionist intellect that black people think differently from one another; it is also clear that the time for undiscriminating racial unity has passed. A conversation, a serious exchange between black men and women, has begun in a new arena, and the contestants defy the mold. Nor is it as easy as it used to be to split along racial lines, as the alliances and the coalitions between white and black women, and the conflicts among black women, and among black men, during the intense debates regarding Anita Hill's testimony against Clarence Thomas's appointment prove.[3]

Morrison believed that the controversy of the Thomas–Hill affair opened up space for serious deliberations about previously silenced social issues, and she worked to fill the space with serious discussion. Her edited volume, *Race-ing Justice, En-gendering Power: Essays on Anita Hill, Clarence Thomas, and the Constructing of Social Reality*, represents an attempt at civilized intellectual intervention into public life in America. Morrison invited a group of academics to offer their commentary on the implications of the controversies surrounding the Thomas appointment to the Supreme Court. She and they attempt to speak about these matters "without the barriers, the silences, the embarrassing gaps in discourse." Their successes are very real.

The collection opens with an impassioned letter from Judge A. Leon Higgenbotham Jr. to Clarence Thomas. In the letter, Higgenbotham reminds Thomas of his debt to those who preceded him, of his connectedness, whether he wants to recognize it or not, to those who have struggled against racism in American society.

When I think of your appointment to the Supreme Court, I see the result of not only your own ambition, but also the culmination of years of heartbreaking work by thousands who preceded you. I know you may not want to be burdened by their sacrifices. But I also know that you have no right to forget that history. Your life is very different from what it would have been had these men and women never lived. That is why today I write to you about this country's history of civil rights lawyers and civil rights organizations; its history of voting rights; and its history of housing and privacy rights. This history affected your past and present life.[4]

There has been much controversy about the unorthodox positions of black conservatives. From their point of view, they are the real critical intellectuals, questioning unexamined liberal orthodoxies. Their liberal and radical critics question the legitimacy of their positions. Higgenbotham tries to circumvent the limitations of both the liberal and the conservative views. He adds the dimension of the history of the civil rights movement into what is often a dogmatic ideological discussion.

A New Deal–Great Society liberalism is the dominant political orientation in the black community. This is the orientation of the leadership of the major civil rights organizations, of the leadership of the black churches and of the great majority of the African-American population across the socio-economic spectrum. It is, with qualifications and elaborations, the position of Higgenbotham.[5] Although there are, of course, differences of opinion among such liberals on many issues, there is a broad consensus that the problems black America faces require resolute government action: from programs to support the nurturing of underprivileged youth, such as Headstart, to those that are focused on the care for indigent elderly, such as Medicaid. The legacies of slavery, as liberals see them, require concerted political attention. The approved primary end of affirmative action is to overcome the consequences of past discriminations. Extensive support for public education is understood as the only way the younger generation will be able to make it, despite all the obstacles a racist society will present. Various sorts of special programs for disadvantaged youth are appreciated as the alternative to the disproportionate incarceration of young African-American men.

Thomas, along with other black conservatives, challenges this dominant liberal consensus concerning the causes and remedies of the problems facing black America. They see the degradation of the black underclass as a moral crisis. Drug abuse, teenage pregnancy, the fantasies of "gangster rap," and the realities of gang violence and black on black crimes are understood as being primarily the result of the loss of a central moral compass within the black community. Conservatives look for the causes of the crisis in urban America, and they underscore the negative effects of government paternalism and the breakdown of individual responsibility in the African-American community. Past racism is not denied, but the answer to the problems of the community is seen in self-help, voluntary community associations, and individual initiative.[6]

For liberals, the conservative position is not without its appeal. It is well understood that there are important conservative undercurrents in the African American community, from the support of traditional morality and the recognition of the importance of the family, to the emphasis on self-help and independence by both the traditional black churches and the Nation of Islam. The problems arise when the articulation of the conservative position seems to be formulated with the express purpose of currying favor with white conservatives, with the clear purpose of advancing individual interests against the interest of the black community.

Thomas was vulnerable to such suspicions. His changing political orientation is not that unusual. People in their maturity do often hold political positions quite different from those of their youth. But there has been a ruthlessness in Thomas's transformation. An infamous case in point was when he ridiculed his own sister in a public address to a conservative audience on the problem of welfare dependency. He contrasted his own career with that of his sister. He progressed through hard work and individual initiative, according to his account, while she did not, because she became dependent upon the state for welfare. She even would complain vehemently if her welfare check was not in the mail on time. He spoke about himself and his sister using the most coarse of conservative stereotypes, which in itself is hard to understand from a man who claims to be a strong supporter of family values. Human complexity always involves more than such stereotypes will allow, and it seems odd in the extreme that anyone would put his own sister in such a stereotypical narrative, even if it were essentially true. But in the case of Emma Mae Martin, Thomas's sister, the narrative did not apply. She was only on welfare temporarily. She usually held two minimum-wage jobs to support her four children. She was on welfare for the short time that she nursed her aunt who had suffered a stroke and who usually cared for her children.[7] Thomas had strongly suggested to a conservative audience that his sister was a prime example of all that is wrong with the black family, confirming preconceived hostilities. In fact the details of her travails belie racist imaginations, and this Thomas did not reveal. With such a track record, liberals could and do easily dismiss his conservatism as the promotion of an opportunistic ideology. He appears to be a man with few scruples, with no sense of honor.

Yet Higgenbotham, in his open letter, overlooks this to address a more important issue, of great principled and pragmatic import. He views Thomas's conservative position as being worthy of respect, and he addresses Thomas himself with respect. He just asks Thomas to remember those on whom his advancement has relied, to recognize the accomplishments of the man he has replaced on the bench and his thousands of co-workers in the struggle for civil rights.

Higgenbotham is trying to penetrate the myth of absolute individual responsibility, while he is not denying that independent judgment and individual initiative are to be respected. Unlike the more conventional liberal critics of Thomas, he operates under the assumption that Thomas's intellectual position is worthy of respect, yet, with concreteness, he engages in a fundamental practical criticism of that intellectual position. This is civil discourse of the most refined sort, markedly different from Malcolm's rhetorical style, but supportive of the sort of deliberation the *Autobiography* opened.

Higgenbotham reveals the mythical aspects of radical individualism as it pertains to Thomas and his career and his interpretation of the law. Thomas's accomplishments never could have been realized without the victories of the civil rights movements, including the adoption of affirmative action. He would not have gone to the schools that he did. He would not have had the job opportunities, been permitted to live where he lives, and to marry whom he did. (Before the civil rights movement, in his home state of Virginia, Thomas's inter-racial marriage would not have been legal.) It may be true that Thomas is the author of his accomplishments, but he wrote his script within a societal context, authored by many others. Higgenbotham wants Thomas to recognize this and to act accordingly. He adds the dimension of time and serious reflection to the partisan controversies between liberal and conservative political positions.

BETWEEN MEDIA POLITICS AND ACADEMIC PROFESSION

Higgenbotham's is a classic intellectual intervention. He writes as an expert jurist to the general public, through a published open letter. Using common sense and the vernacular, he simultaneously appeals to Thomas and establishes grounds for the public to be critical of Thomas's subsequent actions. While implied in the form of his letter is the hope that Thomas will see the reason of the appeal to historical consciousness and temper the harshness of his judicial opinions, implied as well is the critical judgment that if he does not, the pursuit of justice will be undermined. Higgenbotham does not ask of Thomas the expression of racial solidarity in the form of agreement with the dominant liberal consensus among blacks. He no more expects complete political consensus among blacks than he would expect such a consensus among whites, but he does point out that Thomas shares his fate with other African-Americans, and it would be foolish to act without a conscious awareness of this. Individual and collective responsibility and fate are linked, though they are not identical.

Open letters addressed to the general public, by prominent intellectuals, have an antique quality. It was around such an intervention in the famous Dreyfus case in France that the term intellectual was first coined.[8] In the age of the electronic mass media, intellectual appeal is much less likely to take such direct form. A text without significant interaction with the electronic mass media does not reach the general public. An unmediated occurrence, without media follow up, without the interaction between the text and the media, may not, in the full sense, be public at all. Indeed, the publication of Higgenbotham's letter in a collection of readings reveals how the serious general reader, as the concerned citizen, may be reached nowadays: in interaction with media-dominated discussion, through academic forms. The other articles in the collection more accurately reveal the relationship between intellectual activity and public life in the age of mass electronic media. They are written by academics addressing the general reader, as media consumer. The commentary offered is of events perceived through the media. They assume media-based knowledge of the Thomas confirmation hearings, trying to interpret them in a more knowledgeable way, deconstructing their apparent meaning, criticizing the actions of the principals of the event and its aftermath.

Affirmative action was strikingly evident in the Thomas–Hill affair, especially as it was instituted at Yale University. Yale's African-American best and brightest were the key actors. Before the advent of affirmative action, there was no such group. After, there is. This led to banal commentary. Clarence Thomas, Anita Hill, and John Doggett (Hill's chief debunker) are representatives of a new black upper middle class, impressive graduates of Yale Law School. They are strikingly articulate and authoritative in their demeanor.

The controversy, in their persona, in a perverse sense reveals the progress of black America. It has joined the establishment.

But is there a link between this sort of progress and the way it was achieved? Is the integration of members of an oppressed group into a structure of oppression a form of liberation, or a new, more subtle and effective form of oppression? Is the perversity of the progress revealed in the case more significant than the progress itself? There was little room for these questions in the mass media. They did not fit into the melodramatic storyline of "he says, she says." They also are not the way affirmative action is usually conceived.

Michael Thelwell presents his own alternative melodrama to correct this. He remembers a meeting he had with a prominent Yale professor in 1968. At that time, according to Thelwell, "as a consequence of other young blacks' dying in the burning cities of this nation, black students were, for the first time, being admitted to Ivy League universities in something slightly better than token numbers."[9] The professor was very pleased and impressed with this; Thelwell had his doubts. The professor appreciated that Kingman Brewster, the President of Yale University, had a grand plan: "fully and completely" to integrate the nation's establishment in one generation. For the professor, this would be a remarkable accomplishment, a realization of social justice with unprecedented rapidity. But Thelwell, realizing the injustices of the overall social structure which includes this establishment into which a new black elite was being integrated, was not impressed. The integration of a black elite into the system of their oppression was "neither desirable, progressive, nor as benign" as his professor suggested.

In retrospect, from the point of view of the Thomas confirmation hearings, Brewster's grand plan has become to a significant degree a reality. Thelwell mentions General Powell, Justice Thomas, Governor Wilder of Virginia, the head of the Ford Foundation, the chairman of the New York Bar Association, and many heads of public universities, and division chiefs of a number of Fortune 500 companies, as clear indications that blacks in significant numbers have joined the establishment. Yet, rather than celebrating, he judges that his initial pessimism about the grand plan has been confirmed. This, he points out, is especially evident in the Thomas confirmation hearings:

there they were in full display, Yale Law's blackest and brightest, in their full tunnel vision, expedient, careerist splendor. Young black conservatives on the make, evincing not a scintilla of obligation to anything save naked self-advancement unmediated by any principle – moral, political, or intellectual – that was visible to the naked eye. Thank you, Kingman Brewster, wherever you are.[10]

Thelwell worried in the late sixties, and continues to worry now, about the content of affirmative action initiatives. He underscores the significant difference between overcoming exploitation, and integration into a system of exploitation. Thirty years ago, he wanted not only admittance of African-Americans into the halls of Yale. He wanted, as well, the establishment of a program of study into African-American culture and history. Now, he underscores what happens when people think of entrance into the elite, of individual advancement, as the primary end of the educational enterprise – Associate Justice Clarence Thomas, who outflanks the existing right wing of the court, who stands in opposition to political attempts to right the wrongs of the institutions, practices, and legacies of racism in America. This, to Thelwell's mind, is not progress.

He questions the political neutrality of affirmative action, a criticism from the left, through a fictive depiction of the precursors of the present black conservatives and a striking contrast between them and the earlier black conservative, Booker T. Washington, ("Sure, he bowed and scraped, 'Tommed' if you will... but he usually returned from these journeys into self-abasement with another class-room, science lab, dormitory, or teacher to place in service to our youth"[11]). The affirmative action at Yale helped make compliant black professionals. Thelwell maintains that the black conservative intellectuals are exclusively concerned with their own individual advancement. The fact that Anita Hill is from this same group, according to Thelwell, explains why African-Americans were strikingly not sympathetic to her case. Both Hill and Thomas do not challenge the prevailing order of things, but in fact help it function smoothly. This is made evident in small, and subtle, and in large, and not so subtle, ways.

Supreme Court nominee, Judge Clarence Thomas, was repeatedly referred to as Clarence during the confirmation hearings by his own advocates, in contrast to the earlier practice of referring to Judge Bork and Judge Ginsberg. Through the mode of address, the black man is kept in his place.

President Bush's insistence that race had nothing to do with the nomination was such an affront to common sense that it begged the intelligence not only of the American public, but of the nominee himself. He played their game to the point that he used the charge of racism to defend himself from the accusations of a black woman.

When Thomas defended himself against a "high-tech lynching," it was unclear who was the alleged perpetrator of the crime. The charge of racism was used as a defense against the charge of sexism, and, in the process, both were compromised. Senator Strom Thurmond, the segregationist candidate for President in 1948, expressed his dismay and outrage that Clarence was the victim of "scu'lous attacks." This was race talk through the looking glass, a discussion about racism in which major political racists led a cynical attack against a purported free-floating racism.

A new form of racism was being formed, or at least crystallized, during the course of Thomas's confirmation, epitomized, as Thelwell underscores, by David Duke's strong endorsement of the Thomas appointment. How better to sustain racism than by having a representative of the victims to be a chief enforcer of the racist order? This is the underside of contentless affirmative action, of integration without the transformation of the order of things. Thelwell wonders: "Perhaps if President Brewster had it to do over he might well have diverted a fraction of those resources to some politically informed black faculty and a few meaningful courses in black history. Who knows?"[12]

The new racism – neo-racism? post-modern racism? – is the racism of strategic silences and of subtle innuendo. It appears alongside the pretense of racial justice and has a special language. It was dramatically revealed in the nomination of Thomas and in his self-defense during the confirmation hearings. Claudia Brodsky Lacour examines neo-racist linguistic exchanges. She reveals the odd use of the term, "racism," and the implications of the usage for the "undoing of justice," in the naming and confirming of Thomas, a man who was clearly not qualified for the Supreme Court. From Bush's assertion that Thomas was the "best qualified man for the job" to Thomas's self-defense against a "high-tech lynching," racism was an implicit and explicit speech act. The threat that one could be labeled a racist silenced critics, while the labeling of one's critics as racists was effectively disarming.[13]

In Clarence Thomas, as Lacour puts it, "the anti-quota president found his quota of one." Thomas's supporters were ready to use the charge of racism to defend their candidate. As a strong opponent of affirmative action, Thomas was also an unacknowledged beneficiary of it. He moved around this point by presenting his success story as being the result of hard work and the strong role model of his grandfather. Indeed, his grandfather was used strategically to avoid one of the chief contradictions in Thomas's public profile.

If affirmative-action clearly aided Thomas in the past, supporting and aiding antiaffirmative-action policies was just as clearly helping him in the present, and the only witness called upon to resolve this salient contradiction in "character" was Thomas's grandfather.[14]

Under the influence of the unspoken word "racism," Biden [the Chairman of the proceedings] allowed Thomas to invoke his grandfather whenever Republican senators invited him to, or whenever questions from the Democratic side became slightly more difficult to side-step.[15]

The potential charge of racism during the course of the proceedings made the examination of positions on the issue of race and judicial policy impossible to examine. This was most clearly evident when the charges of Anita Hill were brought forward.

The charge of high-tech racism was brought against no one in particular. It was, as Lacour underscores drawing upon the work of J. L. Austin, a speech act in which the utterance does something, rather than stating something. The charge of racism is used instrumentally to disarm, and it did so even more effectively than Thomas's invocation of his humble origins and road to success. The racism charge, with no evidence or even clear referent, was pitted against the concrete and specified charges of sexual harassment, and it prevailed. No one in this political drama could afford to be labeled a racist, so they were quieted by the potential connection between themselves and the charge. The racists, such as Thurmond and Duke, could present themselves as the defenders of racial justice, and those who would have liked to question this odd state of affairs, such as Biden, found themselves corralled, unable to speak.

The intersection of race and gender makes this situation even more complicated and volatile. Many of the authors in the Morrison collection attempt to address this complication. They all attempt to go beyond melodrama, seeking to name the problem and understand its dimensions. The use of race against gender, it is remembered, has a long history in America, dating back to the involvement of women in the abolitionist movement before the civil war, and the tensions that existed between the early feminists and the freed slaves after emancipation. The odd way that feminism became a white issue and racial justice became identified as a male one is examined. How this complicates the relationships among African-American men and women, and between African-Americans and whites is considered. Attempts are made to explain the support for Thomas in the black community. This is justified, by Thelwell, and strongly condemned, by Patricia Williams.[16] A field for discussion and judgment is constructed, facilitating a more informed debate of the issues of race and gender raised by the hearings.

We observe, then, in the Morrison collection, reflective intervention into American public life on the difficult problems of race. The authors are members of their society, concerning themselves with issues on the minds of ordinary people and of political leaders. They are acting as intellectuals. Their engagement involves a careful consideration of the critical dimensions of a media event, asking telling questions of the event based on historical and theoretical reflection. This is the way that the intellectual reaches, or at least tries to reach, the general public in the media age.

The authors in the collection do not write as professionals to professionals. Rather, they attempt to write as informed citizens to their fellow citizens. Their success is an open question. It is determined both by factors under their control and by factors which go well beyond their control. They can formulate their criticism in such a way that it is understandable and accessible, or they can formulate it in the specialized language of the academy and sectarian politics. Yet, even if they choose to reach out beyond the sequestered worlds of academic life and the political margins, as Russell Jacoby would wish and most of the authors in the collection do, they can be lost in the noise of media spectacle.

In a media-saturated public life, theirs may be the quiet, telling voice of critical reason, informing broad public discussion, cutting through the blinders of media logic and commercial pressures, but this, it must be conceded, is unlikely. There is little doubt that the vast majority of the citizens who observed and talked about the Thomas hearings know nothing about the Morrison collection or similar intellectual reflections. They are overwhelmed by the images of the mass media and have little time or inclination for anything else. Sometimes it seems that the be all and end all of public life in the media age is the thirty-second sound bite. Anything more serious and sustained is apparently marked for oblivion.

Yet, it is a mistake to draw from this appearance the conclusion that intellectual interventions are, therefore, necessarily of no or little public importance. Such works do have potential readership among those who wish to pay more attention and who shape public opinion: from professors and students in the academy, to political leaders and their staffs, to journalists and columnists, to educated citizens in many professions. For such people, ideas, at least sometimes, do matter, and have consequences for them and the broader public. The relatively slow world of intellectual life, even in the media age, does sometimes shape broad political currents. This has been most tellingly evidenced in the work of the neo-conservatives, which laid the groundwork for the so-called Reagan Revolution. The small world of such journals as *Commentary* and *Public Interest* provided the intellectual rationale for the new conservative politics of the eighties. In the nineties, the serious intellectual consideration of race may provide the possibility of addressing the American dilemma as it has not been in a generation.[17]

Realizing this possibility, obviously in large part, is beyond the control of intellectuals such as the authors in the Morrison collection. They can only hope that they will be effective, if they address problems of the day, clearly and seriously, drawing upon sustained learning and reflection. Broader political currents will determine whether their work will actually reach the public and be effective. But, there are indications that favorable currents are again flowing, and a real opportunity exists for public intellectuals addressing the problems of race. There appears to be a growing awareness among Americans that our special dilemma is still with us, and that there is a need to go beyond both the conventions of the prevailing racial order and the provocations to that order such as those Malcolm X presented a generation ago. As I write this chapter, the Million Man March has just taken place in Washington, DC. The concerns and interpretations surrounding that event point to a pressing need for inter-racial understanding and racial justice, for intellectuals to address pressing social problems. This raises complexities concerning the formation of a public space for the discussion of difficult social problems beyond the confines of the academy and relatively independent of the influences of the mass media. I will return to this issue in the conclusion of our inquiry. But before proceeding to this crucial topic, we must spend a little more time with the intellectual reflections concerning the Thomas confirmation and the problems of gender in the United States and abroad.

ON THE ACADEMIC MARGINS

I turned to the essays in *Race-ing Justice, En-gendering Power* because they exemplify how intellectuals can successfully contribute to democratic life. But they are not without problems. Some of them actually fail to address the general public, and they fail in telling ways. They are artifacts more of the insular world of the academy, than of the consequential world of the general society. Race and gender conflicts, as they presented themselves at the Thomas confirmation hearings, become topics used to make academic points, rather than to inform public discussion.

For Homi K. Bhabha, the Thomas–Hill confrontation provides an occasion to launch a generalized critique of the notion of a common culture and of multiculturalism, in the name of post-structuralist theory of domination and resistance. Debates about multiculturalism and the devastations of the "inner city," its crime, drugs, and systems of punishment, are the façades, the spectacles, that overshadow the devastation of everyday life of American minorities. They present the ideological rationale for domination. Whether one is committed to the conservative position of a unified common culture or a multicultural one, commitment hides domination. The authenticities of the multicultural, the claims of alternative others, can be used against one another in the officially recognized multicultural order, just as the domination of a unified "hegemonic" culture has been utilized in the past. This, according to Bhabha, is what happened in the Hill–Thomas confrontation. The illusions of humanism, of the world understood in terms of human intentions and ideals, are revealed to be façades for an underlying reality, an underlying genealogy of power.

Difference which should be the basis of resistance, to the radical post-modernist's mind, came to serve the powers. The difference of race prevailed over the difference of gender. The relatively privileged Hill revealed the sexist domination in the work place, but the difference of race overwhelmed her testimony. Yet, because Thomas fought testimony with metaphor, because he defended himself using the claim of his minority status using the full metaphoric powers of that status, i.e. "the high-tech lynching," he implicitly revealed the truth of sexual harassment.

The very system of truth and falsity within which he operates, as part of the common culture, is founded on the evasion of the endemic reality of women's exploitation. And, likewise, Anita Hill must be believed not because she was personally speaking the truth, but because her affective language is symptomatic of the collective "sexual" condition of working women...The empowerment of women is itself like the process of metaphor: a transformative act of the political imagination that makes new connections, breaks boundaries, maps rare sources of sensibility, and embodies other, unsettling regimes of truth.[18]

The truth of the matter, from the point of view of the distanced critic, is determined by the order of governance. The Thomas–Hill controversy becomes an enactment of a larger canvas of the workings of power. If this interpretation is true, it represents a radical insight not only into the true meaning of the Thomas–Hill controversies, but into the working of racism and sexism in America and beyond.

Yet, there is a problem here. The conditional proposition is intrinsically misleading. Interpretations are not a matter of truth, though some intellectuals, such as Bhabha, seem to think that they are. Although the pretense of a true interpretation plays well in the fields of radical politics and in academic culture, such interpretation turns away from democratic publics.

There is a fundamental confusion in Bhabha's essay. He turns the reader away from political judgment and deliberation and toward the pursuit of truth, broadly speaking: from politics to philosophy. The esoteric knowledge of the theorist reveals that the consequences of the actions of such principals as Thomas and Hill go beyond their control and intentions. Without the tool of theory, it is not possible to know what is really happening. This is the exclusive property of the critical theorist. The script written by the distanced observer of events is confused with the events. Acting subjects appear in the theorist's accounts as characters playing roles assigned to them by theory, not of their own making.[19] As philosophy replaces politics, the philosopher apparently rules, or should rule. The theorist, then, is positioned to have one of two possible relationships with the lay public: as philosopher king or as remote critic.

From the point of view of democracy, remote criticism is clearly preferable. The terrors of the twentieth century are a legacy of theorists running wild: relatively successful peasants labeled as "Kulaks" became class enemies deserving of starvation; Jews labeled as racially degenerative people, became worthy of extermination. And the tyranny of theory does not only come in totalitarian forms. The neo-conservative push to deregulate and de-statize economic and social life, without consideration of the immediate consequences, is a more contemporary case in point. Neo-conservatives deduce from theories of such economists as Hayek and Friedman and ignore the consequences of their actions as they affect public life. Theory empowered, rather than experience, becomes the defining guide to political action, and in the process not public deliberation but the dictates of the theoretical seer become the guide for the public. When empowered, and close to the public space, the theorist is dangerous for democracy.

The remoteness of Bhabha, as a radical critic, is, then, not an unfortunate circumstance, given his approach to truth in politics and his apparent understanding of his access to the truth. He has presented the correct reading of the Thomas confirmation hearings, and history in its inscrutable way marches on with the critical theorist as our guide. It is clearly better for democracies for such theorists to be separated in the academy, as Plato was, than to be in the center of public activity, as was the case of Lenin.

In the academy, such theoretical positioning is politically harmless, and it may even be professionally advantageous. The professional revolutionary armed with the true knowledge of history presents an alternative tradition of inquiry and becomes a conventional professional disciplinarian. The tradition competes with others for space in professional journals and at professional conferences. The radical comes to imagine that the success in such competitions has real political consequences. Conservative critics also imagine that the consequences of these theoretical developments are of great significance. Cultural wars about political correctness are fought.

Interesting academic works do come from this. Bhabha's interpretation of the hearings suggests that a Foucaultian understanding of discipline, combined with a Gramscian understanding of the hegemony of ideologies, can provide insights into the workings of racism and sexism in America in general, and in the Thomas hearings in particular. This in turn could be presented to the public in such a way that it could inform democratic deliberation. It is the mode of address and not the message of the address that reveals a dogmatic turn. It is in fact the conception of the role of the intellectual that is at issue. There must be a basis for the relationship between the intellectual and public life other than the intellectual's possession of truth. The experience of this sad century tells us that the vanguard party is a bankrupt strategy. The intellectual should meet the public on equal grounds. Using the vernacular is an obvious way this can be achieved. A judicious skepticism about theory is clearly in order. The theoretically informed expert is rightly the object of suspicion, both with the great tragedies of the twentieth century and with its little failures (the false promises and unforeseen consequences of liberal reforms) in mind.

CHAPTER 10

Why is there no feminism after communism?

If the intellectual's role is to provoke serious discussion about pressing social problems in public and not to bring truth to the world, as I have maintained, we can recognize the wisdom and limitations of both the civil society and the subaltern position, the importance of civility and subversion. Intellectuals who cultivate a civil public realm do provide the time and the place for deliberations and may reap remarkable fruit, as the experience of East and Central Europeans has demonstrated. These intellectuals, though, must realize that restrictions on deliberations, concerning who can deliberate and about what, may turn the ideal of civil society into its opposite, into a mechanism of constraint, a façade of freedom working to enforce the silencing of subjects (as topics and as people). Yet, the advocates of the silenced subjects should be aware that the speech of the subaltern must be heard and considered in a civil fashion. They must demand their right to speak, but they must convince and not simply declare their position, if democracy is to be practiced. Malcolm X's political position unsupported by a commitment to a free public sphere leads to profoundly undemocratic political positions such as those of Farrakhan and Jeffries. These positions present stark but limited alternatives: Orientalism versus Occidentalism, patriarchy versus matriarchy, one sort of class rule or another, one sort of racial domination or another. On the other hand, the commitment to civil society and civil discourse, unquestioned, without disruptions such as those of Malcolm, becomes a force for the subjugation of the marginal, in the US particularly the continued functioning of racism.

The normal partisan and academic approach to an intellectual conflict, such as the one between the civil society advocates and their opponents, is to choose sides and marshal all the support one can to establish the priority of the chosen position. It is quite possible to reveal that civil society in Eastern Europe was the ideology of new class intellectuals. It is equally possible to dismiss Said as a disgruntled Palestinian ideologist. With these dismissals, though, the contribution each position can make to invigorate deliberation would be lost. There are good reasons to take seriously both the civil society position and the position of the subversives, even though they apparently conflict. Lived experience, as well as theoretical justification, point in the direction of both positions. However, the two positions can be balanced not theoretically, but only politically, if democracy is to be sustained. Here we consider how these issues are addressed in debates about feminism. The changed situation of women in post-communist Europe provides a strategic field to examine these issues. It has intrinsic interest, especially for those who are immediately involved, but it also reveals a great deal about the relationship between the public and identity as it is experienced in developed democracies, and about the role intellectuals can play in shaping the relationship between identity and the democratic public.

THE STORY OF CIVIL SOCIETY FROM A FEMINIST PERSPECTIVE

The achievement of a free public life in Eastern and Central Europe is one of the great accomplishments of the twentieth century, proof, from the point of view of this inquiry, that intellectuals matter. But this is not a Hollywood tale with a nice happy ending, the defeat of communism with everyone involved living happily ever after. The collapse of the totalitarian orders and the development of a free public life have meant for a lot of people increased suffering and disorientation, economic hardships, and even war. While this, in my judgment, has as much to do with the chaos of disorder as with the nature of the regimes that have replaced the orders of previously existing socialism, many of those affected have responded to their new situation with nostalgia for the old order. They are motivated by a rejection of social and economic reforms, ushering in the ascendence of the post-communist parties in Eastern Europe and the communists in Russia. Incredibly high expectations have been followed by incredibly low despair, challenging the newly constituted democracies' capacities to accommodate political discontent. Nonetheless, at least as of this writing, the economic discontent and the nationalist antagonisms that are observable all around the old bloc have not undermined the public commitment to democracy on the part of the major political actors. In contrast to the rhetoric of the inter-war period on the political left and right, there is little intellectual agitation against parliamentary democracy, and few principled pressures waged against the formation of free civil societies. Although governments and the political elites are uncertain about the democratic rules of the game, and there have been efforts to control the "inconvenient" aspects of public freedom, from subtle to not so subtle forms of censorship, to the vicious use of government controlled media to wage war in the former Yugoslavia, the ideals of a free public life and democracy are supported across the political spectrum, across the former Soviet bloc with very few marginal exceptions. Given the history of the region, this is amazing, even with all the backsliding and the tragedy. But the miraculous accomplishment does have limits, and the limits raise important theoretical and practical questions. Especially striking among the limits is the deteriorating status of women.

Men and women have fared quite differently under the communist order and the orders that are replacing the old regimes. All suffered under totalitarian control, but along with the suffering there were advances of various sorts: from the spreading literacy to improvements in public health for the bulk of the population. From the point of view of certain central feminist concerns, the communist orders presented real opportunities for women and significant social advances. Women were included into official life to a degree unknown in these societies traditionally. The vast majority of women left the confines of the home for gainful employment. Pre-school child care was broadly available. Political participation in state and party institutions was at a high level, much higher than in the pre- or post-communist political experience. Reproductive rights, including the right to abortion, were, for the most part, officially supported. And when it came to unofficial life, women also played a central role. The informal networks of friends and family, in which the authority of women has been high, were a key to the workings of the quiet and assertive resistance to the communist orders. Private circles took on an importance unknown in free societies, and in the societies where open resistance developed, these private circles played central roles in the making of the democratic opposition. A great deal of respect and accomplishment were thus achieved by women, not only thanks to officialdom, but also in opposition to it. To be sure, women along with men suffered from the failures of the communist orders, but women apparently had much to lose, and did indeed lose much, with the collapse of the previously existing socialist order.

The advances of that order were less than they appeared. The participation in the workplace tended not to represent an emancipation from the obligations of the household, but an addition to those traditional obligations with a new set of obligations. The participation of women in political organizations tended to be as tokens, symbols of the ideology of equality, but not with any real exercise of political power, and, in fact, these organizations had less to do with self-determination and freedom and more to do with political discipline and control. Child care facilities tended to be quite poor, and actual access to them often required bribes and favor exchange which made them costly, not free. They functioned like the public medical care where "tips" were required for decent treatment. And as for reproductive rights, abortions were available, but often as the only means of birth control.

Nonetheless, women are bearing a heavy burden in the so-called transition to democracy. They are experiencing a disproportionate level of unemployment. Their rights to abortions are threatened. A rebirth of traditionalism uses them to symbolize the values of home, hearth, and religious revival. They have lost social services. Their number has drastically dropped in parliamentary institutions. They still struggle with the burdens of the second shift, and they have experienced high rates of domestic violence and, in the war zones of the former Yugoslavia, they have been subjected to systematic campaigns of rape as acts of war.[1]

In addition to this well-known list of burdens, the very act of constituting the new democratic polities has involved gross injustices to women democratic heroes. This has been most striking in the case of Poland. There, the functioning of the Solidarity underground depended on the work of women. They were key figures in the workings of the underground press, led some of the regions of underground Solidarity, and were in large part the underground network of transportation and communication that could not be repressed by the communist authorities. Yet, with very few exceptions, they almost immediately dropped out or were forced out of public life when a more open society was achieved. They themselves have been silent about the contributions they have made. One case illustrates the oddity of the situation.

Danuta Winiarska led the Lublin region's Solidarity underground. She knew that no one would take her seriously as a woman, so she invented an imaginary man whom she claimed to represent. She acted in his name and coordinated the underground's action. After about a year, she found that she could no longer work without the physical presence of "Abramczyk." At that time, she arranged for an acquaintance, recently released from political internment from another region of Poland, to play the Abramczyk role. After the collapse of communism, he actually gave interviews describing his leadership of the Lublin region, without even mentioning his "loyal assistant" Winiarska.[2]

The marginalization of Winiarska's political engagement after the fall of communism was anticipated by the form of her public engagement in the opposition. She, like many women oppositionists, worked in the shadows, not visible to the general public, reinforcing traditional notions about the place of women. Her male puppet's pretense to have had an opposition life of his own making was but an extension of Winiarska's decision to act behind the scenes, and this is being further extended by her decision, along with the majority of other women democratic oppositionists, not to tell the story of their political accomplishments. As far as they are concerned, theirs was a supporting role required at the moment, not worth retelling.

This, then, clearly is not fertile grounds for feminism. If the most politically active and effective women do not take credit for their actions, it would seem that feminism does not have much chance to develop. Even one former woman oppositionist who has broken this general rule and made an effort to tell this story of political accomplishment, Joanna Szczesna, does not consider herself to be a feminist,[3] underscoring the oddity of the situation. In a world where women have accomplished a great deal and experience injustice, there is an open hostility to feminism.

Contrary to official propaganda of the communists, there was significant gender injustice in the old system, and contrary to the hopes of democrats and liberals, of civil society advocates,[4] the injustice not only has not disappeared during the so-called democratic transition, but in certain ways has even intensified: with the loss of even the pretense of the ideal of sexual equality, and the real or at least threatened loss of reproductive rights. Under the communists, equality was a fiction that justified political oppression, for women and men generally, and for women particularly. The oppression of women was part and parcel of the oppression of the society as a whole. With democratic reforms, the oppression is more the outcome of the workings of the society, as it moves against the ideals of equality, and as traditionalisms of various sorts reassert themselves. This would seem to be a most fertile ground for a feminist movement, but there is none, or more precisely, the feminism that does exist is of a relatively marginalized elite, with little broad-based societal support, not even supported, as we have noted, by accomplished women activists.

WHY IS THERE NO FEMINISM IN CENTRAL EUROPE?

If the existence of feminism depended only on the existence of gender injustice, and the need to address it, feminism would be a thriving enterprise in Central Europe. But much more is involved. The injustice must be collectively perceived, and the way of acting on the perception would have to take a certain form, conducive to the development of a feminist worldview.[5] There is an opening for intellectual intervention, which can, though, easily lead to misunderstanding and resentments. This involves both the strange characteristics of the situation of women in Central Europe and the equal oddities of Western feminism as a political orientation and movement. Telescoping my answer to the somewhat illogical question posed, I believe the absence, or at least relative weakness, of feminism in Eastern and Central Europe has less to do with the "feminine," the present situation of women in that part of the world, and more to do with the "ism," the way the problems of women have been theoretically understood by Western feminists and have been applied to the situation of the former communist countries. The problematic relationship between political intellectuals and the public is at issue, especially as intellectuals transverse the boundaries of political cultures.

Wondering why there is no feminism in Central Europe, ironically, echoes the old socialist concern as to why there is no socialism in America. Both questions suggest a worldview that takes the existence of a certain social and political movement to be natural, its absence needing explanation. Intellectuals raise such questions because of their strangeness, their distance from the concerns and perceptions of their compatriots. Inspired by the insights of a particular political or social theory, a philosophy of history, a political experience elsewhere, they know that something ought to be the case, and that it is not needs explanation. Why, after all, should there have been socialism in America? The assumption was that the socialist movement was the natural outgrowth of the injustices of capitalism. Since it was so, following the insights of Marxist theory and European experience, the task was to explain the absence. Given the general loss of legitimacy of socialism as a systemic alternative to capitalism, the question no longer makes much sense apart from the historical interest involved. Could feminism be like socialism in this way?

The explanations for the absence of feminism in Central Europe among Western feminists include: the theoretical allergies Central European women have to Marxist and psychoanalytically inspired feminism, along with the ignorance of Central Europeans of postmodern and post-structuralist theories, theories central to contemporary feminism,[6] the anti- feminism of oppositionalist politics as it interacted with official politics,[7] and the patriarchal character of the liberal democracy being instituted in that part of the world.[8] Sympathetic observers from the region explain the problem differently. They point out that the family orientation of the men and women of the region does not lead to a sense of intra-gender solidarity. Feminism in one account appears as a manifestation of individualism that is lacking in the region.[9] Feminism appears as a foreign ideology, dangerously looking like other, sometimes unwanted, imports, such as McDonalds, Coca Cola, and Hollywood films.[10] The feminist criticism of private life and the questioning of the responsibilities and prerogatives of women in the private domain seem to cast into doubt the arena of highest accomplishment and value to Central European women and men, who have become convinced that politics is synonymous with corruption and human degradation. The emancipation of women brought by the communists is viewed as a failure, and talk about such emancipation again is viewed with suspicion. For many women, a life dedicated to the family and the home is much more desirable than enforced public engagement. And when those suggesting such engagement are obviously influenced by Marxism, and still seem to speak in its language of liberation, exploitation, and internationalism, as Western feminists do, they are rejected not only as aliens, but as representatives of a worn-out politics which has been central to past oppression. In the words of Laura Busheikin, a Western feminist working for an extended time in Prague, "there's a traditional refusal that is already part of the East European psyche – refusal of propaganda, ideology, political messianism, of big liberatory ideas."[11]

The resistance to feminism involves a reaction against stereotypes of Western feminism and a commitment to traditional ideas about gender relations, and a suspicion of the form, as well as the content, of Western feminism (it is presented too much like the discredited official ideology). A suspicion that feminism is like other anti-liberal emancipatory politics turns women away from it. Yet, as with the old question about socialism, the answers to the question about feminism's absence ignore the presence of the political engagement of women in ways that are somewhat different than those of the West. It assumes that a Western style mobilization is natural and does not pay sufficient attention to the different ways that women are becoming politically engaged. There was a great deal of social agitation against the evils of capitalism in America which did not appear as being sufficiently socialist to European observers. Could Western observers be misunderstanding the engagement of women in Central Europe in a similar way?

WESTERN FEMINISM MEETS CIVIL SOCIETY

There are many Western feminists of goodwill who have done good work with women of the new democracies. These intellectual activists have helped establish centers of Gender Studies, such as the one in Prague. They have provided advise for the establishment of the Rape and Abuse Hotline of the Women Against Violence in the former Yugoslavia. They have sponsored international conferences on the problems women face in the region. Feminist intellectuals, like experts on constitutions, economic development, and the universities, among a great many others (including religious missionaries), are attracted to the region for a variety of motives: some because they see the possibility of spreading the good word, the truth; others because they find the novelty of the political situation of the region to be intellectually interesting, a chance to observe up close, and maybe even influence, monumental historic changes; a few may be open to the notion that the experience of the people in the region has something to teach them about their own theoretical and political concerns and hope for political partnership. A combination of all these motives is usually present.

For those in the region who are most antagonistic to feminism, the image of a new internationale, representing the decadence of the West, or at least its silliness, is most conveniently imagined to characterize Western feminists. They are viewed as being secular missionaries of the left: irresponsible intellectuals viewed as the conservative Paul Johnson depicts the type, only these are women. They appear to be foreign and threatening, and are attacked and dismissed. Those who are deeply conservative, traditionally religious, and nationalist, as in the West, are antagonistic to feminism, and view feminist intellectual interventions in the most negative light. But what about the liberals and the more culturally secular and sophisticated? How do the supporters of the democratic opposition and the ideals of civil society respond to feminist ideas? And how do feminists respond to their response? These questions provide an opportunity to consider the way the ideals of civil society and the critics of these ideals can resolve the incompatibility of their opposing positions politically, but not theoretically.

Mira Marody is a well-established Polish sociologist and social psychologist. On the occasion of an extended visit to the United States, she wrote a reflective essay entitled "Why I am not a feminist." Her essay is not one of those post-feminist attacks on feminism with which we in the West are now quite familiar. Rather hers was an attempt to turn the tables on the "why is there no feminism in the East?" question, by asking the equally interesting question: Why is there feminism in the West? She reformulates the question in an objective social scientific manner, asking:

Under what conditions does a sexual identity become a gender identity? When and why do the differences between men and women stop being perceived by the *individual* as natural and biologically grounded and begin being treated as socially maintained? Is it only a problem of individuals' "enlightenment" or can we point at specific social factors which promote or inhibit the development of "feminist consciousness"?[12]

Her answers to these questions lead to a critical appraisal of what she takes to be the universal claims of Western feminism.

Marody is reacting to what she sees as the unusual aspects of the feminist stance. Any particular position held by women to be in their interests is not necessarily understood as being feminist. Feminism embraces a set of enlightened positions: gender equality in political, economic, cultural, and family life;[13] liberation from what are understood to be patriarchal definitions of women's nature and place;[14] and a questioning of male-centered heterosexual under-standings of sexuality.[15] Marody writes about the problem of feminism without subscribing to this battery of commitments. Rather, she asks what are the social conditions upon which these commitments develop. She understands the problems that women in the post-communist situation face quite differently than would feminists. Thus, for example, she strikingly views the high rate of abortion in a Catholic society, such as Poland, as a significant social problem. She sees it as evidence that "women pay most of the cost of sexual liberation."[16]

Among Western feminists, the problem of abortion is understood as the problem of the right to choose, the right to control one's own body and reproductive fate. My guess is that Marody would agree with their position. But because she judges on the grounds of her compatriots' experience and perceptions, she also sees that the high rate of abortion is a burden upon women, an indication of the nation's neglect of women. She reports that although there is acceptance of extra-marital sex by 60% of the population, and only 3% negatively evaluated giving birth out of wedlock, and divorce was accepted by 40% of the population (all indications of changing sexual attitudes and practices), women are subjected to the traumas of abortion at an extremely high rate. She does not infer from this that abortion should be criminalized, but she does question the interaction between changed sexual practices and a societal neglect of birth control.

Marody takes a historical view. She notes that the women of Poland, like the women of many other places and other times, may be dissatisfied or even rebel against their fate, but they do so against their female fate, not against a society that treats them in unequal ways. They are more concerned with the health and freedom of their families which have been politicized by the communists, with the protection of the private domain against public invasion, than with the protection of their own individual rights against the injustices of the family itself. To her mind, Western feminism is predicated upon an individualistic point of view which is foreign to Polish concerns. Western feminists, no doubt, see in Marody's position one that justifies patriarchy. She does seem to assume the individual autonomy of men and only question the autonomy of women. She overlooks the often brutal conditions of family life. But who is to say that focus on the family and the protection of private life against public incursions is mistaken, especially when the people who seek the protection have experienced the systematic invasion of privacy for two generations or more?

Marody concludes with a challenging observation:

For American feminists, the most important goal in life seems to be the defense of their right to socially supported individual development. On the contrary, Polish women have a tendency to subordinate their own individual development to family goals, which they try to achieve by using private methods and tricks. Both attitudes contain in themselves their own negation. In Poland, we observe a growing disorganization of family life which accumulates socially neglected problems of individuals, whereas many American feminists seem to pay for the equality of their social rights with increasing private problems, a great many of which have their source in the disintegration of their families. Whatever may be said about the future of women in both societies, I cannot agree that a solution to their problems lies in the forced choice between [the] individual's rights and happy family life.[17]

It is hard to imagine any serious feminist, from the West or the East, believing that such a forced choice is the solution, given the nature of family commitments in Eastern Europe. To be sure, the traditional structure and power relations of the family have been the subject of feminist critiques, but, there is room within the feminist position for an appreciation of the deep and enduring relationships of the family. Nonetheless, the way the family is understood by Marody is problematic from a feminist point of view. It embodies patriarchy, which feminists know must be confronted if women's rights are to be successfully pursued. Yet, talk about different sorts of family relations, which such a confrontation implies, from the East European point of view, seems to be not only undesirable, but dangerously utopian. There is a real theoretical impasse. From the point of view of the feminist West, the common sense of the ordinary East European, which Marody reports and agrees with, is sexist; from the East European point of view, the feminist critique of the family, along with its theoretical resemblance in form and content to discredited ideologies, is unacceptable. For reasons based in lived experience, feminism, even when addressing the real concerns of women, does not provide a way of understanding or acting in the world, especially when it comes wrapped in a theoretically question-able package. Consider, further, the intervention of Josef Skvorecky on the issue of sexual harassment and date rape.

Skvorecky is a distinguished émigré Czech novelist and cultural and political activist. The author of the acclaimed *The Engineer of Human Souls* and *The Bass Saxophone,* he has also played a major role as the head of a Czech publishing house, 68, that helped keep Czech literature alive during the most repressive period of the communist regime. His works have often focused on the cultural distance between the political East and the political West. In an article he wrote for the Czech weekly *Respekt,* "Can there be Sex without Rape?,"[18] he continues his task of cross-cultural commentary.

His opening sentence summarizes his position: "The worst thing that can happen to a good idea is to have some fanatic, à la Lenin, make it the basis of an ideology." He purports to value the fundamental wisdom of feminism, recognizing that the equal treatment of women in all aspects of private and public life is a worthy idea, but he maintains that this idea has been transformed into the notion of the superiority of women. He provocatively writes about the new ideology of "lesboid feminism" which views sexual intercourse as a crime. It expands, to his mind unacceptably, the unambiguous definition of the crime of rape, in which sexual intercourse has been forced on a woman by physical violence. Two new sorts of rape have been added to the traditional understanding (in which the signs of physical coercion by a stranger can be clearly discerned): when a woman having sexual relationship with a man is physically forced to have sex with him when she does not desire it, and when a man uses verbal coercion, without even touching the woman, until she agrees to have sex. This is the way that Skvorecky understands acquaintance rape and date rape. He believes that seduction and rape have come to be confused by these new feminist understandings. He makes some troubling comments about Mike Tyson, Clarence Thomas, and American male bonding, declaring "So it is no wonder that in North America, more and more young men would rather go for a beer than on a date." He concludes that "It is no wonder that among girls one increasingly hears the lament, 'Why is it that all men I come into contact with are either wimps, married or fairies?' "

The article plays to the anti-feminist prejudices and homophobia of the Czech audience, and, as should be expected, was viewed quite negatively by the feminists of Prague.[19] It seemed to them that Skvorecky's piece was part of a trend to print anti-feminist articles to intimidate people, an attempt to prevent feminism from influencing

Czech women. Taken together with articles that celebrate the contribution of traditional women to history, the negative articles, it seems to the local feminists, are aimed at convincing women that they have a considerable stake in the traditional order of society. They further worry that the discussions about feminist issues, which are very new to the Czech public, are being framed by the antagonistic Skvorecky, who is a major cultural figure on the Czech cultural landscape. His authority comes from his work as an oppositionist public intellectual and a distinguished novelist. The hero of the dissident civil society works against the struggles of Czech feminists.

The cultural editor of *Respekt* maintains that she published the article in order to provoke public discussion, and she was pleased that the article did indeed open public debate about the issues of feminism. But the journal's critics point out that this debate is one that is distorted by the unequal authority of the competing voices. The prevailing attitudes toward feminism and the authority of feminism's critic make a free and open discussion next to impossible. The Czech feminists realized that if the article was published in Canada, where Skvorecky is a Professor of Literature at the University of Toronto, his "bluntly stated sexist views" would have been met with protest and derision, Laura Busheikin reports. While in the Czech Republic his critics have little power to criticize his position head on, in the West political correctness might not allow for the open discussion of Skvorecky's position, Busheikin seems inadvertently to imply. The point is that in both North America and in Eastern and Central Europe, open intellectual discussion about the issues and problems feminism presents is not an easy matter. The existence of a newly formed or a well-established civil public life does not automatically do the trick.

Skvorecky's position on date rape and acquaintance rape may be old-fashioned and incorrect. Indeed, his representation of feminism reveals a fundamental misogyny and is particularly unfortunate because of the way he collapses feminism as a general phenomenon into its most radical and objectionable form (from the point of view of his readers). He erases the liberal element that is a core component of the feminist tradition. He has unleashed a backlash to feminism without there even being a movement to react against. Here we have a corollary to the anti-semitism without the Jews that has been characteristic of the political culture of Central Europe after the Holocaust. Nonetheless, there is something to his argument. There are ideological tendencies in the feminist movement. There are those who call for a purity of position and view all who are opposed as enemies, those who understand the family exclusively as a repressive institution and those who crusade against pornography, who view all concerned with freedom of speech as complicit in rape.[20] As someone who has suffered from the abuses of ideology, it should not be surprising that Skvorecky reacts so strongly to these tendencies among feminists, and feels a responsibility to address the public on the subject. That he has done so in an awkward, even a hateful, manner, in a way that may serve to undermine the capacity of feminism to establish itself, has to do with the gulf between the experience that gave rise to feminism in the West and the experience of the general public and the intellectuals of the former communist countries. There is a political gulf which separates people of goodwill and guarantees misunderstandings and tensions. The ideals of a free public life in civil society do not seem to have room for feminism.

Marody's analysis and Skvorecky's polemics thus suggest that the gulf between feminists and Central European democrats is unbridgeable, apparently confirming what some radical critics maintain with assurance, that liberal democracy is a form of oppression, in this case patriarchy, something to be dismissed or overthrown, part of the problem not the solution. But if we look closer at the activities of feminist intellectuals in the region another conclusion does seem in order.

WOMEN INFORM CIVIL SOCIETY

The resistance to feminism in the new democracies of Central Europe has an organizational dimension, along with the already discussed ideological dimension. This also involves a reaction to communist experience. Supporting the official ideology, there was an elaborate institutional system, which brought the official truth into the everyday life of ordinary people. These were the structures of mass mobilization, the infamous conveyor belts of official ideology: from official industrial unions to peasant associations, to writers' unions, to peace and women's movements. Women activists seem to be reluctant to establish a centralized women's organization or movement, especially one which is unified through an agreed-upon ideology, because they fear that it would resemble the organizations and movements of the recent past. Without the experience of totalitarianism, feminists in the West are much less reluctant to establish national and international coordination of political action. Yet, it is striking that women intellectuals of the new democracies, nonetheless, are developing organized responses to the new problems they are facing. There are dozens of women's resource centers, women's studies programs, and research institutes throughout the former Soviet Bloc: in Hungary and the Czech Republic, and in Estonia, Tajikistan, Ukraine, and beyond.

The form and normative commitment of these responses in Central Europe seem to be informed by the culture of the democratic opposition to the communists, and in an important way seem to keep that culture alive. As Elzbieta Matynia has observed:

in the course of the 1990s, in Warsaw, Budapest, Prague, and Bratislava - places where the political scene is more and more frequently looked upon with disappointment and disgust – one has also been able to detect the reemergence of a public – spirited ethos exemplified more often than not by certain individual women and women's groups in parliaments and beyond. Such an ethos combines the experience and civic commitment of former dissidents (from the democratic opposition of the 1970s and 1980s) with the readiness to address imaginatively the unfamiliar challenges of new political and economic circumstances. These women are beginning to be respected by both the broader public and the political elites either because of – or in spite of – their commitment to women's issues.[21]

In Hungary and Poland almost immediately after the fall of communism, reproductive rights were challenged. Women first organized to defend these rights in and outside of parliament. Publications followed, first focusing on the specific experiences of women under communism. Women realized that the dream to join Europe provided leverage for the articulation of grievances. Just as the Helsinki agreement had provided an opening for the pursuit of human rights in the seventies and eighties, the standards of the European Community and the Council of Europe concerning the equality between men and women are used to press for change in constitutional arrangements. The immediate success of these efforts may not be assured, but neither were the activities of the Helsinki Watch Committees of the late seventies.

The Meeting Place and Foundation ROSA in Prague, supported by the Gender Studies Center, provoke public discussions about the problems of elderly and divorced women. These groups also support a hotline and resource center for female victims of violence. Women are brought together in conferences, seminars, and lectures, and they work to put on the political agenda the special problems of women.

In Bratislava, the women's journal, *Aspekt*, with filial connections to the Public Against Violence, the major pro-democratic anti-nationalist movement of the immediate post-1989 period, works to accomplish the same end of enriching public deliberations in Slovakia.

In Hungary, two significant national associations concern themselves with the issues of women. The Association of Hungarian Women was formed in 1989, as a successor of the Women's Council, which was an old communist conveyor. The Feminist Network includes a small number of Westerners as active and visible members. The first group provokes distrust because of its too intimate connections with the past, the second because of its too intimate connections with the West. But the latter group is adopting a new strategy, becoming a network of projects with some distance from the foreign and ideological sounding label of feminism. They are turning increasingly to more straightforward descriptive names and activities, such as Women for Women Against Domestic Violence and the Women's House. Apparently by adopting this approach, there is an attempt to reach beyond the relatively narrow circles of academia and the urban cultural elite to which these groups are generally confined. Feminist intellectuals are trying to meet the public on its terms, eschewing vanguardism.

In Poland, the legacy of the oppositional civil society seems to be a factor that extends the influence of women's groups, Matynia reports. Discussion about women's issues in Poland are less driven by Western experience, more an outgrowth of indigenous issues. The controversies with the Church, particularly over the question of abortion, are central. Women's groups are related through horizontal structures, reacting against communist organizational principles and recreating the principles of organization of Solidarity, both legal and underground. Women played a key role in the organizational activities then, and women with experience of organizational action are concerning themselves with women's issues now. National organizational activities are constrained by the complicated authority of the Catholic Church in Polish life, with the population often at odds with the Church in its attitudes to political questions, but unwilling to defy the Church openly and in an organized and coordinated fashion. The decentralized organization of women leads to some limited influence in parliament, the development of a wide range of cultural initiatives, and the attempt to defend women against unjust economic burdens. The goal is to enter civil society as a coordinated group of voluntary associations, and support and shape civil society in the process.

Matynia concludes:

women's movements are gaining a firm foothold in much of East and Central Europe, stimulating growth and development of civil society. If successful, they may not only get women's issues onto the official agendas of their respective governments and parliaments, but they may also influence the very process of democratization in their societies.[22]

The expectation that feminism could be imported to Eastern and Central Europe with the same ideological and organizational form and content, not surprisingly, has not been sustained, but women's movements are developing as a part of the indigenous political culture. These movements are informed and supported by Western feminists and feminism, but, as this happens, the movements have something to say to their Western colleagues. Their activists' allergy to ideology is not only an idiosyncrasy of the victims of communism, which make them unreceptive to good Western theory. It has meaning and is a criticism of the ideological foundations and tendencies of at least some Western feminists. Their understanding that an identity movement contributes to and does not work against the ideal of civil society also is an important insight.

But a serious set of problems remains: are the initiatives mentioned here and the dozens, if not hundreds, of similar initiatives definitive of the situation of women and feminism in the emerging democracies of Eastern and Central Europe? Or is the observable deterioration of the status of women definitive? Is the optimism of Matynia warranted? The way one answers these questions is, to be sure, a matter of sensibility as much as a matter of evidence, but there are disturbing patterns that must be recognized.

The emergence of an open civil society and the free public life in the former communist societies has included, as we have already observed, a diminishing status of women. This provides the opening for the interpretation that the diminishing status of women in the emerging democracies is a necessary part of the structures of liberal democracies. This argument has taken on rather stale Marxist and anti-liberal forms. Capitalism can do no good, and the collapse of communism is nothing more than an ascendence of capitalism. A free public life and civil society are but façades for the underlying realities of capitalism. Patriarchy is a necessary component of an abhorrent retrogressive social formation. But this interpretation also can be presented with care and challenges both our understanding of the situation of women after the fall of communism and our understanding of the possibility of intellectual action in democratic society.

Peggy Watson argues that the emergence of the autonomous public sphere is based on the political differentiation of post-communist societies.[23] Under communism, men and women were equally disenfranchised. They equally lacked political citizenship. The absence of women in political life, after the fall of communism, entails the mobilization of difference between men and women which was irrelevant under communism. This, she argues, should be understood as part of a more general process which includes the emergence of nationalism and ethnic strife. People used to be all in the same boat, equally disempowered by communist domination, and now some are taking the helm and some are being thrown overboard.

Contrary to civil society theorists, Watson emphasizes that "civil society mobilizes those self-same differences which subvert its universal ideal."[24] She takes as telling that the emergent zones of free public life include men and not women. The transformation of public and private assigns women exclusively to the private zone. The democratization of the countries of Central Europe has meant the empowerment of men, leading to "a rise of masculinism." But as women are marginalized, systematically excluded from the public sphere, the opportunity for feminism emerges, as well. The traditional social inequalities between men and women which the communists did not transform, now are institutionalized in redefined public and private spheres, politicizing subordination, but also resistance to subordination. The distance between Western feminists and their Eastern counterparts would seem then to be diminishing. Thus, while Matynia sees the rise of women's groups as an outgrowth of the democratic oppositions in Eastern and Central Europe, Watson sees these developments as a movement against the male democratic intellectuals in power. Matynia points to the need to extend the project of civility among the former civil society advocates, while Watson seeks to subvert the civility of these very same advocates.

Matynia emphasizes the commitments that male and female democratic activists share to the opening of a free public sphere and a civil society, while Watson maintains that the actually emerging public space excludes women as part of a continuing and recurring social process. The political implications of these contrasting diagnoses are great. Matynia points to the legitimate expansion of the democratic consensus to include the special problems of women. Watson criticizes the patriarchal character of the emerging political consensus, as we have seen revealed in the writings of Marody and Skvorecky, and points to the need for feminist solidarity in opposition to the political consensus. With an appreciation of the deliberative contribution of intellectuals to political life, it becomes clear that the theoretical resolution of Matynia's and Watson's competing analyses is not desirable. The tension between their competing positions should be articulated and addressed politically, not resolved theoretically. Intellectuals and scholars, such as Watson and Matynia, will have competing positions to present, opening time and space for deliberation. It is the purview for the political actors to act and resolve the tensions in their competing positions. Learning from both positions in the case of feminism in Eastern and Central Europe, they will act within the legal framework of the emerging democracies, extending Matynia's approach both in their acceptance of the legitimacy of the new democratic orders and in their activities of coalition building with and against the new authorities, and, working with the approach of a Watson, they will attempt to forge a new understanding of the nature of contemporary and historical patriarchy and the need to subvert it through a feminist consciousness and social movement.

A major political problem is how to act upon the insight that a civil consensus concerning the rules of the democratic game must be in place, and that this consensus must be subverted for its potential exclusivities. As we observe the resistance to Western feminism after communism in Central Europe, we must realize that this balancing act is ongoing, and that this is not a bad thing, particularly where democratic institutions and culture are new and most fragile.

CONCLUSION: DEMOCRACY AND DIVERSITY

I have had the opportunity to view up close the dilemmas of feminism after communism in a special Graduate Institute co-ordinated by the Transregional Center for Democratic Studies at the New School for the Social Research. This has proven to be an unusual center for cultural and political exchange. Graduate students and junior faculty from the former Soviet bloc meet senior faculty and graduate students from the former free world, primarily the US. Because of the regular attendance of Ann Snitow, an American feminist and prominent organizer of the Network of East–West Women, an unusually large group of young feminists from the region attend the seminar. Because of the work of the New School in the region, some of the most promising young democratic intellectuals from around the old bloc also attend. The two groups are by no means mutually exclusive, but the feminist challenge to the proponents of civil society is more present than is usual in similar educational and intellectual gatherings in the region.

Yearly, Snitow and I are sure to have a discussion about the issue of identity politics and democratic culture. This has led to public dialogues. We reach, it seems to me, no definitive conclusions, only sensitizing doubts about our most fundamental political commitments.

I started these discussions with a sure sense that democracy is a significant end in itself, that politics is about public freedom, and that righting social inequalities, such as those of class, race, nation, and gender, should not be allowed to overwhelm the primary commitment of maintaining a free public space for the pursuit of public freedom. These are themes of the courses I have taught at the Institute, variously named "Democratic Culture," " Civil Society and the Public Sphere," and "The Political and Social Theory of Hannah Arendt." In fact, the normative commitment to public freedom is one I learned simultaneously from my observations of the democratic opposition in Central Europe and from reading the work of Arendt. The power of opposition action and her political theory have convinced me that the first principle of a free politics has to be maintaining the space for freedom.

Snitow is respectful of this position. Yet, she winces when I assert my ideas strongly and declare that I am against all "isms." She is aware how the experience of totalitarianism can lead to such a position, but she questions the idea that the public domain for freedom must take priority over social questions. Such reasoning seems to suggest that women should remain respectful and accepting of their place. She, as a veteran of the New Left and the early struggles of the second wave feminist movement of the sixties and seventies, cannot accept the idea that addressing the women's question must be deferred, and, as a student of women's history, she is well aware that this has been a pattern of political alliances of women dating back, at the very least, to the time of the French and American revolutions. While I affirm the fundamental wisdom of Arendt when she observed how the social question undid the French Revolution, Snitow knows that the problem with modern revolutions, as far as women are concerned, is that the revolutionaries all too frequently overlook the question of the emancipation of women after its use as a theme for mobilization has passed. She is understandably as suspicious of the "Velvet" and "Self-Limiting" revolutions of Central Europe, in this regard, as the veterans of the anti-communist struggles are of the grand narratives of liberation and emancipation. She further argues strongly and convincingly that the way the society addresses the situation of women has a significant impact on its democratic potential. When women are treated as equals with equal rights, democracy is something beyond a slogan. When women are treated as lesser beings, the claims of democracy are justifications for injustice.

But because we met in this special institute in Cracow, with a remarkable group of young democrats and feminists, our dialogues went beyond the assertion of opposing positions, with hopes of clarification and synthesis. They involved, rather, a search for ways to criticize one's own position, so that the insights of the other could be fully appreciated. In this way men and women from Eastern and Central Europe who were highly skeptical of the idea of feminism seriously studied it, realizing that civility must leave room for subversion, and students of the left from the US, Canada, Western Europe, and Latin America learned to be a little bit more skeptical about their political correctness and ideological commitments, realizing the importance of civility alongside subversion, of open discussion, of freedom of speech, and of a non-authoritarian relationship between intellectuals and the general public.

Snitow and I are still having our discussion. This chapter is my most recent contribution to it. The action of non-ideological women activists in Eastern and Central Europe underscores how the ideals of civil society and the pursuit of women's rights are in fact mutually compatible. It is, of course, not the case that this is a new wisdom from the political East. Much of feminism in the West points in the same direction.[25] But some do not, and the dramatic situation of women in the postcommunist orders suggests why we should proceed with caution when echoes of totalitarian certainty can be heard and when intellectuals, feminists among them, claim to know the situation of the masses better than do ordinary people.

CHAPTER 11

Conclusion: civility and subversion in cynical times

We see, then, intellectuals contributing to democratic society. They are people concerned about gender injustice and the problems of race, with the importance of cultural freedom and the continuities of tradition, people who defend Western civilization and people who radically question this civilization. They are distinguished by the abnormal attention they pay to their critical faculties. They use their specialized skills and knowledge to address and constitute public life. They contribute to society's capacity to deliberate about its problems. Some address themselves to elites, some to broader publics. They do so by both cultivating civil society and subverting the constraints of common sense. They promote a civil consensus, and they subvert the limitations of conventional wisdom. They are talk provokers.

Intellectuals have long been with us, but it is in modernity that they find themselves in a relatively stable position in independent cultural institutions. It is worth working for this independence, as our colleagues in post-communist Europe know. It makes it possible to sustain deliberations in a modern social order. But the independence of cultural institutions also entails problems. They can become distanced from the society at large and make it difficult for intellectuals to contribute to public life, as has sometimes been the case in American universities. Specialized languages, not understandable to the lay public, are used to sustain the authority of the professional. Political rhetoric develops, as is the case with political correctness, which has little to do with the concerns of the greater society. It becomes difficult for the academic intellectual to contribute to public life beyond the university.

But difficult does not mean impossible, and intellectuals and intellectual debate are not completely confined to and limited by the university. This is most evident and pressing in the United States in the attempts to talk about race in a consequential fashion. We see that the intellectuals' contributions to the discussions about race have appeared from within, as well as outside, the university. They have disrupted and constituted civil discussion. They work in and against the mass media, in and against the conventions of academia. While the media constrain what the intellectuals can do in contemporary democracies, confining them to certain topics and certain ways of presenting their positions on the problems of race, the media also make it possible for intellectuals, from Malcolm X to today's academics, to address a general public about race problems.

When it comes to the issues of race and gender, disruption of ongoing discourses may be as important as the support of a discursive civil society. Intellectuals subvert the conventions of race and gender talk so that the problems of race and gender can be discussed. Yet, in order to avoid demagoguery and the invention of new dogmas, intellectuals also invent and maintain civilized public discussion, as the creation of a free public life in the totalitarian context of Eastern and Central Europe and the reception of feminism in that part of the world underscore.

We see that the intellectuals still have somehow managed to act in support of democratic projects. As they play with or against the media, they continue to inform public discourse. The dissidents directly challenged the communist orders, and intellectuals who reflected on their activity helped reintroduce the idea of civil society as a project of public action that suggests alternative non-totalized views of the good society, from conservative, liberal, and radical points of view. Means to unite people of disparate positions and to enable them to confront each other have been made available through such intellectual action. The feminist intellectual discussion in Eastern and Central Europe, as in Western Europe and North America, opens the possibility of addressing the problems that women face which have gone unaddressed without this discourse. People in the democracies of Central Europe now notice the diminished role of women in public life, and there are suggestions that the trend is being reversed, as the special concerns women have about the issue of abortion cannot be easily ignored. In the aftermath of the life and autobiography of Malcolm X, the accepted tolerance the society has for institutionalized racism, the awareness that the prevailing practices of social life often reinforce racism, is broadly understood. He forced us to talk about such things. Even discourse about political correctness, for and against, has provided the opportunity for academic intellectuals to discuss important problems concerning the facts of diversity in the contemporary world and the desirability of cultivating and reconsidering the Western cultural inheritance. When intellectuals take some time and comment on the headlines of the day, such as the Thomas–Hill affair, they can provide a means for the thoughtful public to consider the deeper dimensions of media performances. Their intervention does in fact help constitute and form the thoughtful public. Both John Dewey and Walter Lippmann in their writing constituted the public after the eclipse which they both perceived, and Mills and Said did the same.

Intellectuals can and should help their compatriots talk. Yet, we know that not any sort of talk will do, not all talk is supportive of democratic life. The talk needs to open public deliberations and democratic contestation, avoiding the formulas of ideology. Much of the agitation of the intellectuals in this century led away from democracy in that it, at least implicitly, assumed the superiority of the intellectual as a political and moral agent, and much of the sociological accounts of intellectual life took such a stance as natural. When intellectuals imagine that they can provide the definitive position of a specific class or of a specific society, when they assign for themselves the role of solving society's problems (and not more modestly framing and interpreting them), they move against the ideals of democratic life. Intellectuals are tempted to substitute philosophy for politics, science for democracy, and observers of intellectuals take this to be the fundamental intellectual role. The twentieth century provided long and hard experiences of such ideological temptations, from the most tragic, in the form of Soviet Marxism and Nationalist Socialism, to the mildly disappointing, such as the "intelligence work" that Walter Lippmann thought would solve the problems of an ill-informed public opinion. We have come to be disillusioned with the grand narratives of class and racial liberation and emancipation, as the promises of technocratic solutions to modern problems have lost their attraction. Both the vanguard revolutionary, the professional politician, and the technocrat, the political intellectual as expert, are not model figures for the democratic intellectual.

This has led to a sense that intellectuals no longer are of any consequence, a sense amplified in Eastern and Central Europe by the conviction that the time of the intellectual dissidents is over. It would seem that without the grand emancipatory narratives and the technocratic dreams, and with the end of communism and its heroic opposition, the instrumental actions of the entrepreneur, the engineer, and the bureaucrat are all that remain. There are needs for knowledge experts in the pursuit of capitalist accumulation, technical progress, and administrative coordination, but there is no great need for intellectuals.[1] Yet, if that deliberation is required for democracy, and in short supply, the appearance of contemporary irrelevance of the intellectuals is belied.

We observe that through their works, in theater performances and commentaries, newspaper editorials, autobiographies, open letters, book collections, magazine articles, and radio and television appearances, intellectuals continue to contribute to democratic society, and that this, at least implicitly, is desired by their contemporaries. By subverting common sense, the intellectual helps empower the marginal. Those on the margins benefit, support, and seek such intellectual action. By civilizing differences, the intellectual establishes common ground for public life. Those who have difficulty dealing with each other, who cannot find a way to act in concert, seek this type of intellectual action.

I have attempted in these pages to show that intellectuals matter, that they have contributed to the capacity of citizens to talk, to deliberate, about their common problems, by civilizing contestation and subverting common sense. My major task, as I understand it, has been to show that intellectuals can and do have a special role to play in the life of democracy. In making the argument for talk, I have argued against other roles. I trust that the reader has been challenged to think differently about the sociology of the intellectuals: to hesitate when claims are made for and by intellectuals engaging in projects of direct political action, *but also* to question assertions concerning the political irrelevance of intellectuals.

The sense of irrelevance comes with a lack of appreciation of the value and difficulty of talk. I have argued for the importance of talk in societal life and the centrality of intellectuals as promoters of talk. Here, in conclusion, I should concede that the colloquial idea of talk should be used with caution. I have wanted to show that the intellectual's role is not grandiose, that it is not very different from what all citizens do when they consider the problems they face in their private as well as in their public lives, but I know that deliberation is no easy matter, and that when I have referred to talk, I have been abbreviating a very complicated cultural and political set of activities.

Open discourse about complicated problems in differentiated and heterogeneous societies is a pressing problem. Much gets in the way of constituting such discourse, such talk. In the period of the cold war, it was possible to simplify the issues involved, to turn them into ideological formulas. On the left, for those sympathetic to the socialist bloc or to a project of socialism other than that of the politics and culture of actually existing socialism, it could seem that the injustices of capitalism and its structures of domination were the primary obstacles to a free public life. When Habermas concluded his classic early work, *The Structural Transformation of the Public Sphere*, he was arguing that the liberal public sphere was disintegrating primarily because of the internal political and economic forces of capitalism. Because free discourse was being turned into a commodity, the possibility of a free public life was receding. Cultural debate was being replaced by cultural consumption. Habermas himself in his later work recognized that there were many other less totalized obstacles to free public life, and that the transformation of the public was not only that of decline.[2] And we, along with him, must realize that education, the law, the media, and other social institutions can both support and undermine the possibilities of free discourse in social orders with a modern economy.

On the other side of the old ideological divide, for those on the right side of the cold war, for those with ideas of a fundamentalist anti-communism, it should be now clear that capitalism alone does not set us free; it does not assure a free and open public. The free circulation of commodities does not automatically guarantee the free circulation of ideas. As we have seen, intellectual provocation of free discussion faces many obstacles even when fundamental structural conditions for a free politics, culture, and economics are in place.

While the economic and political pressures within the university remain very real, the progress of academic freedom nonetheless has been considerable. Yet, the forces of professionalism, at every level of university life, discourage intellectual life in the university, and the very freedom of the university, as it distances academics from the everyday experience of society, lends irrelevance to their intellectual debates, as we have seen in the case of political correctness. An interesting dilemma has been revealed. The condition of independence of the university from the primary concerns of the socialist left and the anti-socialist right, the workings of capitalism and of statism, has worked to undermine academic contributions to societal deliberation. This suggests that the problems of the deliberation deficit are much greater than the conventional cultural positions of the traditional left and right would ever allow; neither overcoming the injustices of capitalism nor socialism solves the problem.

Such complication is especially striking when we keep in mind the problems of the media. The media loom large when it comes to the sense that intellectuals no longer matter, and clearly the problem goes beyond the question of ownership, whether it be of private corporations or of the state. The possibility of sustaining deliberations in societies which use the mass media as the way to communicate with themselves is a serious question. We have observed the ideal of societal deliberations first in the classical instance of the intellectual, in face to face interaction in the life of Socrates, as he moved about the market, spoke to people, reasoned. Later, deliberations shifted. We have seen the life of intellectuals become a component part of the project of modernity, in relatively independent cultural institutions, as they address a general public. The intellectual becomes a normal component of societal life, based in relatively autonomous cultural institutions, addressing a general public, contributing to societal deliberations. Here, the idea of the public, or at least its image, is archetypically found in the world of letters, in the coffee houses and taverns of the eighteenth century, as readers and writers come to exchange opinion about matters of public concern. This is the public implied in Kant's reflections on the enlightenment. It is the location of Habermas's "bourgeois public sphere." He presented his concern for the decline of the public sphere from within the tradition of critical theory, the position of Horkheimer and Adorno, yet it is notable that a good deal of his and their negative judgment seems to have been reserved for the art (and philosophy), the communications, of the "age of mechanical reproduction," as Walter Benjamin put it. Theirs was a reaction against the electronic media, against photography, radio, movies, and television, and now it would be lodged, no doubt, against the new media of computerization. There is, in this response to the new media and public life, a sense of despair which very much parallels Lippmann's concern for the collapse of public opinion as a democratic force. In Lippmann, this involves, as we have seen, a conservative response, but such a response also has radical manifestations, such as that of the critical theorists.[3] They question whether an independent public life can be constituted in and through the mass media.

For many more postmodern observers of media culture, this negative response is understood as being fundamentally mistaken. They dismiss its basic premise, that media culture represents a fundamental threat to cultural capacity and political critique.[4] The works of media culture, from this point of view, are not simply produced by an industry of manipulation. The products of the media are, as well, received and interpreted by differentiated audiences which use culture for their own purposes.

Studies of popular culture do show how the apparent objects of media manipulation have been appropriated by their consumers to create zones of autonomy, of popular and critical sensibility.[5] Following the perspective of such studies, the critical intellectual works within and not against popular media culture. Indeed, the culture of the old elite, including the work that Habermas and Adorno most valued, is understood as being part of the problem, not the solution.

Andrew Ross in his study of intellectuals and popular culture even goes so far as to label those who are concerned with the autonomy of culture, set apart from popular media, the very institutional grounds we have observed as being necessary for the emergence of independent intellectual life, as a "reactionary consensus of the left and the right" which includes "unreconstructed voices on the left."[6] The followers of the sensibilities of Lippmann, and Adorno and Habermas, contribute to a new rearguard consensus. At the forefront, Ross sees "new intellectuals" who use their positions in society to develop a critical politics based on race, gender, ethnicity, and sexual orientation, and use the new technologies in pursuit of their politics. From this point of view, the intellectual should engage media culture, and use it to undermine the hegemony of the dominant culture. The intellectual should operate against domination, not against the institutions of popular media culture. To confuse popular culture with domination is to miss popular resistance and to justify the institutions of domination as they function in the sphere of refined culture.

But those who celebrate the potential of the actually existing works of the mass media, such as Ross, are too sanguine about the culture industry. Somehow labeling the products of multinational corporations as popular culture does not seem accurate, and giving emphasis to the critical potential in the products of the culture industry, which undoubtedly is there, seems to overlook the profound challenge they present to developing an informed understanding of the world about us, and the difficulty of developing discussions about this understanding. As we have observed in our examination of Lippmann, Dewey, Mills, and Said, the intellectual's relationship to the public is a crucial and problematic aspect of the life of a democracy. When popular culture is conflated with mass culture, when the intellectual is understood as a popular culture vanguardist, it comes to seem that the most authentic and vibrant public life appears in the mass media. Stanley Aronowitz declares, with no apparent irony, that as the public is an endangered species, hope for a public life is to be found in Oprah Winfrey and Phil Donahue, who have "managed to transform the most degraded of TV genres, daytime talk TV, into vociferous sounding boards for discontent."[7] This position fails to draw the distinction between the intellectual and the entertainer, between empty talk and deliberation. There may be serious discussion that does occasionally appear on talk TV, but this is hardly what primarily occurs on the programs, and the notion that these programs represent the best of public life that can be found in the US, even with the low level of American political debate and all the problems with electoral politics, is undoubtedly wrong. Aronowitz's judgment makes sense only when informed discourse is confused with talk performance; important distinctions concerning cultural quality are not made. When they are made, the room for the intellectual would appear to be small indeed.

Thus, both those who deny that the mass media provide any possibility for public deliberation, and those who confuse the mass media with the public, point to the difficulty of being an intellectual in societies where the mass media prevail, i.e., in contemporary democracies. The critics of media culture perceive that intellectuals are impotent in resisting the power of the media, but in suggesting that there is little that they can do in mass democracies, they promote resignation and cynicism. Because the more optimistic postmodern contention that the intellectuals successfully function in the media is unconvincing, this also suggests that there is little that intellectuals can do.

Yet, we have observed that by following either of these contrasting positions, a great deal of salient intellectual and democratic activity is overlooked. The work of intellectuals must be examined much more carefully. The way they interact with and react against the media, indeed act through the media, makes it possible for them to both promote civility, as Toni Morrison and her collaborators did in transforming empty media talk about race and gender into civil discourse about enduring and perplexing problems, and to subvert consensus, as did Malcolm X when he used his power of the sound bite to subvert the racist common sense of his day, and as the popular film revival of his autobiographical story gives his intellectual position a new subversive life.

Things look hopeless only when the focus is on the grand outlines of culture and politics following overly romantic historical scripts, only when we focus on the headlines of "progress" or of "decline and fall," and not on the details of the political story of democracy as it is constituted by conflict and compromise in particular social settings, both beyond the media and through the media. While intellectuals as leaders of major political forces, resisting the powers of mass culture or using those powers against the hegemonic powers of capitalism and the state, are not easily found, intellectuals are observable in and outside of the media as they help civilize conflicts that the media present too starkly and subvert media consensus on societal problems that the standard practice of the media buries.

The importance of the intellectual as a democratic figure is especially evident when we bear in mind the post-cold war situation of politics and culture. While there does seem to be a world-wide consensus for democracy at the end of the twentieth century, when overt opposition to democratic principles has become a rarity, there is, nonetheless, a crisis in political culture. Inherited accounts, both from the left and from the right, of the way things are and why they must change, Mannheim's ideologies and utopias, have become unconvincing. In the aftermath of the cold war, a sense of political incoherence and meaninglessness is observable world-wide, and people have become cynical about the actions of those in power and those who oppose power. Cynicism has become central to international political culture, a direct consequence of our deliberation deficit. It has become strikingly difficult to sustain concerted action for change or for maintaining social order. Both civil and the subversive intellectual projects, in this global context, are pressingly needed, as the marginal seeks a voice, and the voices seek a way to understand each other.

For the intellectuals to do their jobs properly now, for the intellectuals to answer the questions posed by Socrates, the gadfly of the Athenian agora, for intellectuals to provoke talk and help society to overcome the deliberation deficit, they must address the problems posed by today's cynical political culture. Cynicism not too long ago was a pretty common thing, serving the powers of the old communist and the old anti-communist orders,[8] but now it serves confusion and this poses pressing new problems for intellectuals.

Cynicism "then," the cynicism in the former Soviet bloc and the former "free world," was supported by the political configuration of the cold war. The lies people told themselves and told each other were linked to the power struggles of the period. They made sense with reference to these struggles. During the cold war, there was an understanding in the United States that some of the most brutal dictatorships were included within the so-called free world. To paraphrase Orwell, slavery had become freedom. This kind of cynical usage made sense because it was set within the Manichean contest between the United States and the Soviet Union. People became accustomed to official lies linked with top secrets, and as they became accustomed to this usage, they also came to expect domestic lies as well. This was especially the case in the politics of race. As the civil rights movement made substantial progress in overturning the legal supports of racism and as overt racism became socially unacceptable, more elliptical measures were politically enacted to express a racist political stance. A cynical set of codes has been used to communicate racist messages in apparently non-racist ways. Equal rights for whites became the slogan of racist supremacy.

There has been a coherence in these cynical practices, as there was in the cynicism in the existing socialist societies. People used their cynicism strategically and with significant mutual understanding. Although this made open public debate about pressing social and political problems difficult, if not impossible, when the difficulties were overcome, the results could be spectacular. Thus, intellectuals who dared to speak the truth in Eastern and Central Europe played such a key role in the demise of the communist system, and the truth tellers among American writers, most prominently Toni Morrison, by poetically revealing the existential and historical dimensions of American racism, also have had profound cultural, if not political, impact.

In the recent past, cynicism was part of a whole which people came to recognize. In the old Soviet bloc, the whole and the recognition were enforced by the repressive apparatus of the Party-state. In the West, the whole was less reliably enforced and the recognition less certain, but it existed nonetheless. People went along with the cynicism of the powers when it came to geopolitics, in electoral politics and in some aspects of the politics of everyday life. The cynicism of both the East and the West supported the functioning orders of actually existing capitalism and socialism.

The appropriate critical intellectual response to this attitude has been to reaffirm principle, to make discriminations between the lame and the convincing, to follow Vaclav Havel's advice, to "live in truth," i.e., to speak and act in public according to perceived truths.[9] This is the clear intellectual response to the generalized cynicism by the conservative, who is concerned about the cynicism which erodes the social order and the wisdom of custom and habit, and by the social critic, who perceives that cynicism has become an obstacle to change.

Speaking truth to power also could take a decidedly subversive form. Malcolm X, in his rudeness, created his own media circus. He opened up the possibility of considering aspects of race relations which up to that point had not been publicly discussed. His life, autobiography, and accounts of his life occurred within the context of a relatively stable political culture and were thus acted upon, with mutual understanding, by those both for and against his position and symbolism. The coherence of intellectual critics was supported by the coherence of the powers that be and their relationships.

Things are different now. Understanding is not easily forthcoming. The cynical structure has changed, leading from implicit under-standings supporting domination and its opposition, to explicit confusions undermining both the powers that be and their oppo-nents. The cold war is with us no more, and the politics of left and right no longer help organize political action and opinion. Cynicism is still with us, but it is of a free-floating sort. The two superpowers no longer face each other in sublimated moral combat, and the coherence in the logics of the political left and the political right now is less compelling than their incoherence.

With the collapse of communism and anti-communism, a generalized cynicism detached from organized political culture is upon us. It is the cynicism of the unaffiliated and the confused, not of either the critic or the apologist. We hear so much today about the cynicism in American society, and elsewhere, not because cynicism is particularly new or has increased, but because it has changed. It is still a significant problem, but it is a problem in a new way.

People continue to be cynical, believing that beneath public appearances there exists an underlying reality, but they have no sense of what the nature of that reality might be. It no longer is fundamentally structured by the communist and the anti-communist powers. Only narrow self-interests and a disordered set of ideologies remain. Confusion is ubiquitous. It comes in the most malignant and in relatively benign forms, from the civil wars of Eurasia and Africa to the American election campaigns. But the attempts to explain the confusion do not make coherent sense. There are the attempts of xenophobia and a broad variety of neo-nationalisms and of neo-communism, of market magic and of the benevolent state. Cynicism becomes the strongest of explanations, reducing all politics to business (i.e. "they are all in it for themselves") or going, as well, in the opposite direction: all business is reduced to politics (i.e. "it's all a matter of who you know").

We seem to be observing a cast of characters who are performing together on the same stage, playing different scripts. It is unclear how the performances relate, and all too clear that performance and not real public interaction is being observed. This is how the political leaders with easy answers gain their appeal. And even they are confusing. The public seems to demand easily understood answers to complex political problems, and the politicians naturally deliver them the demanded goods. Yet, once these are delivered, it is all too clear that they are shoddy products, further indicating that politics is a corrupted enterprise. The situation is assured to produce profound disappointments, and it is self-generating. There is a need for intellectuals to provide alternatives.

Today's intellectual works within a cynical framework of confusion, between the false promise of ideology and the fractured minor narratives of the identity and interest of specific groups in society, in the shadows of the electronic and mass media. Inherited common sense remains subordinating to the marginal, but this subordination is not accomplished through cultural institutions and practices which are broadly viewed as being legitimate. A major intellectual and political task is to link the problems of identity and interest to specific group experiences, and to show how the experiences, identity, and interests relate to other experiences, identities, and interests. The voices of the subaltern must be articulated in the way that Edward Said reveals, the subversive task, but they also must be related in a meaningful way, allowing for concerted action beyond the politics of identity, be it based on gender or sexuality, race or ethnicity, class or nationality, the civil task. It is most important that the task of civility is pursued along with the task of subversion if the generalized societal cynicism of the confused is to be overcome. If not, the specific claims of the subaltern become but another interest group to be cynically dismissed.

The grand narratives of the past told women and racial minorities how their specific interests would be realized in the grand scheme of things, how they would come to be realized when the masses led by the proletariat and its vanguard came into power, for example. When the revolution would come, some on the left could believe, everything would be better. The progressive peoples of the world would unite, and overthrow all that is repressive. For those on the right, it could be imagined that the same would be achieved when the nation defended its honor or when the evil communists from within and without would be defeated. The democratic liberal approach could link happiness to progress, as the democratic conservatives could invest in the power of tradition and morality. Master orientations, even if not master narratives, in these demo-cratic orientational variants, also brought together a multitude of dreams and expectations. A notable disadvantage of these modern approaches to politics, as with the more totalized approaches, is that they tended to silence the concerns of subordinate groups, or their concerns were considered not as they understood them, but as the more dominant did.[10] The specific complexities of human experi-ence in its multiplicity would be homogenized or rejected as other. Thus, Said's critique of Orientalism. But, we should remember that there was an advantage to the old dominant paradigms, as well. They helped ordinary people make sense of the world, as they explained how the different concerns of people were connected; how the concern, for example with the environment, was connected with the concern for the state of education and the concern for racial and gender justice and the end to class exploitation. It is exactly this kind of linking which is missing in contemporary politics, making for the incoherence of our political scene. Truth telling, by itself, without the framing of the modern political narratives, can be confusing.

The incoherence can be and has been addressed, momentarily and instrumentally, using the crafts of media manipulation and high-tech political mobilization, presenting suggestions of what a post-modern tyranny might be. In contrast to modern tyranny (recall this is how Hannah Arendt conceived of totalitarianism), the key to mobilization on the post-modern political stage of our day is not ideological purity linked with coercion, but intellectual confusion and isolation, linked with minimal ideological and maximal techno-logical coordination. The political leader expresses the sentiments of population segments which feel disenfranchised, powerless to under-stand a world beyond their comprehension. The segments are not united by a singular political position, a meaningful political orienta-tion, but by a combination of specific appeals, often not notably rational, sometimes even hidden from each other. Hence, the politics of Zhironovsky, Le Pen, Perot, and company.

Without central principles, without the prevailing political tradi-tions of the modern era, politics develops chaotically. There are only momentary strategies. There are no generally agreed upon ideas to help people act in concert. It does seem unlikely that intellectuals will contribute to democratic society in this context. Grounds for pessimism surely do exist. The voices of the intellectuals hardly are audible in the noise of mass culture and politics. We have to listen very carefully to Morrison, Higgenbotham, and company to develop an understanding of a media event such as the Thomas confirmation hearings, going beyond the formulas of melodrama and horse racing. Intellectuals have a hard time sustaining themselves in the universities, with their dominant commitments to professionalism, and the intellectual outside the universities is an endangered species. The pressures for commercial expression, easily marketable to target audiences, do not allow for the vibrant intellectual life of the inter-war period, and the intellectual responsibility of professional associ-ations is an archaic remembrance unknown to today's professionals. The project of the consumer society seems to have been achieved. That which caused fear for the conservative, Walter Lippmann, and the radical democrat, John Dewey, has come to pass. The public good has become identified with the availability of consumer goods. The possibility of questioning this is not of interest to the general public. Such questioning is all but silenced by the workings of the power elite, as Mills understood, and the unchallenged nature of the hegemonic ideology, as Said has revealed. Although I am uncomfortable with this pessimistic view, I must admit that it is well grounded. The quality of public debate has not improved. The power of media manipulation seems to increase every day. The very notion of public deliberations seems to be foreign. The need for the intellectual is great, but the need as much as the social figure is not broadly recognized.

Yet, everywhere we turn we hear the complaint that there is a paucity of new ideas, a need for social and political vision, a desire for a sensible approach to the problems of the day. This means, in my opinion, that the public wants intellectuals to do their work. New ideas come from the critical distant view of the intellectual, from informed public discussion, from a position not completely defined by the logics of political power and the economy. The unacknowledged recognition that the intellectuals are necessary to democratic life today may not be the grounds for optimism about the successful practice of intellectuals, but it does suggest some room for action, some basis for hope. Substantiated by our findings, our observations of intellectuals provoking public deliberations, as they both civilize differences and undermine common sense, this hope is an invitation to the democratic intellectual.

POSTSCRIPT: REFLECTIONS ON AN EXCHANGE
WITH ADAM MICHNIK

The implications of the changed cynical culture for democratic intellectuals became apparent to me in an interaction I had with Adam Michnik, a leading civil intellectual in previously existing socialism and now a leading journalist intellectual in post-communist Poland. This exchange substantiates the conclusions of our inquiry. It suggests that the invitation to intellectuals to cultivate civility, as they subversively provoke, is one that can be answered.

In the fall of 1994 in New York City, Michnik presented a lecture to my university, the New School for Social Research. His talk was entitled: "Dignity and Fear: A Dialogue with a Friend from Belgrade." Inspired by an essay by Nebojsa Popov, he delivered an open letter to "his friend" about the problems of nationalistic hatred. He spoke as one critical intellectual to the other, commending Popov, a severe critic of Serbian excesses, for saying no to xenophobic horrors. "The intellectual must never fail to defend his own nation when it is threatened by its own people."

I listened to his talk with deep admiration. Here was one of the true intellectuals of our times, commending a colleague for taking a stand against a great injustice. Echoes of Zola and the Dreyfus affair were clearly discernible, the intellectual committed to truth against the prejudices of the ignorant. Indeed, it was people like Michnik during the communist period who reminded us that intellectuals can still matter. In Havel's terms, and with Havel, he spoke the truth and acted upon it, and, in the process, he helped create a democratic movement that ultimately helped to defeat the cynical powers of totalitarianism.

Yet, as Michnik spoke, I was struck by doubt, a doubt which served as a stimulus for this study of the intellectual in democratic society. Somehow, it seemed that speaking the truth to power was not enough or even of primary concern in our confusing times. I asked him if he thought that the intellectual still had a role to play. I asked him if he thought that the simple acts of speaking the truth in public, writing articles, and delivering open letters were effective ways to oppose the threats of xenophobic nationalism in the post-communist world.

He gave the expected answer. It is not, he counseled, a question of effectiveness. When Thomas Mann wrote his famous letter to the

Rector, he did not consider whether his protest would have an impact. He simply acted with honor and honesty. He spoke the truth, the primary responsibility of the intellectual according to Michnik. At the same time that Mann composed his letter, most Germans were adapting themselves to the rising power of Nazism, with varying degrees of enthusiasm. Yet, while Mann could not possibly be effective in that political climate, it is important, nonetheless, that he told the truth in his letter.

This was classic Michnik, a classical response of an intellectual with great public authority, achieved on the printed page and in a prison cell. But there are problems with his stated position. On strictly ethical grounds his position is admirable, but from a more sociological point of view, problems become apparent. Prominent intellectuals should, no doubt, continue to dedicate themselves to the pursuit of truth and address the public. Yet, in the present cynical environment, it has become quite easy to take a political stance, make a grand gesture, based on a perceived truth, but the meaning of the stances and the gestures are far from clear. It is far more difficult to help people who oppose, and do not understand each other, to engage in common public actions. Because confusion and its cynicism are central problems, the actions of intellectuals probably need to take on new forms, or at least a different and finer sociologically strategic dimension. The task is not only to speak truth to the powers, but also to set up the conditions for such address to occur, to provide the time and space for public deliberations, the central thesis of our inquiry. The task is not only subversion, but also civility.

Here is the irony of Michnik's answer to my question. He is a man who has tended to the civilizing dimension with great distinction. He is a person who has spent much of his life civilizing political, intellectual, and religious differences in Poland. One of the constituting documents of the democratic opposition in Eastern and Central Europe was Michnik's book, *The Church and The Left.*[11] In it, he proposed what previously seemed to be illogical: that the secular non-communist left and those affiliated with the conservative religious Church had much in common and ought to find a way to talk about their commonalities, without abandoning their differences. His suggestion went against the long-established conventions of Polish and European political culture, in which the forces of enlightenment and faith have confronted each other in a way that has been definitive for their identities. The book, to say the least, was controversial: among his friends on the left, because it seemed to be overly self-critical and unclear in its political commitments,[12] and among those on the right, because he presumed to judge the religious on his own irreligious grounds. While the specifics of these controversies are not our immediate concern, Michnik's general strategy is.

It is interesting to note that Michnik has repeated this approach throughout his career as a public intellectual, both as an oppositionist and as a political commentator in post-communist Poland. In the eighties, despite his fundamental opposition to the National Democrats of the first part of this century, he published an appreciative portrait of its leader Roman Dmowski, and in the nineties, he has worked with former communists in an attempt to de-ideologize the democratic discourse after communism.[13] Michnik has taken the narratives of the Church and the left, of the independent Polish socialists (of Pilsudski) and the National Democrats (of Dmowski), and of the post-communist and post-Solidarity parties, and attempted at different times to make a coherent politics possible among those who differ: before the fall of communism, a democratic opposition, after the fall of communism, a non-authoritarian alternative to the totalitarian left and to the newly emerging nationalist right. He has not tried to eradicate the identity of the societal actors whose stories he appreciates, but he has tried to tell their different stories in ways that they come to be seen as compatible at least for a period of time. The secular left and the Catholic Church are different, but for a time their concern for human rights and dignity in opposition to communism made enough sense that they were capable of acting in concert. The Polish nationalists and the Polish liberals and socialists tell their histories in opposition to each other, but the integrity of their opposing stories constituted a political pluralism in the opposition which embodied the idea of pluralism in an open society. Former communists and former oppositionists have faced each other as jailers and jailed, but they now have a common interest in the rule of law and sound economic policies in the post-communist period.

Thinking about Michnik's speech and his actions, it becomes clear that there is a contradiction between what he has accomplished as an intellectual and how he has accounted for intellectuals. It seems to me that we learn more about the role of the intellectual in our cynical times from what he has done, than from what he said that night in New York. He portrayed in his lecture the intellectual as the subversive, the agent of the unpleasant truth that must be told, essentially the portrait presented to us by Sartre and Said. But Michnik has been, most remarkably, the intellectual as the agent and voice of civility, and his life indicates how powerful and important civility can be. It is not the case that ours is a time when subversion is no longer needed. Common sense and practices still cover the irrational and the unjust. But, given cynicism and confusion, it is clearly the time when the civility that intellectuals such as Michnik can bring is desperately needed by both the subversive intellectuals and the authorities who seek to serve democracy.

Notes

I INTRODUCTION: THE INTELLECTUALS AT CENTURY'S END

1 For a theoretically informed description of the role of the intellectual in modern society see Ron Eyerman *Between Culture and Politics: Intellectuals in Modern Society*, Cambridge, Mass.: Blackwell, 1994; for a history of intellectual life in the United States, see Lewis Perry, *Intellectual Life in America*, Chicago: University of Chicago Press, 1989.

2 See Neil Postman, *Amusing Ourselves to Death: Public Discourses in the Age of Show Business*, New York: Penguin, 1985.

3 This perception of the need to make distinctions between entertainment and serious culture is a key to Hannah Arendt's criticisms of mass culture. Her analysis, I believe, stands ever more firmly the test of time; see her "Crisis in Culture," in Hannah Arendt, *Between Past and Future*, New York: Penguin, 1980. The informed reader will note my debt to Arendt in her approach to the problem of intellectuals and their relationship with democracy and free politics.

4 Vladimir Lenin, *What Is To Be Done?*, trans. S. V. and Patricia Utechin, Oxford: Clarendon Press, 1963; Karl Mannheim, *Ideology and Utopia*, trans. Louis Wirth and Edward Shils, New York: Harcourt, Brace and World, 1963; and Julian Benda, *The Treason of the Intellectuals*, trans. Richard Aldington, New York: Norton, 1969.

5 See Alan Riding "How the Peasants Lit the Fires of Democracy," *The New York Times*, February 27, 1994, p. 5, and Alma Guillermoprieto, "Zapata's Heirs," *The New Yorker*, May 16, 1994, pp. 52–63.

6 Alexis de Tocqueville explored this tension in the second volume of his *Democracy in America*, trans. George Lawrence, ed. J. P. Mayer, New York: Anchor Books, 1969; see specifically the first book of this volume.

7 Gordon Wood, *The Radicalness of the American Revolution*, New York: Knopf, 1992.

8 Herbert Gans, *Popular and High Culture: An Analysis and Evaluation of Taste*, New York: Basic Books, 1974.

9 See Hilton Kramer, "Art and its Institutions: Notes on the Culture War," *The New Criterion*, 12, 1, 1993: pp. 4–7.

10 Irving Howe, "Toward an Open Culture," *The New Republic*, 190, March 5, 1984, pp. 25–9.

11 Richard Hofstadter, *The Paranoid Style in American Politics and Other Essays*, Chicago: University of Chicago Press, 1979, and *Anti-Intellectualism in American Life*, New York: Vintage Books, 1962, and Pierre Bourdieu, *Distinction: A Social Critique of the Judgment of Taste*, Cambridge, Mass.: Harvard University Press, 1984.

12 See Andrew Ross in his *No Respect: Intellectuals and Popular Culture*, New York: Routledge, 1989, and Stanley Aronowitz, *Roll Over Beethoven: The Return of Cultural Strife*, Hanover: Wesleyan University Press, 1993.

13 José Ortega y Gasset, *The Revolt of the Masses*, trans. Anthony Kerrigan, ed. Kenneth Moore, Notre Dame, Ind.: University of Notre Dame Press, 1985.

14 See Max Horkheimer and Theodor Adorno, *The Dialectic of the Enlightenment*, New York: Herder and Herder, 1972; Jurgen Habermas, *The Structural Transformation of the Public Sphere: An Inquiry into a Category of Bourgeois Society*, trans. Thomas Burger with Frederick Lawrence, Cambridge: The MIT Press, 1991: and Hannah Arendt, "The Crisis in Culture: Its Social and Political Significance," in Hannah Arendt, *Between Past and Future*, New York: Penguin, 1980, pp. 197–227.

15 See Michael Rogin, *Ronald Reagan: The Movie, and Other Episodes in Political Demonology*, Berkeley: University of California Press, 1987.

16 See Edward S. Herman and Noam Chomsky, *Manufacturing Consent: The Political Economy of the Mass Media*, New York: Pantheon Books, 1988.

17 See Postman, *Amusing Ourselves to Death*.

18 For a cogent argument against this confusion see Richard Rorty, "The Priority of Democracy to Philosophy," in his *Objectivity, Relativism, and Truth*, New York: Cambridge University Press, 1991, pp. 175–96.

19 See Hannah Arendt, *The Origins of Totalitarianism*, pp. 460–82, and "Truth and Politics," in *Between Past and Future*, pp. 227–64. For a more recent set of reflections that parallel the ones presented here see Jean Bethke Elshtain, *Democracy on Trial*, New York: Basic Books, 1995.

20 See Morris Dickstein, *Double Agent: The Critic and Society*, New York: Oxford University Press, 1992, for an interesting account of the tradition of literary criticism which attempts to do justice to literature as it engages in social criticism, avoiding ideological and academic cant.

21 I examine this in the post-communist situation in Central Europe in my book: *After the Fall: The Pursuit of Democracy in Central Europe*, New York: Basic Books, 1992.

22 The case of Malcolm X is analyzed in detail in chapter 8. For an excellent account of the politics of Martin Luther King Jr, see Taylor Branch, *Parting the Waters: America in the King Years 1954 – 1963*, New York: Simon and Schuster, 1988.

2 WHO ARE THE INTELLECTUALS?

1 This is most thoroughly studied by Hofstader in his *Anti-Intellectualism in American Life*.

2 See Aleksander Gella (ed.), *The Intelligentsia and the Intellectuals*, London: Sage, 1976.

3 Russell Jacoby, *The Last Intellectuals*: *American Culture in the Age of Academe*, New York: Basic Books, 1987.

4 Paul Johnson, *Intellectuals*, London: Weidenfield and Nicolson, 1988.

5 See Alvin Gouldner, *The Future of the Intellectuals and the Rise of the New Class*, New York: Seabury, 1979, and S. Martin Lipset, *Political Man*, New York: Doubleday, 1960.

6 In a modern accessible fashion, i.e. in the fashion of an intellectual, I. F. Stone reflects on these issues in his *The Trial of Socrates*, New York: Anchor Books, 1989. The following account of the trial draws primarily from Plato's dialogue, *Apology*, translated by Benjamin Jowett in *The Dialogues of Plato*, New York: Bantam Books, 1986.

7 With some qualification, this seems to be the position of Stone.

8 For a presentation of this position see Werner Jaeger's classic:, *Paideia: The Ideals of Greek Culture*, New York: Oxford University Press, 1943, particularly vol. II, "In Search of the Divine Center," pp. 1–86. For historical background of the issues involved see J. B. Bury and Russell Meiggs, *A History of Greece: To the Death of Alexander the Great*, fourth edition, London: Macmillan, 1975, especially pp. 356–65.

9 See Georg Simmel, "The Stranger," in *Georg Simmel: On Individuality and Social Forms*, trans. and ed. Donald Levine, Chicago: University of Chicago Press, 1971.

10 For a synthetic account of the relationship between the major sociological traditions see Donald Levine, *Visions of the Sociological Tradition*, Chicago: University of Chicago Press, 1995. The basic positions of the theorists cited can be found in the following works: Karl Marx, *The German Ideology*, London: Lawrence and Wishart, 1965; Max Weber, *Economy and Society*, ed. Guenther Roth and Claus Wittich, trans. Ephraim Fischoff *et al.*, New York: Bedminster Press; Simmel, *Georg Simmel: On Individuality*; Emile Durkheim, *Division of Labor in Society*, New York: The Free Press, 1984; Talcott Parsons, *The Social System*, Glencoe: The Free Press, 1951; Jurgen Habermas, *The Theory of Communicative Action*, trans. Thomas McCarthy, Boston: Beacon Press, 1987; Niklas Luhmann, *The Differentiation of Society*, New York: Columbia University Press, 1982. For a reconsideration of differentiation theory from the point of view of democratizing potential see Hans Joas, *The Creativity of Action*, Chicago: University of Chicago Press, 1996, especially, pp. 233–44.

11 I refer here to the new sociological social history which seeks to "bring the state back in," and to those researchers who polemicize with this position. For representative surveys of these studies see Peter Evans,

Dietrich Rueschemeyer, and Theda Skocpol (eds.), *Bringing the State Back In*, New York: Cambridge University Press, 1985; Theda Skocpol (ed.), *Vision and Method in Historical Sociology*, New York: Cambridge University Press, 1984; and Ira Katznelson and Aristide R. Zolberg (eds.), *Working Class Formation: Nineteenth-Century Patterns in Western Europe and the United States*, Princeton: Princeton University Press, 1986. For a strong argument for this kind of sociology see Charles Tilly, *Big Structures, Large Processes, Huge Comparisons*, New York: Russell Sage Foundation, 1985.

12 See Horkheimer and Adorno *Dialectics of the Enlightenment*; Walter Benjamin. *Illuminations*, ed. Hannah Arendt, trans. Harry Zohn, New York: Schocken Books, 1969; and Habermas, *The Theory of Communicative Action*.

13 For an overview of Foucault's position see *The Foucault Reader*, ed. Paul Rabinow, New York: Pantheon Books, 1984.

14 Jean-Paul Sartre, "A Plea to Intellectuals," in his *Between Existentialism and Marxism*, trans. John May, London: New Left Review Books, 1974.

15 Immanuel Kant, "An Answer to the Question: What is the Enlightenment?" in *Kant: Political Writings*, ed. Hans Reiss, New York: Cambridge University Press, 1970, pp. 54–60.

16 See Habermas, *The Structural Transformation of the Public Sphere*. For an alternative account of the performative qualities of public life see Richard Sennett, *The Fall of Public Man*, New York: Knopf, 1977.

17 See Georg Lukacs, *History and Class Consciousness*, Cambridge, Mass.: The MIT Press, 1971.

18 Mannheim, *Ideology and Utopia*. For an excellent explication and critique of Mannheim's position see Paul Ricoeur, *Lectures on Ideology and Utopia*, ed. George Taylor, Chicago: University of Chicago Press, 1986.

19 George Lundberg, *Can Science Save Us?*, New York: Longman Green, 1961.

20 At a conference held soon after the fall of communism, comparing the revolutionary dynamics of 1989 in Eastern and Central Europe with those of America in 1789, I heard a prominent conservative rational choice theorist express this colorful judgment.

21 Gouldner, *The Future of the Intellectuals and the Rise of the New Class*; George Konrad and Ivan Szelenyi, *The Intellectuals on the Road to Class Power: A Sociological Study of the Role of the Intelligentsia in Socialism*, New York: Harcourt, Brace, Jovanovich, 1979; Zygmunt Bauman, *Legislators and Interpreters*, Cambridge, Mass., Polity Press, 1987.

22 See James Coleman, "The Rational Reconstruction of Society," 1992 Presidential Address, *American Sociological Review*, 58, 1, February, 1993.

23 The distinction I am making here concerning the proper spheres of talk and instrumental action, I realize, parallel's Habermas's analysis of life world, where open discussion is central, and system, where instrumental action and interaction are key. I prefer to use the categories of action as a matter of practical discernment, to be determined by actors with

competing insights and sensibilities, rather than to consider them as distinct spheres of social order. This preference, no doubt, is a matter of both personal sensibility and scholarly project, i.e. to study the role of the intellectual in democratic society.

24 See *The Coleman Report on Public and Private Schools: The Draft Summary and Eight Critiques*, Virginia: Educational Research Service, 1981.

25 He develops this position in his *Ideology and Utopia*.

26 See for example, Johnson, *Intellectuals*, and Edward Shils, *The Intellectuals and the Powers, and Other Essays*, Chicago: University of Chicago Press, 1972.

27 See Chaim Waxman, *The End of Ideology Debate*, New York: Funk and Wagnalls, 1968.

28 See, for example, Daniel Bell, *The End of Ideology: The Exhaustion of Political Ideas in the Fifties*, New York: The Free Press, 1962.

29 See Daniel Bell, *The Coming of Post-Industrial Society*, New York: Basic Books, 1976.

30 Alberto Melucci, *Challenging Codes: Collective Action in the Information Age*, Cambridge, Cambridge University Press, 1996.

31 See Ross, *No Respect*.

32 This is the remarkable position taken by Michel Foucault in his reflections on the praxeological legacy of Kant, see Michel Foucault, "What is Enlightenment?" in *The Foucault Reader*.

3 THE CIVIL INTELLECTUAL AND THE PUBLIC

1 I have attempted to show how this is in fact a democratic development, for better and for worse, in *The Cynical Society: The Culture of Politics and the Politics of Change in American Life*, Chicago: University of Chicago Press, 1991.

2 Robert A. Dahl, *Democracy and Its Critics*, New Haven: Yale University Press, 1989.

3 The debate between Dewey and Lippmann has become a classic, a key exchange between two intellectual giants. For an account of the significance of the exchange in the understanding of populism see Christopher Lasch, *The Revolt of the Elites and the Betrayal of Democracy*, New York: W. W. Norton and Company, 1995; for an account of the exchange as it informs an understanding of the institutional problems of American society see Robert Bellah, Richard Marsden, William Sullivan, Ann Swidler and Steven Tipton, *The Good Society*, New York: Knopf, 1991.

4 For an excellent telling of Lippmann's biography see Ronald Steel, *Walter Lippmann and the American Century*, New York: Little Brown and Company, 1980.

5 See Robert Westbrook, *John Dewey and American Democracy*, Ithica: Cornell University Press, 1991.

6 Walter Lippmann, *Public Opinion*, New York: The Free Press, 1965, first published in 1922, and John Dewey, *The Public and Its Problems*, Chicago: Swallow Press, 1980, first published in 1927. In the following analysis, the citations are taken from these editions.

7 This is a particularly important insight. It goes a long way in explaining the puzzle of Ronald Reagan, who was both remarkably ignorant about the details of public affairs and one of the most powerful and successful (on his own terms) Presidents in American history. See Rogin *Ronald Reagan*, and Garry Wills, *Reagan's America: Innocents at Home*, Garden City: Doubleday, 1987.

8 In *The Cynical Society*, I attempt to show that even worse than the intervention of the political machine are the political interventions of a disorganized ideological politics of the left, and the post-modern media- and computer-based politics of the right.

9 It is Westbrook's convincing contention that Dewey's work on education and schooling, like a great deal of his philosophy, is best understood through his democratic public philosophy. See *John Dewey*.

10 See Westbrook, *John Dewey*, and Cornell West, *The American Evasion of Philosophy: A Genealogy of Pragmatism*, Madison: University of Wisconsin Press, 1989.

11 See Adam Gopnik, "Read All About It," *The New Yorker*, December 12, 1994, pp. 84–102.

12 See Michael Walzer, *Interpretation and Social Criticism*, Cambridge, Mass.: Harvard University Press, 1987, and *The Company of Critics: Social Criticism and Political Commitment in the Twentieth Century*, New York: Basic Books, 1988.

4 THE SUBVERSIVE INTELLECTUAL AND THE PUBLIC

1 C. Wright Mills, *The Sociological Imagination*, New York, Oxford University Press, 1959.

2 For a discussion of the interconnection between Mills's life and sociology see Irving Louis Horowitz, *C. Wright Mills: An American Utopian*, New York: The Free Press, 1983.

3 C. Wright Mills, *The Power Elite*, New York: Oxford University Press, 1956, p. 3. All citations below are taken from this edition.

4 C. Wright Mills, "The Social Role of the Intellectual," in *Power, Politics and People: The Collected Essays of C. Wright Mills*, ed. Irving Louis Horowitz, New York: Oxford University Press, 1963, p. 299.

5 See James Miller, *Democracy is in the Streets: From Port Huron to the Siege of Chicago*, New York: Simon and Schuster, 1987.

6 See my *The Cynical Society*.

7 Dmitri Shalin, "Postmodernism, and Pragmatist Inquiry: An Introduction," *Symbolic Interaction*,16, 4: 1993, pp. 303–31.

8 Jean-François Lyotard, *The Postmodern Condition*, trans., Geoff Ben-

nington and Brian Massumi, Minneapolis: University of Minnesota Press, 1984.

9 See Edward Shils, *The Constitution of Society*, Chicago: University of Chicago Press, 1982, for an analysis of the working of society as an interaction between the center and its periphery.

10 For an expression of dismay about the development of a centerless United States, see Arthur M. Schlesinger Jr, *The Disuniting of America: Reflections on a Multicultural Society*, New York: W. W. Norton, 1992. For a sociological celebration of the demise of a central public domain see Steven Siedman, *Contested Knowledge: Social Theory in the Postmodern Era*, Cambridge, Mass.: Blackwell, 1994.

11 This is the position of radical feminists such as Dorothy Smith. See her *The Conceptual Practices of Power: A Feminist Sociology of Knowledge*, Boston: Northeastern University Press, 1990. It is also the position of advocates of Afrocentrism and black nationalism. See, for example, Molefi K. Asanti, *Malcolm X as a Cultural Hero and Other Afrocentric Essays*, Trenton: Africa World Press, 1993.

12 For a general account of the issues being raised here see two volumes edited by Craig Calhoun: *Social Theory and the Politics of Identity*, Cambridge, Mass.: Blackwell, 1994, and *Habermas and the Public Sphere*, Cambridge, Mass.: The MIT Press, 1992.

13 Edward Said, *Orientalism*, New York: Vintage Books, 1994, p. 333.

14 Bernard Lewis, *Islam and the West*, New York: Oxford University Press, 1993.

15 See, for example, Gayatri Spivak, *The Post Colonial Critique: Interviews, Strategies, Dialogues*, New York: Routledge, 1990, and Carol A. Breckenridge and Peter van der Veer, *Orientalism and the Post Colonial Predicament*, Philadelphia: University of Pennsylvania Press, 1993.

16 Said makes this point not only in *Orientalism* but also in much of his literary and political commentaries, see *The World, the Text and the Critic*, Cambridge, Mass.: Harvard University Press, 1983, and *Culture and Imperialism*, New York: Knopf, 1993.

17 Edward Said, *Representations of the Intellectual*, New York: Pantheon, 1994, p. 20.

18 *Ibid.*, p. 22.

19 *Ibid.*, p. 53.

20 *Ibid.*, p. 63.

21 *Orientalism*, p. 335.

22 For a clear presentation of Mills's Deweyan position on the role of interlocking publics as opposed to mass society, see his *Power Elite*, pp. 298–324.

23 For critical accounts of the sentiment of the French intellectual left in the post-war period see Tony Judt, *Past Imperfect: French Intellectuals 1944–1956*, Berkeley: University of California Press, 1992 and Bernard-Henri Lévy, *Adventures on the Freedom Road: The French Intellectuals in the 20th Century*, London: Harvill Press/Harper Collins World, 1995.

24 Said, *Orientalism*, p. 342.
25 See *Representations of the Intellectual*, pp. 50–1.
26 See his *The Question of Palestine*, New York: Times Books, 1979.
27 These issues will be discussed in greater detail in chapter 7.
28 See David Harvey, *The Condition of Postmodernity*, Cambridge, Mass.: Blackwell, 1990.
29 For a subtle set of reflections on the theoretical implications of globalization see Alberto Melucci, *The Playing Self: Person and Meaning in the Planetary Society*, Cambridge: Cambridge University Press, 1996.
30 He asserted this position directly at a public lecture at New York University, December 1995.
31 There are by now a whole series of works that deal with the fact that our political culture no longer makes sense in the way it did even in the most recent past. My contribution to these reflections can be found in *After the Fall*. Noteworthy contributions to this genre include: Ralf Dahrendorf, *Reflections on the Revolution in Europe: in a letter intended to have been sent to a Gentleman in Warsaw*, New York: Times Books, 1990; Hans Magnus Enzensberger, *Civil Wars: From L.A. to Bosnia*, New York: The New Press, 1990; and Anthony Giddens, *Beyond Left and Right: The Future of Radical Politics*, Stanford: Stanford University Press, 1994.
32 In Saul Bellow, *It All Adds Up: From the Dim Past to the Uncertain Future*, New York, Penguin, 1995, p. 170.
33 See Francis Fukuyama, *Trust: Social Virtues and the Creation of Prosperity*, New York: The Free Press, 1995, Enzensberger, *Civil Wars*, and Samuel Huntington, "The Clash of Civilizations?" *Foreign Affairs*, 72, 3, 1993: p. 22–49.
34 I develop this position in *Beyond Glasnost: The Post-Totalitarian Mind*, Chicago: University of Chicago Press, 1989, *The Cynical Society*, and *After the Fall*.
35 See Todd Gitlin, *The Twilight of Common Dreams: Why America is Wracked by Culture Wars*, New York: Metropolitan Books, 1995.
36 Hannah Arendt's major works on political theory include: *The Origins of Totalitarianism*; *Between Past and Future*, New York: Penguin, 1980; *On Revolution*, New York: Penguin, 1977; and *The Human Condition*, Garden City: Doubleday, 1959.

5 THE CIVIL SOCIETY IDEAL

1 I present my account of this in *Beyond Glasnost* and *After the Fall*.
2 Of particular concern is the relative importance of the intellectuals in the political transformation. Some scholars, such as Roman Laba and Lawrence Goodwin, want to downplay the importance of intellectuals, while the dominant point of view, emphasized by such observers as Timothy Garton Ash, Lawrence Weschler and many others, including myself, have recognized the special role of intellec-

tuals and the special importance of the cooperation between intellectuals and the workers. See Roman Laba, *The Roots of Solidarity: A Political Sociology of Poland's Working-Class Democratization*, Princeton: Princeton University Press, 1991; Lawrence Goodwyn, *Breaking the Barrier: The Rise of Solidarity in Poland*, New York: Oxford University Press, 1991; Timothy Garton Ash, *The Polish Revolution: Solidarity*, New York: Vintage Books, 1985; and Lawrence Weschler, *Solidarity: Poland in the Season of Its Passion*, New York: Simon and Schuster, 1982.

3 One notable exception to this generalization is in post-war Italy, where debates on the left, inspired by Gramsci, did involve a consideration of the problem of civil society.

4 Adam Seligman, *The Idea of Civil Society*, New York: The Free Press, 1992; Ernest Gellner, *Conditions of Liberty: Civil Society and Its Rivals*, New York: Penguin, 1994; and Jean Cohen and Andrew Arato, *Civil Society and Political Theory*, Cambridge, Mass.: The MIT Press, 1992.

5 At this time, I lived in Poland and often heard concerns expressed about imminent food price increases, along with the certainty that the workers who struck in 1970 would not take them lying down.

6 For an overview of KOR see Jan Josef Lipski, *KOR: A History of the Workers' Defense Committee in Poland, 1976-1981*, Berkeley: University of California Press, 1985.

7 See Jadwiga Staniszkis, *Poland's Self-Limiting Revolution*, Princeton: Princeton University Press, 1984.

8 Adam Michnik "The New Evolutionism," in his *Letters from Prison and Other Essays*, trans. Maya Latynski, Los Angeles: University of California Press, pp. 135–48.

9 Leszek Kolakowski, "Hope against Hopelessness," *Survey*, 17, 1, 1971: 37–52.

10 Discussions with Andrew Arato have been most helpful in piecing together this account. He and Jean Cohen have worked on the concept of civil society and its relationship with social theory in a way that consistently builds upon the insights of Central European intellectuals and political activists.

11 See Edward Shils, "The Virtues of Civil Society," *Government and Opposition*, 26, 2, 1991: 3–20, and Michael Walzer. "The Idea of Civil Society," *Dissent*, Spring 1991: 293–304.

12 This was the prevailing position of modernization theory inspired by the work of Talcott Parsons. See his *The System of Modern Society*, Englewood Cliffs: Prentice Hall, 1971.

13 See, for example, G. M. Tamas, "A Disquisition on Civil Society," *Social Research*, 61, 2, 1994: 205–22.

14 The democratic challenge is for citizens to judge the relative weight to be given to each of these institutions and to determine how they are to be connected. Such judgment is left to democratic decision.

15 This is something that Richard Neuhaus has been arguing forcefully. See his *Naked in the Public Square*, Grand Rapids: Mott Media, 1984.

16 Telling critiques of academic fashions and their distance from public life can be found in Russell Jacoby, *Dogmatic Wisdom: How the Cultural Wars Divert Education and Distract America*, New York: Doubleday, 1994, and David Bromwich, *Politics by Other Means: Higher Education and Group Thinking*, New Haven: Yale University Press, 1992.

6 THE INTELLECTUALS AND THE POLITICS OF CULTURE AFTER COMMUNISM

1 The developmental connection between the small theatrical movement and the transformations of 1989 is documented in my books, *On Cultural Freedom: An Exploration of Public Life in Poland and America*, Chicago: University of Chicago Press, 1982, *Beyond Glasnost*, and *After the Fall*.

2 For an overview of this theater movement, see my "Student Theater in Poland," *Survey*, 2, 99, 1976: 155–78.

3 These interviews were conducted throughout the country in 1973 and 1974 in connection with my research which led to the publication of *The Persistence of Freedom: The Sociological Implications of Polish Student Theater*, Boulder: Westview, 1980.

4 This was strikingly apparent to me during visits to the opposition network in Prague in the late eighties. In an underground seminar, my book *Beyond Glasnost* was discussed. The greatest controversy emanated from my analysis of Kundera as a novelist of the "post-totalitarian mind." For an account of this meeting see my *After the Fall*.

5 Milan Kundera, *The Art of the Novel*, New York: Grove Press, 1988, and *Testaments Betrayed: An Essay in Nine Parts*, New York: Harper Collins, 1995.

6 Art of the Novel, p.144.

7 *Ibid.*, p. 4.

8 *Ibid.*, p. 162.

9 *Ibid.*, p. 163.

10 *Testaments Betrayed*, pp. 146–7.

11 *Ibid.*, p. 58.

12 This is the major move analyzed in my *Beyond Glasnost*. In that work I analyze closely the poetry of the Polish poet Stanislaw Baranczak and the novels of Kundera as a manifestation of an aesthetic which takes as its major project independence from totalitarian culture.

13 See, for example, George Konrad, *Antipolitics*, New York: Harcourt Brace Jovanovich, 1983.

7 THE UNIVERSITY

1 See Thomas Bender, *New York Intellect: A History of Intellectual Life in New York City, from 1750 to the Beginning of Our Times*, Baltimore: The Johns Hopkins University Press, 1987, for an interesting historical account of the non-academic nature of intellectual life in New York from colonial times through the nineteenth century.

2 It is the loss of this situation which is the cause of Jacoby's great lament, see his, *The Lost Intellectuals*.

3 The classic historical work analyzing the implications of the Puritans' quest is Perry Miller's *Errand in the Wilderness*, New York: Harper Torchbooks, 1964.

4 The discussion here about the ironic aspects of the relationship between the development of the American university and religion is informed by the work of George M. Marsden in his *The Soul of the American University: From Protestant Establishment to Established Nonbelief*, New York: Oxford University Press, 1994.

5 See special issue of *Daedalus*, Fall 1993, on the American Research University.

6 For the classic overview of academic freedom from this point of view see Richard Hofstadter and Walter P. Metzger, *The Development of Academic Freedom in the United States*, New York: Columbia University Press, 1955.

7 Marsden, *The Soul of the American University*, pp. 429–44.

8 *Ibid.*, pp. 309–11.

9 For an overview of the political repression of the McCarthy period, see David Caute, *The Great Fear: The Anti Communist Purge under Truman and Eisenhower*, New York: Simon and Schuster, 1978.

10 Thus, for example, at the City College of New York, Professors Leonard Jeffries and Michael Levin, respectively a black racist and a white racist, teach their courses under the protection of academic freedom. For reports on court rulings on Jeffries's and Levin's successful suits against CCNY see Maria Newman, "Court Backs Reinstating of Jeffries to College Post," *The New York Times*, April 19, 1994, Sec. B, p. 3; Richard Bernstein, "Judge Reinstates Jeffries as Head of Black Studies for City College," *The New York Times*, August 5, 1993, Sec. A, p. 1; and Maria Newman, "Free-Speech Decision: Jeffries Victory Shows the Difficulty of Punishing Objectionable Opinions," *The New York Times*, May 16, 1993, Sec. A, p. 33.

11 See Stanley Fish, "There's No Such Thing As Free Speech and It's a Good Thing, Too," in Paul Berman (ed.), *Debating P.C.*, New York: Dell, 1992, pp. 231–45. For a sound overview of the controversies over the issue of free speech in the American University today see Russell Jacoby, *Dogmatic Wisdom*, pp. 29–58.

12 Fish, "There's No Such Thing," p. 233.

13 *Ibid.*, p. 231.

14 Thorsten Veblen, *The Higher Learning in America: A Memorandum on the Conduct of Universities by Business Men*, New York: Hill and Wang, 1957.

15 The difference between the cultural consensus of the university and of the general society is the broader context of the academic cultural wars. For an analysis of this see David Bromwich, *Politics by Other Means*.

16 William Bennett, *The Book of Virtues: A Treasury of Great Stories*, New York: Simon and Schuster, 1993.

17 Newman quoted in D'Souza, *Illiberal Education: The Politics of Race and Sex on Campus*, New York: Vintage Books, 1992, p. 23.

18 See Allan Bloom, *The Closing of the American Mind*, New York: Simon and Schuster, 1987, and Roger Kimball, *Tenured Radicals: How Politics Has Corrupted Our Higher Education*, New York: Harper and Row, 1990.

19 Stanley Aronowitz and Henry A. Giroux, *Postmodern Education: Politics, Culture and Social Criticism*, Minneapolis: University of Minnesota Press, 1991.

20 Robert Hughes presents a clear liberal position in his *Culture of Complaint: The Fraying of America*, New York: Oxford University Press, 1993; see also David Bromwich, *Politics by Other Means*.

21 I first analyzed the consequences of the free speech ideal for the development of autonomous culture in my comparative study *On Cultural Freedom*.

22 William F. Buckley Jr, *God and Man at Yale: The Superstitions of "Academic Freedom,"* Chicago: Henry Regnery and Company, 1951.

23 For criticism of identity politics and PC from the left see Gitlin, *The Twilight of Common Dreams*, and Bromwich, *Politics by Other Means*. For an approach from the point of view of the French left, delving into the philosophical implications of identity politics, see Alain Finkielkraut, *The Defeat of the Mind*, trans. by Judith Friedlander, New York: Columbia University Press, 1995.

24 Benjamin De Mott, *The Imperial Middle: Why Americans Can't Think Straight about Class*, New Haven: Yale University Press, 1992.

25 I believe that the parallel to the totalitarian situation is an exaggeration, but the workings of a kind of official truth are unsettling, see Richard Bernstein, *Dictatorship of Virtue: How the Battle over Multiculturalism Is Reshaping Our Schools, Country, Our Lives*, New York: Vintage Books, 1994.

26 This is a basic theme in Bromwich, *Politics by Other Means*.

27 Levine, *Visions of the Sociological Tradition*. For a highly contentious account of sociology's problems see Irving Louis Horowitz, *The Decomposition of Sociology*, New York: Oxford University Press, 1993.

28 The orientation toward professionalism is built into the origins of the social sciences, see Dorothy Ross, *The Origins of the Social Sciences*, New York: Cambridge University Press, 1991.

8 RACE AND DISCURSIVE DISRUPTION

1 See, William Julius Wilson Jr, *The New York Times*, March 17, 1992, Sec. A, p. 25.

2 Toni Morrison, *Playing in the Dark: Whiteness and the Literary Imagination*, Cambridge: Harvard University Press, 1990; Andrew Hacker, *Two Nations: Black and White, Separate, Hostile, Unequal*, New York: Ballantine Books, 1992; Derrick Bell, *Faces at the Bottom of the Well: The Permanence of Racism*, New York: Basic Books, 1993.

3 Jim Sleeper, *Liberal Racism*, New York: Viking, 1997.

4 In recent years an ascendent group of prominent black public intellectuals have emerged, filling this vacuum, including representatives on the left, such as Cornel West, Henry Louis Gates Jr, and bell hooks, and on the right, such as Shelby Steele and Thomas Sowell. For an interesting recent study provocatively investigating the limits of these intellectuals, especially as they draw upon the legacy of W. E. B. Dubois, see Adolph Reed Jr, *W. E. B. Du Bois and American Political Thought, Fabianism and the Colorline*, New York and Oxford: Oxford University Press, 1997.

5 See Carl Rowan, *Dream Makers, Dream Breakers: The World of Justice Thurgood Marshall*, Boston: Little Brown and Co., 1993.

6 The Autobiography of Malcolm X, as told to Alex Haley, New York: Ballantine Books, 1964.

7 Herbert Marcuse, "Repressive Tolerance," in Robert Paul Wolff, Barrington Moore Jr, and Herbert Marcuse, *A Critique of Pure Tolerance*, Boston: Beacon Press, 1969, pp. 81–117.

8 Indeed, the idea for this chapter comes from an account Gates gives of his mother's reaction to Malcolm, see Henry Louis Gates Jr, *Colored People: A Memoir*, New York: Vintage Books, 1995.

9 See, for example, "Answer to Questions at the Militant Labor Forum," in Malcolm X, *By Any Means Necessary*, New York: Pathfinder, 1970, p. 14–32.

10 At a Paris meeting, November 23, 1964, printed in *By Any Means Necessary*, pp. 117–18.

11 See *The New York Times*, November 18, 1992, Sec. A, p. 1.

12 See Bruce Perry, *Malcolm: The Life of a Man Who Changed Black America*, New York: Station Hill Press, 1991.

13 See bell hooks, "Malcolm X: Consumed By Images," *Z Magazine*, March, 1993: 36–9.

14 See Perry, *Malcolm* and Cornell West, *Race Matters*, New York: Vintage Books, 1994.

9 RACE AND SUSTAINED DELIBERATION

1 Manning Marable, "Clarence Thomas and the Crisis of Black Political Power," in Morrison (ed.), *Race-ing Justice, En-gendering Power: Essays on*

Anita Hill, Clarence Thomas, and the Construction of Social Reality, New York: Pantheon Books, 1992, pp. 61–85. The account of Thomas's careerism draws on this article.

2 David Brock, *Anita Hill: The Untold Story*, New York: The Free Press, 1994.

3 Morrison (ed.), *Race-ing Justice, En-gendering Power*, p. xxx

4 A. Leon Higgenbotham, Jr, "An Open Letter to Justice Clarence Thomas from a Federal Judicial Colleague" in Morrison (ed.), *Race-ing Justice, En-gendering Power*, p. 5.

5 For a detailed elaboration of his political position see A. Leon Higgin-botham, *In the Matter of Color: Race and the American Legal Process*, New York: Oxford University Press, 1978, and A. Leon Higgenbotham, *Shades of Freedom: Racial Politics and Presumptions of the American Legal Process*, New York: Oxford University Press, 1996.

6 See, for example, Shelby Steele, *The Content of Our Characters: A New Vision of Race in America*, New York: Harper Perennial, 1991; Thomas Sowell, *The Economics and Politics of Race: An International Perspective*, New York: W. Morrow, 1983; Glenn Loury, *One by One: Essays and Reviews on Race and Responsibility in America*, New York: The Free Press, 1995.

7 See Nell Irvin Painter, "Hill, Thomas and the Use of Racial Stereo-type," in Morrison (ed.), *Race-ing Justice, En-gendering Power*, pp. 200–14.

8 See Eyerman, *Between Culture and Politics*, pp. 53–63.

9 Michael Thelwell, "False Fleeting, Perjured Chance: Yale's Brightest and Blackest Go to Washington," in Morrison (ed.), *Race-ing Justice, En-gendering Power*, p. 87.

10 *Ibid.*, pp. 89–90.

11 *Ibid.*, p. 93.

12 *Ibid.*, p. 124.

13 Claudia Brodsky Lacour, "Doing Things with Words: Racism as Speech Act and the Undoing of Justice," Morrison (ed.), *Race-ing Justice, En-gendering Power*, p. 127–58.

14 *Ibid.*, p. 129.

15 *Ibid.*, p. 130.

16 See Thelwell, "False Fleeting, Perjured Chance" and Patricia Williams, "A Rare Case Study of Muleheadedness and Men," in Morrison (ed.), *Race-ing Justice, En-gendering Power*, pp. 159–71.

17 For a careful consideration of the intellectual ferment among black intellectuals today, see Manning Marable, *Beyond Black and White:Trans-forming African American Politics*, New York: Verso, 1995, especially pp. 167–73. A most telling instance of academic discourse reaching beyond the purview of the university on matters of race is the work on critical race theory applied to the law. There is an interaction between the work of critical race theorists and the unfolding of the media murder trial of the century, the case of O. J. Simpson. The theorists critically examine the law as an instrument of justice and interpret it, rather, as

an instrument of domination. This is applied to radical theoretical notions of storytelling as a means to subvert the oppressions of legal objectivism and universalism, and to ideas of jury nullification of a racist legal system by African Americans when considering the fate of apparently guilty African American defendants. Jeffrey Rosen argues that these ideas animated the defense strategy of one of Simpson's lawyers, Johnnie L. Cochran Jr, See his "The Bloods and the Crits," *The New Republic*, December 9, 1996, pp. 27–42. For an overview of critical race theory see Kimberle Crenshaw, Neil Gotanda, Gary Peller, and Kendall Thomas, *Critical Race Theory: The Key Writings that Formed the Movement*, New York: The Free Press, 1995.

18 Homi Bhabha, "A Good Judge of Character: Men, Metaphors, and the Common Culture" in Morrison (ed.), *Race-ing Justice, En-gendering Power*, p. 249.

19 The argument developed here directed at Bhabha is informed by the theory of action of Hannah Arendt, see her *The Human Condition*, especially her critique of Marx in chapter 3, pp. 79–135.

10 WHY IS THERE NO FEMINISM AFTER COMMUNISM?

1 This summary statement concerning the situation of women in the former East Bloc is drawn from an essay by Ann Snitow, "Feminist Futures in the Former East Bloc," *Peace and Democracy News*, 7, 3, 1993: 40.

2 Shana Penn, "The National Secret," *Journal of Women's History*, 5, 3, 1994: 55-69.

3 *Ibid.*, p. 64.

4 I am referring here most explicitly to civil society advocates in the West. It is an open question whether the advocates of civil society in the region concerned themselves with the issue of gender justice at all. A lack of serious thought seems to have been the norm; sometimes even open hostility was apparent.

5 For a telling historical study of how it comes to pass that an inequality is perceived by people as an injustice see Barrington Moore Jr, *Injustice: The Social Bases of Obedience and Revolt*, White Plains: M. E. Sharpe, 1978.

6 Jirina Smejkalova-Strickland, "Do Czech Women Need Feminism? Perspectives of Feminist Theories and Practices in the Czech Republic," in Susanna Trnka with Laura Busheikin (eds.), *Bodies of Bread and Butter: Reconfiguring Women's Lives in post-communist Czech Republic*, Prague: Prague Gender Center, 1993, pp. 13–17.

7 Peggy Watson, "Eastern Europe's Silent Revolution: Gender," *Sociology*, 27, 3: 471–87; for a supportive detailed position from Hungary see Joanna Goven, "Gender Politics in Hungary: Autonomy and Anti-Feminism," in *Gender Politics and Post Communism: Reflections from Eastern Europe and the Former Soviet Union*, New York: Routledge, 1993, pp. 224–40.

8   Peggy Watson, "The Rise of Masculinism in Eastern Europe," *New Left Review*, 198, March/April 1993: 71–82.

9   Mira Marody "Why I Am Not a Feminist," *Social Research*, 60, 4, 1993: 853–64.

10 Jirina Siklova, "McDonalds, Terminators, Coca Cola Ads and Feminism?" in Trnka and Busheikin (eds.), pp. 7–11.

11 Laura Busheikin, "Is Sisterhood Really Global? Western Feminism in East Europe," in Trnka and Busheikin (eds.), *Bodies of Bread and Butter*, p. 70.

12 Marody, "Why I Am Not a Feminist," p. 855.

13 This is the great theme of the first wave of feminism in the nineteenth century and the commitment of liberal feminism in the twentieth century. Mary Wollstonecraft's classic, *A Vindication of the Rights of Woman*, New York: Legal Classics Library, 1993, articulates this position, as does John Stuart Mill's *The Subjugation of Women*, London: Longmans, Green, Reader and Dyer, 1869. More recent feminists who focus on this position include such equal rights advocates as Supreme Court Justice Ruth Bader Ginsburg.

14 This is the theme of the second wave of feminism, born in the post-war period. A classic opening salvo in this development was Simone de Beauvoir's *The Second Sex*, trans. and ed. H. M. Parshley, New York: Knopf, 1993. In the United States Betty Friedan's *The Feminine Mystique*, New York: Norton, 1974, opened the way to a new feminism which was accelerated by women activists of the New Left. They greatly expanded the scope and depth of feminist investigation, criticism, and action, considering such issues as the relationship between gender and racial and class injustice, alternative theologies, critiques of the law and scholarship, and educational and social welfare institutions. For an intriguing insider's account of the development of the second wave from the inside, see Ann Snitow, "Gender Diary," in Marianne Hirsch and Evelyn Fox-Keller (eds.), *Conflicts in Feminism*, New York: Routledge, 1990.

15 The classic work is Kate Millett's *Sexual Politics*, New York: Simon and Schuster, 1980. Her position has been further extended from a variety of alternative positions, see, for example, Adrienne Rich, "Compulsory Heterosexuality and Lesbian Existence," *Signs*, 4, 1980: 630–1, Andrea Dworkin, *Our Blood: Prophecies and Discourses on Sexual Politics*, London: Women's Press, 1976, and Ann Snitow, Christine Stansell, and Sharon Thompson (eds.), *Powers of Desire: The Politics of Sexuality*, New York: Monthly Review Press, 1983.

16 Marody, "Why I Am Not a Feminist," p. 857.

17 *Ibid.*, p. 864.

18 Reprinted in *The Prague Post*, November 25-December 1,1992, p. 17.

19 The feminist reaction to the Skvorecky article is reported in Laura Busheikin, "Sex and Czechs," *This* Magazine, March–April 1993: pp. 28–9.

20 See, for example, Andrea Dworkin and Catherine McKinnon, *Pornography and Civil Rights: A Day for Women's Equality*, Minneapolis: Organizing Against Pornography, 1988.

21 Elzbieta Matynia, "Finding a Voice: Women in Post Communist Central Europe," in Amrita Basu (ed.), *The Challenge of Local Feminism*, Boulder: Westview, 1995, pp. 383–4. She has documented the dialogic qualities of the developing women's movements in Slovakia, the Czech Republic, Hungary, and Poland. The discussion of the contribution of feminism to the ideal of civil society here draws heavily upon Matynia's research.

22 *Ibid.*, p. 403.

23 See the already cited articles by Peggy Watson, and her, "Civil Society and the Politicalization of Difference in Eastern Europe," in J. Scott and C. Kaplan (eds.), *Transitions, Environments, Translations: The Meaning of Feminism in Contemporary Politics*, New York: Routledge, forthcoming, and "Gender Relations, Education and Social Change in Poland," in *Gender and Education*, 4, 1/2, 1992.

24 Watson, "Civil Society and the Politicalization of Difference in Eastern Europe."

25 This is especially the case in the writings of Jean Bethke Elshtain, see her *Public Man, Private Woman: Women in Social and Political Thought*, Princeton: Princeton University Press, 1981.

11 CONCLUSION: CIVILITY AND SUBVERSION IN CYNICAL TIMES

1 Edmund Mokrzycki, "Is the Intelligentsia Needed in Poland?" *Polish Sociological Bulletin*, forthcoming.

2 See Jurgen Habermas, "Further Reflections on the Public Sphere," in Calhoun (ed.), *Habermas and the Public Sphere*, pp. 421–61.

3 For the classic account of critical theory's response to mass culture, see Horkheimer and Adorno, *The Dialectic of Enlightenment*.

4 For overviews of the problems of post-modernism and post-modernity as social and political developments, see Zygmunt Bauman, *Intimations of Postmodernity*, New York: Routledge, 1992; Richard Bernstein, *The New Constellation: The Ethical Horizon of Modernity/Postmodernity*, Cambridge, Mass.: Polity Press, 1991; David Harvey, *The Condition of Postmodernity: An Enquiry into the Origins of Cultural Change*, Cambridge, Mass.: Blackwell, 1990; Agnes Heller and Ferenc Feher, *The Postmodern Political Condition*, New York: Columbia University Press, 1988; and Fredric Jameson, *Postmodernism, or, The Logic of Late Capitalism*, Durham: Duke University Press, 1991.

5 Prime examples of this position include: Stuart Hall and Tony Jefferson, *Resistance Through Rituals: Youth Subcultures in Postwar Britain*, London: Hutchinson, 1976; Dick Hebdige, *Subculture: The Meaning of Style*, London: Methuen, 1979; Janice Radway, *Reading the Romance: Women,*

Patriarchy, and Popular Literature, Chapel Hill: University of North Carolina Press, 1984; and Paul Willis, *Common Culture*, Boulder: Westview, 1990.

6 Ross, *No Respect*, p. 211.

7 Stanley Aronowitz, *Roll Over Beethoven: The Return of Cultural Strife*, Hanover: Wesleyan University Press, 1993, p. xi.

8 This is the central theme of my books *Beyond Glasnost* and *The Cynical Society*.

9 I explain this contention in detail in *Beyond Glasnost*, pp. 87–118. See Jan Vladislav (ed.), *Vaclav Havel or Living in Truth*, Boston: Faber and Faber, 1986, pp. 36–122, for Havel's classic formulation. The distinction between the notion of living in truth and of acting to enforce a regime of truth should be noted. The former represents the strategy to avoid official lies that go by the name of official truths. The latter is the order of a despotic official truth.

10 Ira Katznelson, *Liberalism's Crooked Circle: Letters to Adam Michnik*, Princeton: Princeton University Press, 1996.

11 Adam Michnik, *The Church and the Left*, trans. David Ost, Chicago: University of Chicago Press, 1993, originally published in Polish in 1979.

12 Ironically, in David Ost's introduction to his English translation of Michnik's book, he criticizes Michnik on exactly this point.

13 See "Conversations in the Citadel," in Michnik's *Letters From Prison and Other Essays* and a piece co-authored with the post-communist Prime Minister Ciemosiewicz.

Bibliography

Arendt, Hannah. 1951. *The Origins of Totalitarianism.* New York: Harcourt Brace and Company.

1959. *The Human Condition.* Garden City: Doubleday.

1977. *On Revolution.* New York: Penguin.

1980. *Between Past and Future.* New York: Penguin.

Aronowitz, Stanley. 1993. *Roll Over Beethoven: The Return of Cultural Strife.* Hanover: Wesleyan University Press.

Aronowitz, Stanley and Henry A. Giroux. 1991. *Postmodern Education: Politics, Culture and Social Criticism.* Minneapolis: University of Minnesota Press.

Asanti, Molefi K. 1993. *Malcolm X as a Cultural Hero and Other Afrocentric Essays.* Trenton: Africa World Press.

Bauman, Zygmunt. 1987. *Legislators and Interpreters.* Cambridge, Mass.: Polity Press.

1992. *Intimations of Postmodernity.* New York: Routledge.

Bell, Daniel. 1962. *The End of Ideology: The Exhaustion of Political Ideas in the Fifties.* New York: The Free Press.

1976. *The Coming of Post-Industrial Society.* New York: Basic Books.

Bell, Derrick. 1993. *Faces at the Bottom of the Well: The Permanence of Racism.* New York: Basic Books.

Bellah, Robert, Richard Marsden, William Sullivan, Ann Swindler, and Steven Tipton. 1991. *The Good Society.* New York: Knopf.

Bellow, Saul. 1995. *It All Adds Up: From the Dim Past to the Uncertain Future.* New York: Penguin Books.

Benda, Julian. 1969. *The Treason of the Intellectuals*, trans. Richard Aldington. New York: Norton.

Bender, Thomas. 1987. *New York Intellect: A History of Intellectual Life in New York City, from 1750 to the Beginning of Our Times.* Baltimore: The Johns Hopkins University Press.

Benjamin, Walter. 1969. *Illuminations*, trans. Harry Zohn, ed. Hannah Arendt. New York: Schocken Books.

Bennett, William. 1993. *The Book of Virtues: A Treasury of Great Stories.* New York: Simon and Schuster.

Bernstein, Richard. 1991. *The New Constellation: The Ethical Horizon of Modernity / Postmodernity*, Cambridge, Mass.: Polity Press.

1993. "Judge Reinstates Jeffries as Head of Black Studies for City College." *The New York Times*, August 5, Sec. A, p. 1.

1994a. *Dictatorship of Virtue: How the Battle over Multiculturalism Is Reshaping Our Schools, Country, Our Lives*. New York: Vintage Books.

1994b *Dictatorship of Virtue: Multiculturalism and the Battle for America's Future*. New York: Knopf.

Bhabha, Homi. 1992. "A Good Judge of Character: Men, Metaphors, and the Common Culture," in Morrison (ed.), *Race-ing Justice, En-gendering Power*, pp. 232–50.

Bloom, Allan. 1987. *The Closing of the American Mind*. New York: Simon and Schuster.

Bourdieu, Pierre. 1984. *Distinction: A Social Critique of the Judgment of Taste*. Cambridge, Mass.: Harvard University Press.

Branch, Taylor. 1988. *Parting the Waters: America in the King Years 1954-1963*. New York: Simon and Schuster.

Breckenridge, Carol A. and Peter van der Veer. 1993. *Orientalism and the Post Colonial Predicament*. Philadelphia: University of Pennsylvania Press.

Brock, David. 1994. *Anita Hill: The Untold Story*. New York: The Free Press.

Bromwich, David. 1992. *Politics by Other Means: Higher Education and Group Thinking*. New Haven: Yale University Press.

Buckley Jr, William F. 1951. *God and Man at Yale: The Superstitions of "Academic Freedom."* Chicago: Henry Regnery and Company.

Bury, J. B. and Russell Meiggs. 1975. *A History of Greece: To the Death of Alexander the Great*, fourth edition. London: Macmillan.

Busheikin, Laura. 1993a. "Is Sisterhood Really Global? Western Feminism in East Europe," in Trnka and Busheikin (eds.), *Bodies of Bread and Butter*, pp. 69–76.

1993b. "Sex and Czechs." *This Magazine*. March–April 1993: 28–9.

Calhoun, Craig (ed.) 1992. *Habermas and the Public Sphere*. Cambridge, Mass.: The MIT Press.

1994. *Social Theory and the Politics of Identity*. Cambridge, Mass.: Blackwell.

Caute, David. 1978. *The Great Fear: The Anti Communist Purge under Truman and Eisenhower*. New York: Simon and Schuster.

Cohen, Jean and Andrew Arato. 1992. *Civil Society and Political Theory*. Cambridge, Mass.: The MIT Press.

Coleman, James. 1993. "The Rational Reconstruction of Society." 1992 Presidential Address, *American Sociological Review*, 58, 1.

The Coleman Report on Public and Private Schools: The Draft Summary and Eight Critiques. 1981. Virginia: Educational Research Service.

Crenshaw, Kimberle, Neil Gotanda, Gary Peller, and Kendall Thomas. 1995. *Critical Race Theory: The Key Writings that Formed the Movement*. New York: The Free Press.

Daedalus. Fall 1993. Special Issue on the American Research University.

Dahl, Robert A. 1989. *Democracy and Its Critics*. New Haven: Yale University Press.

Dahrendorf, Ralf. 1990. *Reflection on the Revolution in Europe: In a Letter Intended to Have Been Sent to a Gentleman in Warsaw.* New York: Times Books.

de Beauvoir, Simone. 1993. *The Second Sex.* Trans. and ed. by H. M. Parshley. New York: Knopf.

De Mott, Benjamin. 1992. *The Imperial Middle: Why Americans Can't Think Straight About Class.* New Haven: Yale University Press.

de Tocqueville, Alexis, 1969. *Democracy in America*, trans. George Lawrence, ed. J. P. Mayer. New York: Anchor Books.

Dewey, John. 1980. *The Public and Its Problems.* Chicago: Swallow Press.

Dickstein, Morris. 1992. *Double Agent: The Critic and Society.* New York: Oxford University Press.

Durkheim, Emile. 1984. *Division of Labor in Society.* New York: The Free Press.

Dworkin, Andrea. 1976. *Our Blood: Prophecies and Discourses on Sexual Politics.* London: Women's Press.

Dworkin, Andrea and Catherine McKinnon. 1988. *Pornography and Civil Rights: A Day for Women's Equality.* Minneapolis: Organizing Against Pornography.

D'Souza, Denish. 1992. *Illiberal Education: The Politics of Race and Sex on Campus.* New York: Vintage Books.

Elshtain, Jean Bethke. 1981. *Public Man, Private Woman: Women in Social and Political Thought.* Princeton: Princeton University Press.

　1995. *Democracy on Trial.* New York: Basic Books.

Enzensberger, Hans Mangus. 1990. *Civil Wars: From L.A. to Bosnia.* New York: The New Press.

Evans, Peter, Dietrich Rueschemeyer and Theda Skocpol (eds.). 1985. *Bringing the State Back In.* New York: Cambridge University Press.

Eyerman, Ron. 1994. *Between Culture and Politics: Intellectuals in Modern Society.* Cambridge, Mass.: Blackwell.

Finkielkraut, Alain. 1995. *The Defeat of the Mind*, trans. Judith Friedlander. New York: Columbia University Press.

Fish, Stanley. 1992. "There's No Such Thing as Free Speech and It's a Good Thing, Too," in Paul Berman (ed.), *Debating P.C.* New York: Dell, pp. 231–45.

Foucault, Michel. 1984. *The Foucault Reader*, ed. Paul Rabinow. New York: Pantheon Books.

Friedan, Betty. 1974. *The Feminine Mystique.* New York: Norton.

Fukuyama, Francis. 1995. *Trust: Social Virtues and the Creation of Prosperity.* New York: The Free Press.

Gans, Herbert. 1974. *Popular and High Culture: An Analysis and Evaluation of Taste.* New York: Basic Books.

Garton Ash, Timothy. 1985. *The Polish Revolution: Solidarity.* New York: Vintage Books.

Gates Jr, Henry Louis. 1995. *Colored People: A Memoir.* New York: Vintage Books.

Gella, Aleksander (ed.). 1976. *The Intelligentsia and the Intellectuals*. London: Sage.

Gellner, Ernest. 1994. *Conditions of Liberty: Civil Society and Its Rivals*. New York: Penguin.

Giddens, Anthony. 1994. *Beyond Left and Right: The Future of Radical Politics*. Stanford: Stanford University Press.

Gitlin, Todd. 1995. *The Twilight of Common Dreams: Why America is Wracked by Culture Wars*. New York: Metropolitan Books.

Goldfarb, Jeffrey. 1976. "Student Theater in Poland." *Survey*, 2, 99: 155–78.

    1980. *The Persistence of Freedom: The Sociological Implications of Polish Student Theater*. Boulder: Westview.

    1982. *On Cultural Freedom: An Exploration of Public Life in Poland and America*. Chicago: University of Chicago Press.

    1989. *Beyond Glasnost: The Post-Totalitarian Mind*. Chicago: University of Chicago Press.

    1991. *The Cynical Society: The Culture of Politics and the Politics of Culture in American Life*. Chicago: University of Chicago Press.

    1992. *After the Fall: The Pursuit of Democracy in Central Europe*. New York: Basic Books.

Goodwyn, Lawrence. 1991. *Breaking the Barrier: The Rise of Solidarity in Poland*. New York: Oxford University Press.

Gopnik, Adam. 1994. "Read All About It." *The New Yorker*, December 12, pp. 84–102.

Gouldner, Alvin. 1979. *The Future of the Intellectuals and the Rise of the New Class*. New York: Seabury.

Goven, Joanna. 1993. "Gender Politics in Hungary: Autonomy and Anti-Feminism," in Nanete Funk and Magda Mueller (eds.), *Gender Politics and Post Communism: Reflections from Eastern Europe and the Former Soviet Union*. New York: Routledge, pp. 224–40.

Guillermoprieto, Alma. 1994. "Zapata's Heirs." *The New Yorker*, May 16, pp. 52-63.

Habermas, Jurgen. 1987. *The Theory of Communicative Action*, trans. Thomas McCarthy. Boston: Beacon Press.

    1991. *The Structural Transformation of the Public Sphere: An Inquiry into a Category of Bourgeois Society*, trans. Thomas Burger with Frederick Lawrence. Cambridge: The MIT Press.

    1992. "Further Reflections on the Public Sphere." in Calhoun (ed.), *Habermas and the Public Sphere*, pp. 421–61.

Hacker, Andrew. 1992. *Two Nations: Black and White, Separate, Hostile, Unequal*. New York: Ballantine Books.

Hall, Stuart and Tony Jefferson. 1976. *Resistance Through Rituals: Youth Subcultures in Postwar Britain*. London: Hutchinson.

Harvey, David. 1990. *The Condition of Postmodernity: An Enquiry into the Origins of Cultural Change*. Cambridge, Mass.: Blackwell.

Hebdige, Dick. 1979. *Subculture: The Meaning of Style*. London: Methuen.

Heller, Agnes and Ferenc Feher. 1988. *The Postmodern Political Condition*. New York: Columbia University Press.

Herman, Edward S. and Noam Chomsky. 1988. *Manufacturing Consent: The Political Economy of the Mass Media*. New York: Pantheon Books.

Higgenbotham Jr, A. Leon. 1978. *In the Matter of Color: Race and the American Legal Process*. New York: Oxford University Press.

   1992. "An Open Letter to Justice Clarence Thomas from a Federal Judicial Colleague," in Morrison (ed.), *Race-ing Justice, En-gendering Power*, pp. 3–39.

   1997. *Shades of Freedom: Racial Politics and Presumptions of the American Legal Process*, New York: Oxford University Press.

Hofstadter, Richard. 1962. *Anti-Intellectualism in American Life*. New York: Vintage Books.

   1979. *The Paranoid Style in American Politics and Other Essays*. Chicago: University of Chicago Press.

Hofstadter, Richard and Walter P. Metzger. 1955. *The Development of Academic Freedom in the United States*. New York: Columbia University Press.

hooks, bell. 1993. "Malcolm X: Consumed By Images." *Z Magazine*, March: 36–9.

Horkheimer, Max and Theodor Adorno. 1972. *The Dialectic of the Enlightenment*. New York: Herder and Herder.

Horowitz, Irving Louis. 1983. *C. Wright Mills: An American Utopian*. New York: The Free Press.

   1993. *The Decomposition of Sociology*. New York: Oxford University Press.

Howe, Irving. 1984. "Toward an Open Culture." *The New Republic*, March 5, 190: 25–9.

Hughes, Robert. 1993. *Culture of Complaint: The Fraying of America*. New York: Oxford University Press.

Huntington, Samuel. 1993. "The Clash of Civilizations?" *Foreign Affairs*, 72, 3: 22–49.

Jacoby, Russell. 1987. *The Lost Intellectuals: American Culture in the Age of Academe*. New York: Basic Books.

   1994. *Dogmatic Wisdom: How the Cultural Wars Divert Education and Distract America*. New York: Doubleday.

Jaeger, Werner. 1943. *Paideia: The Ideals of Greek Culture*. New York: Oxford University Press.

Jameson, Fredric. 1991. *Postmodernism, or, The Logic of Late Capitalism*. Durham: Duke University Press.

Joas, Hans. 1996. *The Creativity of Action*. Chicago: University of Chicago Press.

Johnson, Paul. 1988. *Intellectuals*. London: Weidenfeld and Nicolson.

Judt, Tony. 1992. *Past Imperfect; French Intellectuals 1944-1956*. Berkeley: University of California Press.

Kant, Immanuel. 1970. "An Answer to the Question: What is the Enlightenment?" in *Kant: Political Writings*, ed. Hans Reiss. New York: Cambridge University Press, pp. 54–60.

Katznelson, Ira. 1996. *Liberalism's Crooked Circle: Letters to Adam Michnik*. Princeton: Princeton University Press.

Katznelson, Ira, and Aristide R. Zolberg (eds.). 1986. *Working Class Formation: Nineteenth-Century Patterns in Western Europe and the United States*. Princeton: Princeton University Press.

Kimball, Roger. 1990. *Tenured Radicals: How Politics Has Corrupted Our Higher Education*. New York: Harper and Row.

Kolakowski, Leszek. 1971. "Hope Against Hopelessness." *Survey*, 17, 1: 37–52.

Konrad, George. 1983. *Antipolitics*. New York: Harcourt Brace Jovanovich.

Konrad, George and Ivan Szelenyi. 1979. *The Intellectuals on the Road to Class Power: A Sociological Study of the Role of the Intelligentsia in Socialism*. New York: Harcourt Brace Jovanovich.

Kramer, Hilton. 1993. "Art and its Institutions: Notes on the Culture War." *The New Criterion*, 12, 1: 4–7.

Kundera, Milan. 1988. *The Art of the Novel*. New York: Grove Press.

    1995. *Testaments Betrayed: An Essay in Nine Parts*. New York: Harper Collins.

Laba, Roman. 1991. *The Roots of Solidarity: A Political Sociology of Poland's Working-Class Democratization*. Princeton: Princeton University Press.

Lacour, Claudia Brodsky. 1992. "Doing Things with Words: Racism as Speech Act and the Undoing of Justice," in Morrison (ed.), *Race-ing Justice, En-gendering Power*, pp. 127–58.

Lasch, Christopher. 1995. *The Revolt of the Elites and the Betrayal of Democracy*. New York: W. W. Norton and Company.

Lenin, Vladimir. 1963.*What Is To Be Done?*, trans. S. V. and Patricia Utechin. Oxford: Clarendon Press.

Levine, Donald. 1995. *Visions of the Sociological Tradition*. Chicago: University of Chicago Press.

Lévy, Bernard-Henri. 1995. *Adventures on the Freedom Road: The French Intellectuals in the 20th Century*. London: Harvill Press/Harper Collins World.

Lewis, Bernard. 1993. *Islam and the West*. New York: Oxford University Press.

Lippmann, Walter. 1965. *Public Opinion*. New York: The Free Press.

Lipset, S. Martin. 1960. *Political Man*. New York: Doubleday.

Lipski, Jan Josef. 1985. *KOR: A History of the Workers' Defense Committee in Poland, 1976- 1981*. Berkeley: University of California Press.

Loury, Glenn. 1995. *One by One: Essays and Reviews on Race and Responsibility in America*. New York: The Free Press.

Luhmann, Niklas. 1982 *The Differentiation of Society*. New York: Columbia University Press.

Lukacs, Georg. 1971. *History and Class Consciousness*. Cambridge, Mass.: The MIT Press.

Lundberg, George. 1961. *Can Science Save Us?* New York: Longman Green.

Lyotard, Jean-François. 1984. *The Postmodern Condition*, trans. Geoff Bennington and Brian Massumi. Minneapolis: University of Minnesota Press.

Mannheim, Karl. 1963. *Ideology and Utopia*, trans. Louis Wirth and Edward Shils, New York: Harcourt, Brace and World.

Marable, Manning. 1992. "Clarence Thomas and the Crisis of Black Political Power." in Morrison (ed.), *Race-ing Justice, En-gendering Power* pp. 61–85.

    1995. *Beyond Black and White: Transforming African American Politics*. New York: Verso.

Marcuse, Herbert. 1969. "Repressive Tolerance," in Robert Paul Wolff, Barrington Moore Jr, and Herbert Marcuse, *A Critique of Pure Tolerance*. Boston: Beacon Press, pp. 81–117.

Marody, Mira. 1993. "Why I Am Not a Feminist." *Social Research*, 60, 4: 853–64.

Marsden, George M. 1994. *The Soul of the American University: From Protestant Establishment to Established Nonbelief*. New York: Oxford University Press.

Marx, Karl. 1965. *The German Ideology*. London: Lawrence and Wishart.

Matynia, Elzbieta. 1995. "Finding a Voice: Women in Post Communist Central Europe," in Amrita Basu (ed.), *The Challenge of Local Feminism*. Boulder: Westview, pp. 374–404.

Melucci, Alberto. 1996a. *Challenging Codes: Collective Action in the Information Age*. Cambridge: Cambridge University Press.

    1996b. *The Playing Self: Person and Meaning in the Planetary Society*. Cambridge: Cambridge University Press.

Michnik, Adam. 1985. *Letters from Prison and Other Essays*, trans. Maya Latynski. Los Angeles: University of California Press.

    1993. *The Church and the Left*, trans. David Ost. Chicago: University of Chicago Press.

Mill, John Stuart. 1969. *The Subjection of Women*. London: Longmans, Green, Reader and Dyer.

Miller, James. 1987. *Democracy in the Streets: From Port Huron to the Siege of Chicago*. New York: Simon and Schuster.

Miller, Perry. 1964. *Errand in the Wilderness*. New York: Harper Torchbooks.

Millett, Kate. 1980. *Sexual Politics*. New York: Simon and Schuster.

Mills, C. Wright. 1956. *The Power Elite*. New York: Oxford University Press.

    1959. *The Sociological Imagination*. New York: Oxford University Press.

    1963. "The Social Role of the Intellectual," in *Power, Politics and People: The Collected Essays of C. Wright Mills*, ed. Irving Louis Horowitz. New York: Oxford University Press.

Mokrzycki, Edmund. Forthcoming. "Is the Intelligentsia Needed in Poland?" *Polish Sociological Bulletin*.

Moore Jr, Barrington. 1978. *Injustice: The Social Bases of Obedience and Revolt.* White Plains: M. E. Sharpe.

Morrison, Toni. 1990. *Playing in the Dark: Whiteness and the Literary Imagination.* Cambridge, Mass.: Harvard University Press.

Morrison, T. (ed.), 1992. *Race-ing Justice, En-gendering Power: Essays on Anita Hill, Clarence Thomas, and the Construction of Social Reality.* New York: Pantheon Books.

Neuhaus, Richard. 1984. *Naked in the Public Square.* Grand Rapids: Mott Media.

Newman, Maria. 1993. "Free-Speech Decision: Jeffries Victory Shows the Difficulty of Punishing Objectionable Opinions." *The New York Times,* May 16, Sec. A, p. 33.

　1994. "Court Backs Reinstating of Jeffries to College Post." *The New York Times,* April 19, Sec. B, p. 3.

Ortega y Gasset, José. 1985. *The Revolt of the Masses,* trans. Anthony Kerrigan, ed. Kenneth Moore. Notre Dame, Ind.: University of Notre Dame Press.

Painter, Nell Irvin. 1992. "Hill, Thomas and the Use of Racial Stereotype," in Morrison (ed.), *Race-ing Justice, En- gendering Power,* pp. 200–14.

Parsons, Talcott. 1951. *The Social System.* Glencoe: The Free Press.

　1971. *The System of Modern Society.* Englewood Cliffs: Prentice Hall.

Penn, Shana. 1994. "The National Secret." *Journal of Women's History,* 5, 3: 55–69.

Perry, Bruce. 1991. *Malcolm: The Life of a Man Who Changed Black America.* New York: Station Hill Press.

Perry, Lewis. 1989. *Intellectual Life in America.* Chicago: University of Chicago Press.

Plato. 1986. *The Dialogues of Plato,* trans. Benjamin Jowett. New York: Bantam Books.

Postman, Neil. 1985. *Amusing Ourselves to Death: Public Discourses in the Age of Show Business.* New York: Penguin.

Radway, Janice. 1984. *Reading the Romance: Women, Patriarchy, and Popular Literature.* Chapel Hill: University of North Carolina Press.

Reed, Adolph, Jr. 1997. *W. E. B. Dubois and American Political Thought, Fabianism and the Colorline.* New York and Oxford: Oxford University Press.

Rich, Adrienne. 1980. "Compulsory Heterosexuality and Lesbian Existence," *Signs,* 4: 630–1.

Ricoeur, Paul. 1986. *Lectures on Ideology and Utopia,* ed. George Taylor. Chicago: University of Chicago Press.

Riding, Alan. 1994. "How the Peasants Lit the Fires of Democracy." *The New York Times,* February 27, Sec. A, p. 5.

Rogin, Michael. 1987. *Ronald Reagan: The Movie, and Other Episodes in Political Demonology.* Berkeley: University of California Press.

Rorty, Richard. 1991. "The Priority of Democracy to Philosophy." in Rorty

Objectivity, Relativism, and Truth. New York: Cambridge University Press, pp. 175–96.

Rosen, Jeffrey. 1996. "The Bloods and the Crits." *The New Republic*, December 9, pp. 27–42.

Ross, Andrew. 1989. *No Respect: Intellectual and Popular Culture*. New York: Routledge.

Ross, Dorothy. 1991. *The Origins of the Social Sciences*. New York: Cambridge University Press.

Rowan, Carl. 1993. *Dream Makers, Dream Breakers: The World of Justice Thurgood Marshall*. Boston: Little Brown and Co.

Said, Edward. 1979. *The Question of Palestine*. New York: Times Books.

  1983. *The World, the Text and the Critic*. Cambridge, Mass.: Harvard University Press.

  1993. *Culture and Imperialism*. New York: Knopf.

  1994a. *Orientalism*. New York: Vintage Books.

  1994b. *Representations of the Individual*. New York: Pantheon.

Sartre, Jean-Paul. 1974. *Between Existentialism and Marxism*, trans. John May. London: New Left Review Books.

Schlesinger Jr, Arthur M. 1992. *The Disuniting of America: Reflections on a Multicultural Society*. New York: W. W. Norton.

Seligman, Adam. 1992. *The Idea of Civil Society*. New York: The Free Press.

Sennett, Richard. 1977. *The Fall of Public Man*. New York: Knopf.

Shalin, Dmitri. 1993. "Postmodernism and Pragmatist Inquiry: An Introduction." *Symbolic Interaction*, 16, 4: 303–31.

Shils, Edward. 1972. *The Intellectuals and the Powers, and Other Essays*. Chicago: University of Chicago Press.

  1982. *The Constitution of Society*. Chicago: University of Chicago Press.

  1991. "The Virtues of Civil Society." *Government and Opposition*, 26, 2: 3–20.

Siedman, Steven. 1994. *Contested Knowledge: Social Theory in the Postmodern Era*. Cambridge, Mass.: Blackwell.

Siklova, Jirina. 1993. "McDonalds, Terminators, Coca Cola Ads and Feminism?," in Susanna Trnka and Laura Busheikin (eds.), *Bodies of Bread and Butter*, pp. 7–11.

Simmel, Georg. 1971. *George Simmel: On Individuality and Social Forms*, trans. and ed. Donald Levine. Chicago: University of Chicago Press.

Skocpol, Theda (ed.). 1984. *Vision and Method in Historical Sociology*. New York: Cambridge University Press.

Sleeper, Jim. 1997. *Liberal Racism*. New York: Viking.

Smejkalova-Strickland, Jirina. 1993. "Do Czech Women Need Feminism? Perspectives of Feminist Theories and Practices in the Czech Republic," in Susanna Trnka and Laura Busheikin (eds.), *Bodies of Bread and Butter*, pp. 13–18.

Smith, Dorothy. 1990. *The Conceptual Practices of Power: A Feminist Sociology of Knowledge*. Boston: Northeastern University Press.

Snitow, Ann. 1990. "Gender Diary," in Marianne Hirsch and Evelyn Fox-Keller (eds.), *Conflicts in Feminism*. New York: Routledge, pp. 9–43.

1993. "Feminist Futures in the Former East Bloc." *Peace and Democracy News*, 7, 3: 40.

Snitow, Ann, Christine Stansell, and Sharon Thompson (eds.). 1983. *Powers of Desire: The Politics of Sexuality*. New York: Monthly Review Press.

Sowell, Thomas. 1983. *The Economics and Politics of Race: An International Perspective*. New York: W. Morrow.

Spivak, Gayatri. 1990. *The Post Colonial Critique: Interviews, Strategies, Dialogues*. New York: Routledge.

Staniszkis, Jadwiga. 1984. *Poland's Self-Limiting Revolution*. Princeton: Princeton University Press.

Steel, Ronald. 1980. *Walter Lippmann and the American Century*. New York: Little Brown and Company.

Steele, Shelby. 1991. *The Content of Our Characters: A New Vision of Race in America*. New York: Harper Perennial.

Stone, I. F. 1989. *The Trial of Socrates*. New York: Anchor Books.

Tamas, G. M. 1994. "A Disquisition on Civil Society." *Social Research*, 61,2: 205–22.

Thelwell, Michael. 1992. "False Fleeting, Perjured Chance: Yale's Brightest and Blackest Go to Washington," in Morrison (ed.), *Race-ing Justice, En-gendering Power*, pp. 86–126.

Tilly, Charles. 1985. *Big Structures, Large Processes, Huge Comparisons*. New York: Russell Sage Foundation.

Trnka, Susanna and Laura Busheikin (eds.). 1993. *Bodies of Bread and Butter: Reconfiguring Women's Lives in Post Communist Czech Republic*. Prague: Prague Gender Center.

Veblen, Thorsten. 1957. *The Higher Learning in America: A Memorandum on the Conduct of Universities by Business Men*. New York: Hill and Wang.

Vladislav, Jan (ed.). 1986. *Vaclav Havel or Living in Truth*. Boston: Faber and Faber.

Walzer, Michael. 1987. *Interpretation and Social Criticism*. Cambridge, Mass.: Harvard University Press.

1988. *The Company of Critics: Social Criticism and Political Commitment in the Twentieth Century*. New York: Basic Books.

1991. "The Idea of Civil Society." *Dissent*, Spring: 293–304.

Watson, Peggy. 1992. "Gender Relations, Education, and Social Change in Poland." *Gender and Education*, 4, 1/2:

1993. "Eastern Europe's Silent Revolution: Gender." *Sociology*, 27, 3: 471–87.

1993. "The Rise of Masculinism in Eastern Europe." *New Left Review*, 198, March/April: 71–82.

forthcoming. "Civil Society and the Politicalization of Difference in Eastern Europe," in J. Scott and C. Kaplan (eds.), *Transitions, Environ-*

ments, Translations: The Meaning of Feminism in Contemporary Politics. New York: Routledge.

Waxman, Chaim. 1968. *The End of Ideology Debate*. New York: Funk and Wagnalls.

Weber, Max. *Economy and Society*, ed. Guenther Roth and Claus Wittich, trans. Ephraim Fischoff *et al*. New York: Bedminster Press.

Weschler, Lawrence. 1982. *Solidarity: Poland in the Season of Its Passion*. New York: Simon and Schuster.

West, Cornell. 1989. *The American Evasion of Philosophy: A Genealogy of Pragmatism*. Madison: University of Wisconsin Press.

1994. *Race Matters*. New York: Vintage Books.

Westbrook, Robert. 1991. *John Dewey and American Democracy*. Ithaca: Cornell University Press.

Williams, Patricia. 1992. "A Rare Case Study of Muleheadedness and Men," in Morrison (ed.), *Race-ing Justice, En-gendering Power*, pp. 159–71.

Willis, Paul. 1990. *Common Culture*. Boulder: Westview.

Wills, Garry. 1987. *Reagan's America: Innocents at Home*. Garden City: Doubleday.

Wilson Jr, William Julius. 1992. *The New York Times*. March 17, Sec. A, p. 25.

Wollstonecraft, Mary. 1993. *The Vindication of the Rights of Women*. New York: Legal Classics Library.

Wood, Gordon. 1992. *The Radicalness of the American Revolution*. New York: Knopf.

X, Malcolm. 1964. *The Autobiography of Malcolm X*, as told to Alex Haley. New York: Ballantine Books.

1970. "Answer to Questions at the Militant Labour Forum," in *By Any Means Necessary*. New York: Pathfinder.

Index